Theory and Practice of
Computation

Theory and Practice of
Computation

Proceedings of Workshop on Computation: Theory and Practice WCTP2017

Osaka University, Osaka   12 – 13 September 2017

Editors

Shin-ya Nishizaki
Tokyo Institute of Technology, Japan

Masayuki Numao
Osaka University, Japan

Jaime D L Caro
University of the Philippines Diliman, Philippines

Merlin Teodosia C Suarez
De La Salle University, Philippines

World Scientific

NEW JERSEY · LONDON · SINGAPORE · BEIJING · SHANGHAI · HONG KONG · TAIPEI · CHENNAI · TOKYO

Published by

World Scientific Publishing Co. Pte. Ltd.
5 Toh Tuck Link, Singapore 596224
USA office: 27 Warren Street, Suite 401-402, Hackensack, NJ 07601
UK office: 57 Shelton Street, Covent Garden, London WC2H 9HE

Library of Congress Cataloging-in-Publication Data
Names: Workshop on Computation: Theory and practice (7th : 2017 : Osaka, Japan) |
    Nishizaki, Shin-ya, editor. | Numao, Masayuki, 1961–   editor. |
    Caro, Jaime D. L., editor. | Suarez, Merlin Teodosia C., editor.
Title: Theory and practice of computation : proceedings of Workshop on Computation:
    Theory and Practice WCTP2017, Osaka University, Osaka 12–13 September 2017 /
    edited by Shin-ya Nishizaki, Tokyo Institute of Technology, Japan, Masayuki Numao,
    Osaka University, Japan, Jaime D L Caro, University of Philippines Diliman, Philippines,
    Merlin Teodosia C. Suarez, De La Salle University, Philippines.
Description: New Jersey : World Scientific, 2018. | Includes bibliographical references and index.
Identifiers: LCCN 2018052950 | ISBN 9789813279667 (hardcover)
Subjects: LCSH: Computer science--Congresses. | Information theory--Congresses.
Classification: LCC QA75.5 .T5255 2017 | DDC 004--dc23
LC record available at https://lccn.loc.gov/2018052950

British Library Cataloguing-in-Publication Data
A catalogue record for this book is available from the British Library.

For any available supplementary material, please visit
https://www.worldscientific.com/worldscibooks/10.1142/11259#t=suppl

Desk Editor: Tay Yu Shan

Printed in Singapore

Preface

Computation should be a good blend of theory and practice. Researchers in the field should create algorithms to address real world problems putting equal weight to analysis and implementation. Experimentation and simulation can be viewed as yielding to refined theories or improved applications. WCTP 2017 is the seventh workshop organized by the Tokyo Institute of Technology, The Institute of Scientific and Industrial Research – Osaka University, University of the Philippines Diliman and De La Salle University – Manila that is devoted to theoretical and practical approaches to computation. It aims to present the latest developments by theoreticians and practitioners in academe and industry working to address computational problems that can directly impact the way we live in society.

Following the success of WCTP 2011–2016, WCTP 2017 was held in Osaka University, on September 12 and 13, 2017. This post-proceedings is the collection of the selected papers that were presented at WCTP 2017.

The program of WCTP 2017 consisted of selected research contributions. It included the most recent visions and researches of 4 talks in work-in-progress session and 17 contributions. We collected the original contributions after their presentation at the workshop and began a review procedure that resulted in the selection of the papers in this volume. They appear here in the final form.

WCTP 2017 required a lot of work that was heavily dependent on members of the program committee, and lastly, we owe a great debt of gratitude to Osaka University, for organizing the workshop.

August, 2018

Shin-ya Nishizaki
Masayuki Numao
Jaime Caro
Merlin Teodosia Suarez

PROGRAM CO-CHAIRS

Shin-ya Nishizaki   Tokyo Insitute of Technology, Tokyo, Japan
Masayuki Numao   Osaka University, Osaka, Japan
Jaime Caro   University of the Philippines Diliman,
                       the Philippines
Merlin Teodosia Suarez De La Salle University – Manila, the Philippines

PROGRAM COMMITTEES

Ken-ichi Fukui   – Osaka University, Japan
Satoshi Kurihara   – The University of Electro-Communications, Japan
Koichi Moriyama   – Nagoya Institute of Technology, Japan
Mitsuharu Yamamoto   – Chiba University, Japan
Hiroyuki Tominaga, Koji Kagawa
                       – Kagawa University, Japan
Shigeki Hagihara,   – Tohoku University of Community Service and
                         Science, Japan
Takuo Watanabe, Masaya Shimakawa
                       – Tokyo Institute of Technology, Japan
Raymund Sison, Jocelynn Cu, Gregory Cu, Rhia Trogo, Ju-
dith Azcarraga, Ethel Ong, Charibeth Cheng, Nelson Mar-
cos, Rafael Cabredo, Joel Ilao
                       – De La Salle University, the Philippines
Rommel Feria, Henry Adorna
                       – University of the Philippines Diliman,
                         the Philippines
John Paul Vergara, Mercedes Rodrigo
                       – Ateneo De Manila University, the Philippines
Allan A. Sioson   – Cobena, the Philippines

GENERAL CO-CHAIRS

Masayuki Numao — International Collaboration Center, The Institute of Scientific and Industrial Research, Osaka University, Japan

Shin-ya Nishizaki — Tokyo Tech Philippines Office, Tokyo Institute of Technology, Japan

ORGANIZING COMMITTEES

Masayuki Numao, Ken-ichi Fukui
– Osaka University, Japan

Contents

Approximation of Two Simple Variations of the Poset Cover Problem

I. Ordanel* , H. Adorna and J. Clemente

Department of Computer Science, University of the Philippines, Diliman, Quezon City, Philippines
* E-mail: ivyordanel@gmail.com

The Poset Cover Problem is the problem where the input is a set of linear orders and the goal is to find a minimum set of posets that generates exactly all the given linear orders.The computational complexity of the decision version of the problem is already known; it is NP-Complete. However, the approximation complexity or approximability of the problem is not yet known.

In this paper, we show the approximability of two simple variations of the problem where the poset being considered are Hammock posets having hammocks of size 2. The first is $Hammock(2, 2, 2)$-Poset Cover Problem where the solution is a set of Hammock posets with 3 hammocks of size 2. This problem has been shown to be NP-Complete and in this paper we show that it is 2.7-approximable. The second variation which is more general than the first one considers Hammock posets with any number of hammocks of size 2 and we show that it is $H(n) - \frac{196}{300}$-approximable.

Keywords: Algorithm, Approximation, Poset, Partial orders.

1. Introduction

In every day life, there are many instances where ordering can be observed. Typically, the orderings are given and the flow of events follow from them. A basic example of this is in making a plan of study. We are given with ordering of the courses in a degree program. There are some courses that have prerequisite courses, say course A is a prerequisite of course B. This means that course A should be taken and passed first before course B can be taken. There are also some courses that have no dependencies on other courses. Let B and C be courses that have no dependencies on any other courses. Hence, a student can take the sequence of courses $A \to B \to C \to D$. Another student can have the sequence $A \to B \to D \to C$. Another student can have the sequence $C \to D \to A \to B$.

In data mining, the problem is the reverse. The given is large sets of sequential data and the goal is to come up with a network model that shows the ordering pattern in the data set. We can find problem like this in many areas. For instance, in neuroscience, neuronal network are constructed from the sequences of individual neuron firings[1]. In chemical engineering, chemical process network or pathways are constructed from studying sequential data of chemical concentrations[2]. In epidemiology, structures of disease spread are constructed from the sequential data of people movement from one location to another[3]. In paleontology, evolutionary ordering of fossil sites are constructed from sequential data about the taxa that occur in each site[4,5]. In systems biology, reaction systems or pathways are constructed from a sequence of concentration, measured from time to time, of the species composing the system[6]. In business, process models are constructed from logs of events in a workflow that are recorded sequentially[7,8]. A simple example of this is the case when the business wants to generate a process model from the logs of purchases of their products. The process model can be used to predict other customers' future purchases and the business could develop marketing campaigns from it.

The intuitive concept of ordering or ranking of a collection of objects or events is formalized in mathematics using poset (partially ordered set). Formally, a poset $P = (V, \leq_P)$ is a pair consisting of a finite vertex set V and a binary relation $\leq_P \subseteq V \times V$ that is reflexive, antisymmetric and transitive. In this paper, we only consider strict poset, written here as $P = (V, <_P)$, where the binary relation is antisymmetric and transitive but irreflexive. An example of strict poset is shown in Figure 1.a. From this point on, all posets being discussed in this paper are strict posets.

The binary relation in a poset is called a partial order since not all pairs need to be related. For the case wherein all pairs are related, the binary relation is called a total order and the poset is said to be a totally ordered set or a linear order. Formally, a linear order $l = (V, <_l)$ is a poset where for all distinct elements $u, v \in V$, either $u <_l v$ or $v <_l u$. Moreover, a linear order $l = (V, <_l)$ is said to be a linear extension of poset P if $<_P \subseteq <_l$. The set of all linear extensions of P is denoted by $\mathcal{L}(P)$. For example, Figure 1.c shows the set of linear extensions of the poset P in Figure 1.a.

Now, back to the problem, the sequential data of events which is basically a permutation of events can then be treated as a linear order. Reconstructing a network model from sequential data can then be translated to reconstructing a partially ordered set (poset) from a set of linear orders. If the goal is to find the minimum number of posets, then the problem becomes the Poset Cover Problem. Formally, the Poset Cover Problem is defined as follows[9]:

POSET COVER PROBLEM
INSTANCE: A set $\Upsilon = \{l_1, l_2, ..., l_m\}$ of linear orders over the set $V = \{1, 2, 3, ..., n\}$.
SOLUTION: A set $P^* = \{P_1, P_2, ..., P_q\}$ of posets where $\bigcup_{P_i \in P^*} \mathcal{L}(P_i) = \Upsilon$ and q is minimum.

The Poset Cover Problem has been shown to be NP-Complete[9]. One of the known approaches in dealing with hard problems like the Poset Cover Problem is to consider simpler cases. The studies in[10–12] attacked the Poset Cover Problem using this approach. They defined different restricted cases of the problem by considering only posets of certain class according to their Hasse diagram such as kite, hammock and leveled posets and/or by considering only specific number of poset.

Another known and seems to be the most successful approach in dealing with hard optimization problems is approximation[13]. In approximation, we find algorithm that gives solution within a factor of optimum. In our knowledge, there are no results yet on the approximation complexity of the problem. However, two algorithms that always return feasible solution to the problem have been devised[14]. There are also approximation results to problems that are closely related to the Poset Cover Problem. The first is the Optimal Bucket Order Problem where the goal is to find a bucket order that fits a set of pairwise preference[15]. The bucket order is the same as the leveled poset mentioned above. A pairwise preference is a probability that a pair (i, j) is in the relation of the bucket order. The study[15] came up with a random 9-approximation algorithm. Another problem is the Poset Dimension Problem, the problem of finding the dimension of a poset, i.e., the minimum integer k such that the partial order can be expressed as the intersection of k total orders. This problem was shown to be NP-Complete[16] and hard to approximate[17].

The results on this paper are on simple variations of the Poset Cover Problem where the posets being considered are Hammock Posets only. The first variation is the Hammock(2,2,2) Poset Cover Problem where the solution is a set of Hammock posets with 3 hammocks of size 2. This problem has been shown to be $NP - Complete$[10] and in this paper we show that it is 2.7-approximable. The second which is more general than the first one is the $Hammock(a_1, a_2, \ldots, a_t), t \geq 0, a_i = 2$ for $i = 1, \ldots, t$. In this problem,

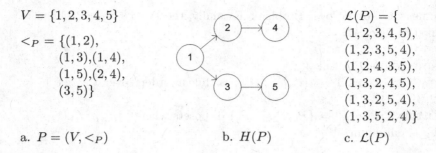

a. $P = (V, <_P)$ b. $H(P)$ c. $\mathcal{L}(P)$

Fig. 1.   Poset P, its Hasse diagram and linear extensions.

the solution is a set of Hammock posets with any number of hammocks of size 2. We show in this paper that this problem is $H(m) - \frac{196}{300}$-approximable where m is the number of linear orders in the input.

2. Definitions

We first define in this section the concepts or notations that are used in the discussion of results.

Definition 2.1. Given a poset $P = (V, <_P)$ and elements $u, v \in V$, u **covers** v, written as $u \prec_P v$ iff $u <_P v$ and there is no $w \in V$ such that $u <_P w <_P v$.

For example in the poset in Fig. 1.a, $2 \prec_P 4$ since $2 <_P 4$ and $\nexists\, w$ such that $2 <_P w <_P 4$. But $1 \not\prec_P 4$ since there is an element 2 where $1 <_P 2 <_P 4$.

Definition 2.2. The **Hasse diagram** $H(P)$ of poset $P = (V, <_P)$ is a directed acyclic graph $G = (V, A)$ having the vertex set V and an edge set $A = \{(u, v) | u \prec_P v\}$.

Figure 1.b shows the Hasse diagram $H(P)$ of the poset P defined in Figure 1.a.

Definition 2.3. A **hammock poset** $P = (V, <_P)$ is a poset where the set V can be partitioned into disjoint subsets $V_1, V_2, \ldots, V_k$ such that for $u \in V_i$ and $v \in V_j$, we have $u <_P v$ iff $i < j$, $|V_1| = |V_k| = 1$ and either $|V_i| = 1$ or $|V_{i+1}| = 1$ for $2 \leq i \leq k - 1$.

A non-singleton V_i in a hammock poset is called a **hammock**. The elements on the single-ton V_i are called **link vertices**. The sequence of the sizes of the hammocks are used to name the hammock poset. The $Hammock(a_1, a_2, \ldots, a_n)$ is the hammock poset where a_i is the size of the ith hammock.

For example, Hammock(2,3) poset is a hammock poset that has two hammocks - the first hammock has size of 2 and the second hammock has size of 3. The hasse diagram of a Hammock(2,3) poset is shown on Fig. 2.

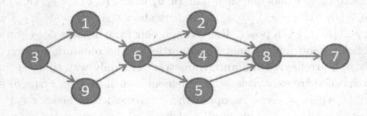

Fig. 2.   Hasse diagram of a hammock poset.

Definition 2.4. Let C be a property of a poset (perhaps C characterizes the Hasse diagram of a poset). A poset on V that satisfies C is called a **C-poset**. The **C-Poset Cover Problem** is the minimization problem where
INSTANCE: A set $\Upsilon = \{l_1, l_2, \ldots, l_m\}$ of linear orders over the set $V = \{1, 2, 3, \ldots, n\}$ and an integer $K \leq m$.
SOLUTION: A poset cover $P^* = \{P_1, P_2, \ldots, P_k\}$ of Υ such that $k \leq K$ and (P_i) is a $C - poset$ for every $P_i \in P^*$.

For example, the Hammock(2,2,2)-Poset Cover Problem is the problem where the solution is a set of Hammock(2,2,2) posets that cover the input set of linear orders.

Definition 2.5. Given $P = (V, <_P)$, vertices a and b are **siblings** if for all $c \in V - \{a, b\}$, $c <_P a$ if and only if $c <_P b$, and $a <_P c$ if and only $b <_P c$.

Definition 2.6. Given a poset $P = (V, <_P)$ and elements $u, v \in V$, u and v are **comparable** if $u <_P v$ or $v <_P u$. On the other hand, u and v are **incomparable**, if $u \not<_P v$ and $v \not<_P u$.

3. Results

Lemma 3.1. *Given posets $P_1 = (V, <_{P_1})$ and $P_2 = (V, <_{P_2})$, if there exists at most one pair $\{a, b\}, a \neq b$ such that $(a, b) \in <_{P_1}$, $(b, a) \in <_{P_2}$ and $<_{P_1} \backslash \{(a, b)\} = <_{P_2} \backslash \{(b, a)\}$, then there exists a poset $P_3 = (V, <_{P_3})$ where $<_{P_3} = <_{P_1} \backslash \{(a, b)\} = <_{P_2} \backslash \{(b, a)\}$ and $\mathcal{L}(P_3) = \mathcal{L}(P_1) \cup \mathcal{L}(P_2)$.*

Proof. If there is no such pair $\{a, b\}$, then $P_1 = P_2 = P_3$. The theorem obviously follows.

Suppose there exists one such pair $\{a, b\}$ where $(a, b) \in <_{P_1}$, $(b, a) \in <_{P_2}$ and $<_{P_1} \backslash \{(a, b)\} = <_{P_2} \backslash \{(b, a)\}$. We first show that $P_3 = (V, <_{P_3})$ where $<_{P_3} = <_{P_1} \backslash \{(a, b)\}$ is a poset. Removing a pair from a poset does not affect the irreflexive and antisymmetric properties of the remaining pairs. This means $<_{P_3}$ is irreflexive and antisymmetric. The only way that $<_{P_3}$ is not transitive is if there exist at least one element x such that $(a, x), (x, b) \in <_{P_3}$ or $(b, x), (x, a) \in <_{P_3}$. Now, suppose there exists such element $x \in V$ such that $(a, x), (x, b) \in <_{P_3}$. This implies that $(a, x), (x, b)$ are also in $<_{P_1}$ and $<_{P_2}$. By transitive property of posets, $(a, b) \in <_{P_2}$. This contradicts the antisymmetric property of $<_{P_2}$ since (b, a) is also in $<_{P_2}$. In a similar way, we can also show that there exists no x such that $(b, x), (x, a) \in <_{P_3}$.

Next, we show that $\mathcal{L}(P_1) \cup \mathcal{L}(P_2) \subseteq \mathcal{L}(P_3)$ and $\mathcal{L}(P_3) \subseteq \mathcal{L}(P_1) \cup \mathcal{L}(P_2)$.

To show the first part, let the linear order $L_1 \in \mathcal{L}(P_1) \cup \mathcal{L}(P_2)$. Then, it is either $L_1 \in \mathcal{L}(P_1)$ or $L_1 \in \mathcal{L}(P_2)$. Suppose $L_1 \in \mathcal{L}(P_1)$. This means that $<_{P_1} \subseteq <_{L_1}$. Since $<_{P_3} \subseteq <_{P_1}$, then $<_{P_3} \subseteq <_{L_1}$. This implies that $L_1 \in \mathcal{L}(P_3)$. In a similar way, we can show that if $L_1 \in \mathcal{L}(P_2)$, then $L_1 \in \mathcal{L}(P_3)$. Thus, $\mathcal{L}(P_1) \cup \mathcal{L}(P_2) \subseteq \mathcal{L}(P_3)$.

To show the second part, let the linear order $L_2 \in \mathcal{L}(P_3)$. By definition, $<_{P_3} \subseteq <_{L_2}$. Since a is incomparable to b in P_3 and every pair of distinct elements in L_2 are comparable, then it is either $(a, b) \in <_{L_2}$ or $(b, a) \in <_{L_2}$. If $(a, b) \in <_{L_2}$, then $<_{P_3} \cup \{(a, b)\} \subseteq <_{L_2}$. This implies $<_{P_1} \subseteq <_{L_2}$. Thus, $L_2 \in \mathcal{L}(P_1)$. On the other hand, if $(b, a) \in <_{L_2}$, then $<_{P_3} \cup \{(b, a)\} \subseteq <_{L_2}$. This means $<_{P_2} \subseteq <_{L_2}$. Thus, $L_2 \in \mathcal{L}(P_2)$. In either cases, $L_2 \in \mathcal{L}(P_1) \cup \mathcal{L}(P_2)$. Hence, $\mathcal{L}(P_3) \subseteq \mathcal{L}(P_1) \cup \mathcal{L}(P_2)$. $\square$

The previous lemma tells us a condition when can two posets be combined into single poset such that the linear extension of the new poset is the union of the two combined posets. On the other hand, the following lemma is somewhat the reverse of the previous one. It tells us a condition when a single poset can be decomposed in two posets such that the union of the linear extensions of the two poset is the same as that of the single poset.

Lemma 3.2. *Given a poset $P = (V, <_P)$ and $x_i, x_j \in V$, if x_i and x_j are siblings in P, then there exist posets $P_1 = (V, <_{P_1})$ and $P_2 = (V, <_{P_2})$ where $<_{P_1} = <_P \cup \{(x_i, x_j)\}$ and $<_{P_2} = <_P \cup \{(x_j, x_i)\}$ such that $\mathcal{L}(P_1) = \{L \in \mathcal{L}(P) | x_i <_L x_j\}$ and $\mathcal{L}(P_2) = \{L \in \mathcal{L}(P) | x_j <_L x_i\}$. Moreover, $\mathcal{L}(P_1) \cap \mathcal{L}(P_2) = \emptyset$ and $\mathcal{L}(P_1) \cup \mathcal{L}(P_2) = \mathcal{L}(P)$.*

Proof. We first show that P_1 and P_2 are posets. Since $x_i \neq x_j$, then $<_{P_1}$ and $<_{P_2}$ are irreflexive. x_i and x_j are siblings hence they are incomparable. This means there is no (x_i, x_j) nor (x_j, x_i) in $<_{P_1}$ and $<_{P_2}$. Hence, adding (x_i, x_j) or (x_j, x_i) to $<_P$ makes $<_{P_1}$ and $<_{P_2}$ still antisymmetric. Lastly, to show that P_1 is transitive, we just need to show that the addition of pair (x_j, x_i) to transitive relation $<_P$ makes $<_{P_1}$ still transitive. Let $a, b \in V$ where $a <_{P_1} x_i$ and $x_j <_{P_1} b$. Since x_i and x_j are siblings in P, then $a <_P x_j$ and $x_i <_P b$. This implies $a <_{P_1} x_j$ and $x_i <_{P_1} b$. Hence, P_1 is transitive. We can also show that P_2 is transitive in similar way.

Now, let $A = \{L \in \mathcal{L}(P) | x_i <_L x_j\}$ and $B = \{L \in \mathcal{L}(P) | x_j <_L x_i\}$. Next, we show that $\mathcal{L}(P_1) = A$ and $\mathcal{L}(P_2) = B$. Let $L_1 \in \mathcal{L}(P_1)$. Then $<_{P_1} \subseteq <_{L_1}$. Since $<_P \subset <_{P_1}$, then $<_P \subset <_{L_1}$. Hence $L_1 \in \mathcal{L}(P)$. Also, since $(x_i, x_j) \in <_{P_1}$ then $x_i <_{L_1} x_j$. Hence, $L_1 \in A$. On the other hand, let $L_2 \in A$. This means $<_P \subset <_{L_2}$. Also, since $x_i <_{L_2} x_j$, then $(x_i, x_j) \in <_{L_2}$. This implies that $<_P \cup \{(x_i, x_j)\} \subset <_{L_2}$. This means $<_{P_1} \subset <_{L_2}$. Hence, $L_2 \in \mathcal{L}(P_1)$. Thus, $A = \{L \in \mathcal{L}(P) | x_i <_L x_j\}$. In the same way, we can also show that $B = \{L \in \mathcal{L}(P) | x_j <_L x_i\}$.

Next, suppose there exists $L \in A \cap B$. This means that $x_i <_L x_j$ and $x_j <_L x_i$. This contradicts that antisymmetric property of $<_L$. Hence, $A \cap B = \emptyset$.

Lastly, since every pair in L is related, then it is either $x_i <_L x_j$ or $x_j <_L x_i$. Hence, it is either $L \in A$ or $L \in P$. Hence, $A \cup B = \mathcal{L}(P)$. $\square$

Lemma 3.3. *Given a poset $P = (V, <_P)$, if P is a Hammock$(a_1, a_2, \ldots, a_y)$, then $|\mathcal{L}(P)| = a_1! a_2! \ldots a_y!$.*

Proof. Let $n = |V|$.

To form a linear extension l of length n, we first place all the link vertices in order while leaving respective spaces for the hammock vertices. Then place elements of hammock a_1 in the space alloted for a_1. There are $a_1!$ possible arrangement of the elements of hammock a_1. Do this for hammock a_2 to a_y. Hence, by Multiplication Principle, $|\mathcal{L}(P)| = a_1! a_2! \ldots a_y!$. $\square$

The previous lemmas are the main bases of Algorithm 1 that is shown in Fig. 3. There are basically two parts in the algorithm. The first part (lines 1-19) generates P_r^* which is the set of hammock posets having r hammocks of size 2. It is initially P_0^* which is the set of the given linear orders. Every rth iteration of the outer while loop produces P_r^* by combining every possible pair of posets in P_{r-1}^* into single poset. The function *CombinePoset*, which is shown in Fig. 4, determines if the two pairs of poset can be combined into a single poset according to Lemma 3.1. Lines 15-27 of *CombinePoset* further ensure that the combined poset is a hammock poset. On the other hand, the second part(lines 20-22) of Algorithm 1 determines the minimum set of posets from P_r^* that covers the input set of linear orders. Since P_r^* has all the possible hammock posets having r hammocks of size 2 , determining the minimum poset that covers input Υ can then be translated to determining the minimum set cover of Υ using the set of linear extensions of each poset in P_r^* as the collection of subsets. Algorithm 1 uses the Johnson's Greedy Algorithm, which is shown in Fig. 5, to determine the minimum set cover.

INPUT: A set $\Upsilon = \{l_1, l_2, ..., l_m\}$ of linear orders on $V = \{1, 2, ..., n\}$
OUTPUT: A set $P_f^* = \{P_{r_1}, P_{r_2}, ..., P_{r_k}\}$ of Hammock(2,2,2) posets
    where $\bigcup_{P_{r_i} \in P_f^*} \mathcal{L}(P_{r_i}) = \Upsilon$

```
1   P₀* ← {P₀₁, P₀₂, ..., P₀ₘ} where P₀₁ = l₁, P₀₂ = l₂,..., P₀ₘ = lₘ
2   MAX_ITER ← 3
3   for r ← 1 to MAX_ITER do
4       s ← 0
5       for i ← 1 to |P*_{r-1}| do
6           for j ← i + 1 to |P*_{r-1}| do
7               P_temp = CombinePoset(P_{r-1_i}, P_{r-1_j})
8               if P_temp ≠ null then
9                   s ← s + 1
10                  P_{r_s} ← P_temp
11                  L(P_{r_s}) ← L(P_{r-1_i}) ∪ L(P_{r-1_j})
12                  P_r* ← P_r* ∪ {P_{r_s}}
13              end if
14          end for
15      end for
16      if |P_r*| = 0 then
17          return NULL
18      end if
19  end for
20  τ ← {L(P_{r_1}), L(P_{r_2}), ..., L(P_{r_s})}
21  ω ← MinSetCover(Υ, τ)
22  P_f* = {P_{r_k}|L(P_{r_k}) ∈ ω}
23  return P_f*
```

Fig. 3. Algorithm 1.

```
CombinePoset  (P_1 = (V, <_{P_1}), P_2 = (V, <_{P_2}))
 1  if | <_{P_1} | ≠ | <_{P_2} | then
 2     return null
 3  end if
 4  <_{P_3} = <_{P_1} − <_{P_2}
 5  <_{P_4} = <_{P_2} − <_{P_1}
 6  if | <_{P_3} | ≠ 1 and | <_{P_4} | ≠ 1 then
 7     return null
 8  end if
 9  (a, b) ← <_{P_3} [0]
10  (c, d) ← <_{P_4} [0]
11  if a ≠ d or b ≠ c then
12     return null
13  end if
14  P = (V, <_P) where <_P = <_{P_1} − <_{P_3}
15  noPrecCover ← 0
16  noSucCover ← 0
17  for all i ∈ V − {a, b} do
18     if (i, a) ≺_P and (i, b) ≺_P  then
19        noPrecCover ← noPrecCover + 1
20     else if (a, i) ≺_P and (b, a) ≺_P  then
21        noSucCover ← noSucCover + 1
22     end if
23  end for
24  if noPrecCover ≠ 1 or noSucCover ≠ 1 then
25     return null
26  end if
27  return  P
```

Fig. 4.   CombinePoset subroutine.

```
MinSetCover  (U, S = {S_i | S_i ⊆ U, 1 ≤ i ≤ n})
 1  C ← ∅
 2  UNCOV ← U
 3  SET(i) = S_i, 1 ≤ i ≤ n
 4  while UNCOV ≠ ∅ do
 5     Choose j ≤ n such that |SET(j)| is maximum
 6     C ← C ∪ {S_j}
 7     UNCOV ← UNCOV − SET(j)
 8     SET(i) = SET(i) − SET(j), 1 ≤ i ≤ n
 9  end while
10  return  C
```

Fig. 5.   Johnson's Greedy Algorithm for Min Set Cover Problem [18].

We first show that the following claim holds.

Claim 1. : *The output in each rth iteration of the outermost for-loop in Algorithm 1 is $P_r^* = \{P | P$ is $Hammock(a_1, a_2, \ldots, a_r), a_i = 2$ for $i = 1, \ldots, r$ such that $\mathcal{L}(P) \subseteq \Upsilon\}$.*

Proof. For $r = 1$, let P_1^* be the output of the first iteration. Let $P = (V, <_P)$ be a Hammock(2) poset such that $\mathcal{L}(P) \subseteq \Upsilon$ .Let x_1 and x_2 be the elements of the hammock of P. Since P has only one hammock, x_1 and

x_2 are the only incomparable pairs in $<_P$. Moreover, x_1 and x_2 are also siblings. Hence from Lemma 3.2, P is a combination of posets $P_1 = (V, <_{P_1})$ and $P_2 = (V, <_{P_2})$ where $<_{P_1} = <_P \cup \{(x_1, x_2)\}$, $<_{P_2} = <_P \cup \{(x_2, x_1)\}$. This implies that every pairs in V are related in $<_{P_1}$ and $<_{P_2}$. Hence, P_1 and P_2 are linear orders. The first iteration of Algorithm 1 checks on every pair of linear order, say $L_1, L_2 \in \Upsilon$ where L_1 and L_2 that can be combined according to the condition in 3.1. Since, P_1 and P_2 are linear orders in Υ and $<_{P_1} - \{(x_1, x_2)\} = <_{P_2} - \{(x_2, x_1)\}$, then they must be identified by Algorithm as linear orders that can be combined. This is performed in the CombinePoset subroutine of the Algorithm. Moreover, the CombinePoset subroutine also ensures in lines 15-26 that $\{x_1, x_2\}$ form a hammock by verifying if there only exists only one $c \in V$ where $(c, x_1), (c, x_2) \in \prec_P$ and only one $d \in V$ where $(x_1, d), (x_2, d) \in \prec_P$. Hence, $P \in P_1^*$.

Now, suppose the claim is true for $r = k$ that is the output is P_k^* in kth iteration outputs all possible Hammock posets with k hammocks of size 2 whose set of linear extensions are in Υ. Let $P_3 = (V, <_{P_3})$ be a Hammock posets with $k + 1$ hammocks of size 2, i.e., $Hammock(a_1, a_2, \ldots, a_{k+1})$ poset where $a_i = 2$ for $i = 1, \ldots, k+1$ such that $\mathcal{L}(P_3) \subseteq \Upsilon$. Let hammock $a_i = \{x_{i_1}, x_{i_2}\}$. Since x_{i_1} and x_{i_2} are siblings, then P_3 is a combination of posets $P_{i_4} = (V, <_{P_{i_4}})$ and $P_{i_5} = (V, <_{P_{i_5}})$ where $<_{P_{i_4}} = <_{P_3} \cup \{(x_{i_1}, x_{i_2})\}$, $<_{P_{i_5}} = <_{P_3} \cup \{(x_{i_2}, x_{i_1})\}$. Since there are $k + 1$ pairs of siblings in P_3, then there are also $k + 1$ pairs of P_{i_4} and P_{i_5}, $i = 1, \ldots, k + 1$. Note that P_{i_4} and P_{i_5} are hammock posets with k hammocks of size 2. Since $\mathcal{L}(P_{i_4}) \subseteq \Upsilon$ and $\mathcal{L}(P_{i_5}) \subseteq \Upsilon$, then $P_{i_4}, P_{i_5} \in P_k^*$. The iteration $r = k+1$ of Algorithm 1 checks and combines all possible pairs of posets in P_k^* using Lemma 1. Note that $<_{P_{i_4}}$ and $<_{P_{i_5}}$ satisfy the condition of Lemma 1. Hence, combining them by Lemma 3.2, we get P_3. Hence, $P_3 \in P_{k+1}^*$. In other words, the claim is true for iteration $r = k + 1$. $\square$

Theorem 3.1. *Algorithm 1 is a 2.7-approximation for Hammock(2,2,2)-Poset Cover Problem.*

Proof. In Algorithm 1, r goes from 1 to 3 , hence at the end of outermost for-loop (line 16) the value of $P_r^* = \{P | P$ is $Hammock(2, 2, 2)$ such that $\mathcal{L}(P) \subseteq \Upsilon\}$. Algorithm 1 also stores $\mathcal{L}(P)$ for each $P \in P_r^*$. The problem of determining the minimum Hammock(2,2,2) posets that cover Υ can then be translated to the problem of determining the minimum set cover of Υ from subsets $\mathcal{L}(P) \subseteq \Upsilon$ for each $P \in P_r^*$. Hence, determining the approximation ratio of Algorithm 1 is also the same as determining the approximation ratio of minimum set cover.

C^* - optimal solution

C - solution returned by the algorithm

P_i - ith poset selected

1 - cost when P_i is selected

c_y - cost allocated to element y, for every $y \in \Upsilon$ that is covered for the first time by P_i

$$c_y = \frac{1}{|\mathcal{L}(P_i) - (\mathcal{L}(P_1) \cup \mathcal{L}(P_2) \cup \ldots \cup \mathcal{L}(P_{i-1}))|}$$

$$|C| = \sum_{y \in \Upsilon} c_y \leq \sum_{P \in C^*} \sum_{y \in \mathcal{L}(P)} c_y$$

$$\sum_{y \in \mathcal{L}(P_i)} c_y \leq H(|\mathcal{L}(P_i)|) \qquad \text{where H(j) is the jth harmonic number}$$

$$|C| \leq \sum_{P_i \in C^*} H(|\mathcal{L}(P_i)|)$$

$$\leq H(max|\mathcal{L}(P_i)|) \cdot |C^*|$$

$$= H(8) \cdot |C^*| \qquad \text{by Lemma 3.3}$$

$$\approx 2.7|C^*|$$

$\square$

We can actually modify Algorithm 1 to get hammock posets with any number of hammocks of size 2 that could cover Υ. Thus, we have Algorithm 2 as shown in Fig. 6.

Theorem 3.2. *Algorithm 2 is an $H(m) - \frac{196}{300}$-approximation for Hammock($a_1, a_2, \ldots, a_t$)-Poset Cover Problem where $t \geq 0, a_i = 2$ for $i = 1, \ldots, t$ and $m = |\Upsilon|$.*

Proof. We first show that the following claim holds.

Claim 2. *After line 28, $P_q^* = \{P | P$ is Hammock($a_1, a_2, \ldots, a_t$), $t \geq 0, a_i = 2$ for $i = 1, \ldots, t$ such that $\mathcal{L}(P) \subseteq \Upsilon\}$.*

At each rth iteration of the outermost for-loop(lines 3-27), posets that can no longer be combined or paired from P_{r-1} are added to P_q^* and on line 28 the posets from last P_r^* is added to P_q^*. Note that P_r^*'s in Algorithm 2 is generated in the same way as in Algorithm 1, hence by Claim 1, $P_r^* = \{P | P$ is $Hammock(a_1, a_2, \ldots, a_r), a_i = 2$ for $i = 1, \ldots, r$ such that $\mathcal{L}(P) \subseteq \Upsilon\}$. The largest number of hammock of size 2 is $lg|\Upsilon|$ by Lemma 3.3. This is

---

MinSetCover INPUT: A set $\gamma = \{l_1, l_2, ..., l_m\}$ of linear orders on $V = \{1, 2, ..., n\}$

OUTPUT: A set $P_f^* = \{P_{r_1}, P_{r_2}, ..., P_{r_k}\}$ of $Hammock(a_1, a_2, ..., a_t)$-poset, $t \geq 0, a_i = 2$ for $i = 1, ..., t$ where $\bigcup_{P_{r_i} \in P_f^*} \mathcal{L}(P_{r_i}) = \Upsilon$

1   $P_0^* \leftarrow \{P_{0_1}, P_{0_2}, ..., P_{0_m}\}$ where $P_{0_1} = l_1, P_{0_2} = l_2, ..., P_{0_m} = l_m$

2   $MAX\_ITER \leftarrow \lg |\Upsilon|$

3   **for** $r \leftarrow 1$ to MAX_ITER **do**

4     $s \leftarrow 0$

5   **for** $i \leftarrow 1$ to $|P_{r-1}^*|$ **do**

6       $isPaired[|P_{r-1}^*|] \leftarrow$ each index initialize to $false$

7   **for** $j \leftarrow i + 1$ to $|P_{r-1}^*|$ **do**

8         $P_{temp} = CombinePoset(P_{r-1_i}, P_{r-1_j})$

9   **if** $P_{temp} \neq null$ **then**

10           $s \leftarrow s + 1$

11           $P_{r_s} \leftarrow P_{temp}$

12           $\mathcal{L}(P_{r_s}) \leftarrow \mathcal{L}(P_{r-1_i}) \cup \mathcal{L}(P_{r-1_j})$

13           $P_r^* \leftarrow P_r^* \cup \{P_{r_s}\}$

14           $isPaired[i] = true$

15           $isPaired[j] = true$

16   **end if**

17   **end for**

18   **end for**

19   **for** $u \leftarrow 1$ to $|P_{r-1}^*|$ **do**

20   **if** $isPaired[u] = false$ **then**

21         $P_q^* = P_q^* \cup P_{r-1_i}$

22   **end if**

23   **end for**

24   **if** $|P_r^*| = 0$ **then**

25   break

26   **end if**

27   **end for**

28   $P_q^* \leftarrow P_q^* \cup P_r^*$

29   $\tau \leftarrow \{\mathcal{L}(P_{q_1}), \mathcal{L}(P_{q_2}), ..., \mathcal{L}(P_{r_{|P_q^*|}})\}$

30   $\omega \leftarrow MinSetCover2(\Upsilon, \tau)$

31   $P_f^* = \{P_{r_k} | \mathcal{L}(P_{r_k}) \in \omega\}$

32   **return** P_f^*

Fig. 6.   Algorithm 2.

if there is a single hammock poset that covers the Υ. Since $1 \leq r \leq lg|\Upsilon|$, then $P_q^* = \{P | P$ is $Hammock(a_1, a_2, ..., a_t), t \geq 0, a_i = 2$ for $i = 1, ..., t$ such that $\mathcal{L}(P) \subseteq \Upsilon\}$.

Similar to Theorem 3.1, the problem can be translated to the problem of determining the minimum set cover of Υ from subsets $\mathcal{L}(P) \subseteq \Upsilon$ for each $P \in P_q^*$. There are already some refinements of the Johnson's Greedy Algorithm that applies to instance of minimum set cover problem with larger size of subsets. The best approximation algorithm is by Asaf Levin[19] with approximation ratio $H(k) - \frac{196}{300}$ where k is the upper bound of the cardinality of subsets in the input. The largest set of linear extension is

$|\mathcal{L}(P)| \leq 2^{lg|\Upsilon|} = |\Upsilon|$ (by Lemma 3.3). Hence, if $MinSetCover2$ uses the algorithm of Levin, then Algorithm 2 is a $H(m) - \frac{196}{300}$-approximation for $Hammock(a_1, a_2, \ldots, a_t)$-Poset Cover Problem where $t \geq 0, a_i = 2$ for $i = 1, \ldots, t$ and $m = |\Upsilon|$. $\qquad\square$

4. Concluding remarks

In this paper, we have shown results on the approximability of the two simple variations of the Poset Cover Problem. We have shown that the $Hammock(2, 2, 2)$ Poset Cover Problem is 2.7-approximable while the $Hammock(a_1, a_2, \ldots a_t)$ Poset Cover Problem where $t \geq 0, a_i = 2$ for $i = 1, \ldots, t$ is $H(n) - \frac{196}{300}$-approximable. The hammock poset with hammocks of size 2 is one of the simplest classes of posets we could think of. The result of this paper suggests that even for this simple case of the Poset Cover, the approximation ratio is already a function (a harmonic function which is approximately a logarithmic function) on the input size. This somehow gives us an idea on the approximability of the general Poset Cover Problem or to variations using more complex classes of poset.

5. Acknowledgment

I. Ordanel and J. Clemente acknowledge support from DOST-ERDT.
H. Adorna acknowledges support from DOST-ERDT and Semirara Mining Corporation professorial chair.

References

1. A. Lee and M. Wilson, A combinatorial method for analyzing sequential firing patterns involving an arbitrary number of neurons based on relative time order, *Journal of Neurophysiology* **92**, 2555 (2005).
2. C. Wiggins and I. Nemenman, Process pathway via time series analysis, *Experimental Mechanics* **43**, 361 (2003).
3. K. Unnikrishnan, N. Ramakrishnan, P. Sastry and R. Uthurusamy, Network reconstruction from dynamic data, *ACM SIGKDD Exploration Newsletter* **8** (2006).
4. K. Puolamki, M. Fortelius and H. Mannila, Seriation in paleontological data: Using markov chain monte carlo methods, *PLoS Computational Biology* **2** (2006).
5. H. Mannila, Finding total and partial orders from data for seriation, *Lecture Notes in Computer Science* **5255**, 16 (2008).

6. A. Arkin, P. Sheng and J. Ross, A test case of correlation metric construction of a reaction pathway from measurements, *Science* **277**, 1275 (1997).

7. R. Agrawal, D. Gunopulos and F. Leymann, *Mining process models from workflow logs* (Springer Berlin Heidelberg, 1998).

8. W. V. Der Aalst, T. Weijters and L. Maruster, Workflow mining: Discovering process models from event logs, *Knowledge and Data Engineering, IEEE Transactions* **16**, 1128 (2004).

9. L. S. Heath and A. K. Nema, The poset cover problem, *Open Journal of Discrete Mathematics* **3**, 101 (July 2013).

10. P. L. Fernandez, L. S. Heath, N. Ramakrishnan, M. Tan and J. P. C. Vergara, Mining posets from linear orders, *Discrete Mathematics, Algorithms and Applications* **5** (2013).

11. I. Ordanel and P. Fernandez, Reconstructing a tree poset from linear extensions, *Philippine Information Technology Journal* **4**, 18 (2011).

12. G. A. Sanchez, P. Fernandez and J. P. Vergara, Some heuristics for the 2-poset cover problem, *Philippine Computing Journal* **9**, 26 (2014).

13. J. Hromkovi, *Algorithmics for hard problems: introduction to combinatorial optimization, randomization, approximation, and heuristics* (Springer-Verlag Berlin Heidelberg New York, 2001).

14. I. Ordanel and H. Adorna, Two approximation algorithms to the poset cover problem, *Proceedings of the 17th Philippine Computing Science Congress* , 179 (2017).

15. A. Ukkonen, K. Puolamki, A. Gionis and H. Mannila, A randomized approximation algorithm for computing bucket orders, *Information Processing Letters* **109**, 356 (2009).

16. M. Yannakakis, The complexity of the partial order dimension problem, *SIAM Journal on Algebraic Discrete Methods* **3**, 351 (1982).

17. R. Hegde and K. Jain, The hardness of approximating poset dimension, *Electronic Notes in Discrete Mathematics* **29**, 435 (2007).

18. J. David, Approximation algorithms for combinatorial problems, *Journal of computer and system sciences* **9**, 256 (1974).

19. A. Levin, Approximating the unweighted k-set cover problem: Greedy meets local search, *SIAM Journal on Discrete Mathematics* **23**, 251 (2008).

A Polynomial-Time Algorithm for Computing the Translocation Syntenic Distance of Special Graphs

John Robert B. Basiloña*, Maria Rosario T. Gueco, Jhoirene Clemente,

Richelle Ann Juayong, Jasmine Malinao, Henry Adorna, and Jan Michael Yap

*Algorithms and Complexity Laboratory, Department of Computer Science,
University of the Philippines Diliman, Quezon City, 1101, Philippines
E-mail: * basilona.jr.b@gmail.com, maria_gueco@upd.edu.ph, jhoiclemente@gmail.com,
richelleann.juayong@gmail.com, janmichaelyap@gmail.com, hnadorna@dcs.upd.edu.ph*

The Minimum Synteny problem is a well-known NP-hard problem that aims to identify the minimum syntenic distance between two genomes. In this paper, we focus on solving a variant of the problem, called the Minimum Translocation Synteny problem, where we consider the minimum number of translocations to transform one genome to another. We propose a polynomial-time algorithm that computes for the translocation syntenic distances between two genomes with square instances. The MinTranSyn algorithm presents a solution to the translocation syntenic distance problem by using a prioritization method in selecting an index to be isolated and vertices to be translocated. The MinTranSyn algorithm is devised for genomes with square instances having square-connected components. With this, the algorithm presented by Belenzo8 was improved with respect to the number of translocations. We showed the quality of the algorithm is bounded above by the total number of chromosomes in a genome for synteny graphs that are 2-regular, wheel, and acyclic.

Keywords: Syntenic Distance, Translocation Synteny, Minimum Synteny Problem, Computational Biology.

1. Background of the Study

A genome is the entirety of the genetic material of an organism, encoded in DNA and RNA[1]. It is composed of genes and non-coding sequences and evolves through rearrangements. There are more than 3 billion DNA base sets in a genome that is contained in all cells that have a core that we call the nucleus in humans according to the Human Genome Project of the US National Library of Medicine[2]. Chromosomes are molecules of DNA that composes a genome. In a single chromosome, a gene segment could have its order reversed (reversal) or it could be relocated to a different location (transposition) on the chromosome. Between chromosomes, genes can be translocated, fused, or split into two.

Genome rearrangement determines evolutionary distance between genomes. In this study, we compute the evolutionary distance measured by the syntenic distance through translocations, proposed by Ferretti, *et al.*[3]. The syntenic distance is measured as the minimum number of translocations, fusions, and fissions, necessary to evolve one genome to another and computing for it is NP-hard[4]. Common approaches towards measuring syntenic distance is the usage of approximation algorithms[5,6].

In this paper, we focus on a special type of syntenic distance where the number of operations are restricted to translocations. We propose an algorithm that makes use of a prioritization mechanism that integrates the vertex weight and edge distance of the genome's synteny graph in selecting the vertices in which translocations were performed.

2. Preliminaries

Definition 1. [Böckenhauer[7]] Let $G = \{g_1, \ldots, g_m\}$ be a set of genes. A set $\mathcal{G} = \{S_1, \ldots, S_k\}$ is called a genome over G if and only if the following holds:

- For each $1 \leq i \leq k$, S_i is non-empty and $S_i \subseteq G$.
- $\bigcup_{i=1}^{k} S_i = G$.
- For every pair $S_i, S_j, i \neq j, S_i \cap S_j = \{\emptyset\}$.

Each S_i is called a chromosome. We let the set of all possible genome over G be denoted by Γ_G.

Let Γ_G be the set of all genomes over G and $|\Gamma_G| = \sum_{x=1}^{m} {}_mC_x$ where $m = |G|$ and $x = 1, 2, \ldots, m$.

Definition 2. [Böckenhauer[7]] Let $\mathcal{G}_1 = \{S_1, \ldots, S_k\}$ and $\mathcal{G}_2 = \{T_1, \ldots, T_n\}$ be two genomes over a finite set G.

A translocation is a function $\rho : \Gamma_G \to \Gamma_G$ such that the following holds for $\mathcal{G}_2 = \rho(\mathcal{G}_1)$: There exist $i_1, i_2 \in \{1, \ldots, k\}$ and $j_1, j_2 \in \{1, \ldots, n\}$ such that $S_{i_1} \cup S_{i_2} = T_{j_1} \cup T_{j_2}$ and $\{S_i | i \notin \{i_1, i_2\}\} = \{T_j | j \notin \{j_1, j_2\}\}$ hold.

Let $\rho_1, \ldots, \rho_l$ be a sequence of translocations. We use $\mathcal{G}_1 \rho_1, \ldots, \rho_l$ to denote applying this sequence of translocations on a genome $\mathcal{G}_1$.

Definition 3. [Ferretti[3]] The translocation syntenic distance $D(\mathcal{G}_1, \mathcal{G}_2)$ of $\mathcal{G}_1$ and $\mathcal{G}_2$ is the number of translocations necessary to transform $\mathcal{G}_1$ to $\mathcal{G}_2$.

Example 1. Translocation performed two chromosomes:

- Let $\mathcal{G}_1 = \{\{g_1, g_3, g_4\}, \{g_2, g_6, g_5, g_7, g_8\}\}$
- $\rho(\mathcal{G}_1) = \{\{g_1, g_2\}, \{g_3, g_4, g_5, g_6, g_7, g_8\}\}$

3. The Minimum Translocation Synteny Problem

Definition 4. The problem of computing the minimum translocation syntenic distance, the MinSyn problem, is the following optimization problem:

- Input: A finite set G and two genomes $\mathcal{G}_1, \mathcal{G}_2 \in \Gamma_G$.
- Feasible solutions: Every sequence $\rho_1, \ldots, \rho_l$ of translocations satisfying $\mathcal{G}_1 \rho_1, \ldots, \rho_l = \mathcal{G}_2$.
- Costs: For a feasible solution $\rho_1, \ldots, \rho_l$, the costs are $cost(\rho_1, \ldots, \rho_l) = l$.
- Optimization goal: Minimization.

Definition 5. [Böckenhauer[7]] Let G be a finite set and let $\mathcal{G}_1 = \{S_1, \ldots, S_k\} \in \Gamma_G$ and $\mathcal{G}_2 = \{T_1, \ldots, T_n\} \in \Gamma_G$ be two genomes over G where $n \geq k$.

We define $G' = \{1, \ldots, n\}$, $\mathcal{G}'_1 = \{S'_1, \ldots, S'_k\}$ and $\mathcal{G}'_2 = \{\{1\}, \ldots, \{n\}\}$, where

$$S'_i = \bigcup_{x \in S_i} \{j | x \in T_j\}$$

for all $1 \leq i \leq k$. The pair $(\mathcal{G}'_1, \mathcal{G}'_2)$ is then called the compact representation of $(G, \mathcal{G}_1, \mathcal{G}_2)$.

Compact representation is useful when computing syntenic distance *i.e.* distance considering also fusion and fission as genome operations. In Böckenhauer[7], it was proven that the syntenic distance of two genomes $\mathcal{G}_1$ and $\mathcal{G}_2$ is the same as the syntenic distance of their compact representation, $\mathcal{G}'_1$ and $\mathcal{G}'_2$. Because of this property, our algorithm for the minimum translocation synteny problem focuses on using the compact representation of a pair of genomes as input.

Let $I = (\mathcal{G}_1, \mathcal{G}_2)$ be the compact representation where $\mathcal{G}_1 = \{S_1, \ldots, S_n\}$ and $\mathcal{G}_2 = \{\{1\}, \ldots, \{n\}\}$. The synteny graph for I is an undirected graph $Syngraph(I) = (V, E)$ with $V = \mathcal{G}_1$ and $S_i, S_j \in E$ if and only if $i \neq j$ and $S_i \cap S_j \neq \emptyset$ for all $1 \leq i, j \leq k$. (Bockenhauer[7])

Definition 6. [Belenzo, *et al.*[8]] Let $I = (G, G_1, G_2)$ be the compact representation of an input instance. Furthermore, let $G_1 = \{S_1, \ldots, S_n\}$ and $G_2 = \{\{1\}, \ldots, \{n\}\}$. We say that our input instance is a square instance if and only if $n = k$.

Definition 7. [Belenzo, *et al.*[8]] Suppose $I = (G, G_1, G_2)$ be the compact representation of a square input instance, then $Syngraph(I) = (V, E, \Sigma, S)$ is a square synteny graph where $|V| = |\Sigma|$. Let $C_i, 1 \leq i \leq p$, be the connected components of $Syngraph(I)$. $C_i = (V_i, E_i, \Sigma_i, S_i)$ is an undirected graph where:

- $V_i \subseteq V$, $\bigcup_{i=1}^{p} V_i = V$ and $V_i \cap V_j = \emptyset, 1 \leq i, j \leq p, i \neq j$.
- $S_i \subseteq S, S_i$, contains the original mapping of v for all $v \in V_i$, $\bigcup_{i=1}^{p} S_i = S$ and $S_i \cap S_j = \emptyset, 1 \leq i, j \leq p, i \neq j$.
- $\Sigma_i \subset \Sigma$, $\Sigma_i = \bigcup S_i(v)$, for all $v \in V_i$, $\bigcup_{i=1}^{p} \Sigma_i = \Sigma$ and $\Sigma_i \cap \Sigma_j = \emptyset, 1 \leq i, j \leq p, i \neq j$.
- $E_i \subseteq E$ which contains all adjacent edges of v for all $v \in V_i$, $\bigcup_{i=1}^{p} E_i = E$, and $E_i \cap E_j = \emptyset, 1 \leq i, j \leq p, i \neq j$.

Furthermore, we say that $C_i, 1 \leq i \leq p$, is a square component if and only if $|V_i| = |\Sigma_i|$.

We use the compact representation and the resulting synteny graph as input for the minimum translocation synteny problem.

Example 2. Input:
$\mathcal{G}_1 = \{\{g_1, g_3, g_4\}, \{g_2, g_6\}, \{g_5, g_7, g_8\}\}$,
$\mathcal{G}_2 = \{\{g_1, g_2\}, \{g_3, g_4, g_5\}, \{g_6, g_7, g_8\}\}$,
$\mathcal{G}'_1 = \{\{1, 2\}, \{1, 3\}, \{2, 3\}\}$,
$\mathcal{G}'_2 = \{\{1\}, \{2\}, \{3\}\}$.
$D(\mathcal{G}_1, \mathcal{G}_2) = D(\mathcal{G}'_1, \mathcal{G}'_2)$

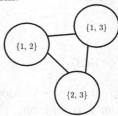

Synteny graph from Example 2

3.1. *On the Prioritization of the Translocation Operation*

Consider the following genomes in compact representation:

- $\mathcal{G}_1 = \{\{1, 2\}, \{3\}\}$
- $\mathcal{G}_2 = \{\{1, 3\}, \{2\}\}$

Generating $\mathcal{G}_2$ without performing translocations would take two (2) steps via fusion and fission. Generating the same genome via translocation would only take one (1) step. In general, translocation is a combination of both fusion and fission in a single-cost step.

3.2. *Existing work on the Minimum Translocation Synteny Problem*

An algorithm for square instances with square connected components, as described in Belenzo, *et al.*[8], using only translocation that runs in polynomial time was devised by Belenzo, *et al.*[8].

This algorithm uses a breadth-first search approach in finding the minimum number of translocations with a running time of $O(n^2)$, for both in time and space. The number of translocations performed is equivalent to the number of vertices, at minimum, and the number of edges, at maximum. However, Belenzo[8] did not device a way to select the starting vertex such that the number of translocations is minimized. Furthermore, the algorithm only considers the indices contained by each vertex in performing translocations.

4. An Algorithm for Translocation Syntenic Distance

The study presents an algorithm called the MINTRANSYN algorithm. A prioritization mechanism is used to select the starting vertex which not only considers the indices inside each vertex but the weight of the edges between the vertices as well. The components, behavior, properties, complexity, and quality of the algorithm is presented in this section.

The MINTRANSYN algorithm goes as follows:

(1) The two genomes, $\mathcal{G}_1$ and $\mathcal{G}_2$, should be in compact representation converted in to their synteny graph forms.
(2) To initialize the MINTRANSYN algorithm we create and initialize lists *IndexCount*, *Matches*, and *VertexCount* where:

- *IndexCount* is the number of vertices in which each index appears.
- *Matches* is the number of common indices every pair-wise combination of vertices.
- *VertexCount* is the number of indices in each vertex.

(3) While Graph G is not equal to the desired Graph G_2, the following are repeatedly done:

(a) Solve for k using *FindK(IndexCount)*.
(b) Find V_i using *VertexMaxScore()*. The starting vertex V_i is used as the initial vertex to be isolated at any given round of translocation. For V_i, we select a vertex that contains the index index k, with the maximum *VertexScore*, where *VertexScore = NumberofVertices + NumberofEdges*.

(c) Find V_j using $VertexMaxMatch()$. The round vertex V_j is the vertex in which translocation is performed against V_i. For V_j, there are two possible cases:

- If only V_i contains k (i.e.: Index k is only present in V_i, and nowhere else in Graph G), we find V_j, a vertex with the maximum number of common indices with respect to Vertex V_i over Graph G.
- Else, if the index k is present in other vertices in Graph G, we find V_j, a vertex that contains k with the maximum number of common indices with respect to Vertex V_i over Graph G.

Through this selection mechanism, we prioritize candidates that contain k with a maximum $VertexScore$ for V_i, and candidates that contain k and has the maximum $ComputeIntersection$ value for V_j, followed by candidates that don't contain k but still has common indices with V_i.

(d) Perform Translocation using $Translocate(G, V_i, V_j)$.

- If only V_i contains k, all other indices in V_i is moved to V_j.
- Else, if the index k is present in V_j, index k is moved from V_j to V_i and all other indices in V_i is moved to V_j.

(e) Increment $TranslocationCount$ by 1.
(f) Recalculate $IndexCount$, $Matches$, and $VertexCount$ in preparation for the next round of vertex selection and translocation using functions $ComputeIndexCount(G)$, $ComputeMatches(G)$, and $ComputeVertexCount(G)$, respectively.

(4) Once the Graph G is equal to the desired Graph G_2, the algorithm exits the while loop, halts, and returns $TranslocationCount$.

4.1. *The MinTranSyn Algorithm Simulated on a 2-Regular Graph*

Figures 1-6 is a simulation that demonstrates the algorithm working an a 2-regular graph. It also shows case where k can not be selected in the initial step and so an arbitrary k is selected instead.

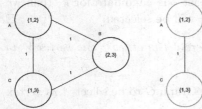

Fig. 1. 2-Regular Graph

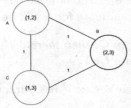

Fig. 2. $k = 1$, $V_i = A$, $V_j = C$.

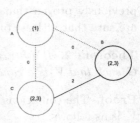

Fig. 3. *Translocation Count* = 1.

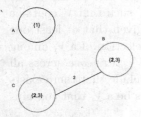

Fig. 4. $k = 2$, $V_i = B$, $V_j = C$.

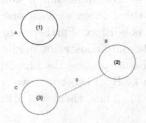

Fig. 5. *Translocation Count* = 2.

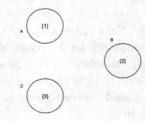

Fig. 6. $G = G_2$.

4.2. *Number of Translocations Performed by the Algorithm*

Theorem 1. *If G is not equal to G_2, then there exists at least one index i in G such that i is a candidate for k.*

Proof. First we discuss the properties of index k. A candidate for k is an index in G that should satisfy the following properties:

- k should be present in at least one vertex in G.
- k should be the index that appears least across all vertices in G.

Given these properties, and that G is not equal to G_2, we are sure that there exists at least one index i that is present in at least one vertex. This fact satisfies the first condition - making the said index i a candidate for k.

To select k, the MYNTRANSYN algorithm chooses a candidate that appears least across all vertices. This data is stored in the *IndexCount* list, computed by the subroutine COMPUTEINDEXCOUNT. Given that we have previously proven that there exists at least one candidate for k, then we are sure that at least one candidate for k will be selected. $\square$

Theorem 2. *If a k exists in G, then there exists at least one vertex V in G such that V is a candidate for V_i.*

Proof. The conditions for a Vertex V in Graph G to be selected as vertex V_i is as follows:

- V should contain the index k returned by the FINDK algorithm.
- V has the highest $VertexScore$.

By Theorem 1, the index k will always exist while G is not equal to G_2, and that k is in G, we conclude that k definitely lies in one of the vertices in G. Therefore, there exists at least one V such that V contains k. This satisfies the first condition. Furthermore, given that at least one candidate for V_i exists, the only constraint in the selection of a V_i among all candidates is that it should possess the highest $VertexScore$ across all vertices in G that contain k. By Theorem 1, we conclude that there exists at least one candidate for V_i. Thus, there will always be a V_i that contains k in G. $\square$

Theorem 3. *If V_i exists in Graph G, then there exists at least one other Vertex V in G such that an edge connecting V and V_i exists.*

Proof. In the compact representation of a genome, an edge exists between two vertices V_1 an V_2 if and only if there exists at least index in V_1 that also exists in V_2. By Theorem 2 we have proven that V_i contains k, an index that appears in at least two vertices, we are sure that there exists at least one other vertex V in G such that it also contains k. Thus, there exist at least one vertex V in G such that an edge is connecting V and V_i. $\square$

Theorem 4. *For every vertex V in G, if there exists an edge connecting V and V_i, where V is not equal to V_i, then V is a candidate for V_j.*

Proof. In a synteny graph of a genome, an edge exists between two vertices if and only if there are common indices amond the two vertices. Furthermore, V_j is the vertex with the most number of common indices with respect to V_i as can be seen in Algorithm MYNTRANSYN. By the definition of k, we know that k is in V_i. Suppose that k only appears in two vertices. Even if it already appears in V_i, we could still conclude that there exists another vertex V in G such that V contains k - therefore an edge exists between

V and V_i. Since the only condition for a vertex to be a candidate for V_j is that there should be an edge that exists between the said vertex and V_i, therefore there exists at least one candidate for V_j. □

Definition 8. An index i is isolatable if it exists in at most two vertices in G.

Theorem 5. *An index i that exists in at most two vertices in G is isolatable in one translocation step.*

Proof. There exists an index k that can be selected such that it appears least across all vertices as proven in Theorem 1. Given that we have such an index, we now look for vertex V_i. Note that V_i always exists by Theorem 2. We know that a vertex V in G exists that contains k. Since V satisfies our condition for V_i, we are able to select our vertex V_i such that it contains k and has the maximum number of indices and edges in total.

By Theorem 4, a round vertex V_j exists such that $(V_i, V_j) \in E$ and k exists in at most 2 vertices of G. Performing a translocation step on V_j which contains k, the following cases can arise:

- Case 1: The index k exist in both vertices V_i and V_j.
- Case 2: The index k exist only in vertex V_i.

In the first case, the translocation step would remove index k from V_j and all other indices in V_i will be transferred over to V_j. In the second case, the translocation step will transfer over all indices that is not k in V_i to V_j. Performing translocation on V_i and V_j would result in isolating V_i as the k would no longer exist in any other vertex and V_i contains only the index k. Therefore, it is isolated from the graph G - making it isolatable in a single translocation step. □

Lemma 1. *If all indices i in Graph G are isolatable, as described in Definition 8, then the number of translocations performed in* MinTranSyn *is* $O(|V|)$.

Proof. By Theorem 5, isolating an index that exist in at most two vertices takes only one step, therefore a graph whose vertices contains indices that exist in at most 2 vertices will take at most n translocations in order for all the indices to be isolated. □

Theorem 6. *For all square instances with square connected components of G, the total number of translocations is $O(|V|)$ if at any given round of translocation, there exists a candidate for k that is isolatable.*

Proof. Consider the following vertices in G: $V_i : \{a, b, c\} \cup l_i, i = 1, 2, \ldots, n$ where $\{a, b, c\}, l_i \subseteq$ of indices in V_i and $\{indices in V_i\} - l_i = \{a, b, c\}$. a, b, and c, are indices common across all vertices $V_1, \ldots, V_n$.

Using Lemma 1, if a vertex V_i contains an index k in l_i that is isolatable, we would have one less index that needs to be isolated upon isolating k. Isolating each index in a subset l_i would take at most $n - 3$ translocation steps leaving us with at most 3 vertices. Isolating the remaining indices would take at most 3 translocation steps. Therefore, the total number of translocations is $n - 3 + 3 = n$. $\qquad \square$

4.3. Time Complexity of the Algorithm

Remark 4.1. The Time complexity of the MINTRANSYN algorithm is $O(n^3)$. For the pseudocode of the MINTRANSYN algorithms and a detailed list of its subroutines, please refer to Appendix A. Table 1 shows the summary of time complexities of the algorithms in the MINTRANSYN algorithm.

Table 1.   Algorithms in MINTRANSYN and their time complexities.

Algorithm	Time Complexity
Algorithm 1 COUNTITEMS()	$O(1)$
Algorithm 2 COMPUTEINTERSECTION()	$O(n)$
Algorithm 3 COMPUTEINDEXCOUNT()	$O(n^2)$
Algorithm 4 COMPUTEVERTEXCOUNT()	$O(n)$
Algorithm 5 COMPUTEMATCHES()	$O(n^2)$
Algorithm 6 FINDK()	$O(n)$
Algorithm 7 TRANSLOCATE()	$O(n)$
Algorithm 8 VERTEXMAXSCORE()	$O(n)$
Algorithm 9 VERTEXMAXMATCH()	$O(n)$
Algorithm 10 MINTRANSYN()	$O(n)$

4.4. On the Performance of the Algorithm

The MINTRANSYN algorithm and Belenzo, *et al.*'s algorithm have a time complexity of $O(n^3)$ and $O(n^2)$ respectively. However, the number of translocations performed by the algorithm by Belenzo[8] varies in the number of Translocations depending on the start vertex. Furthermore, their best case is the the number of vertices, while the worst case is the number of edges.

The prioritization of an index k to be isolated has led to the reduction in the number of translocations in the aforementioned instances. Furthermore, in such instances, the MINTRANSYN algorithm assures that every translocation results in the isolation of an index.

In the case of the MINTRANSYN algorithm, there are instances of the genome wherein Lemma 1 and Theorem 6 are applicable - where the number of translocations are equal or less than the number of vertices. This case includes instances of genomes whose synteny graph is either a 2-regular graph, a wheel graph, or a star graph. Furthermore, it can be shown that the MINTRANSYN algorithm is a more robust algorithm compared to Belenzo, *et al.*'s with respect to the number of translocations. This is seen in Figure 7.

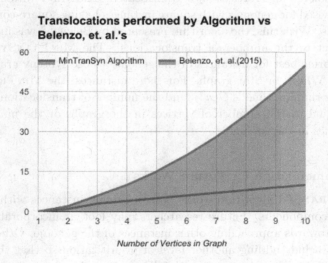

Fig. 7. Comparison of Upper-bounds of Translocations performed by the MinTranSyn Algorithm and the Algorithm by Belenzo, *et al.*[8] for 2-Regular, Wheel, and Star Graphs.

5. Summary

The MINTRANSYN algorithm presents a solution for translocation syntenic distance at a lower number of translocation steps compared to that in literature. Furthermore, by incorporating schemes for selecting starting vertices as well as a prioritization method for selecting index k, vertex V_i and vertex V_j, the algorithm can lessen the number of translocation steps to transform G into G_2.

With respect to having a 2-regular, wheel or a star graph, our proposed MINTRANSYN algorithm will always maintain a stable number of translocations at $O(|V|)$ with a running time of $O(n^3)$. Therefore in comparison to the algorithm by Belenzo[8], the upper-bound of the number of translocations observed for the aforementioned instances has been reduced from $\frac{n^2-n}{2}$ to n, where $n = |V|$ is the number of chromosomes, or indices, in the genome $\mathcal{G}_1$.

6. Conclusion

The MINTRANSYN algorithm presents a solution to the translocation syntenic distance problem by using a prioritization method in selecting an index to be isolated and vertices to be translocated. The MINTRANSYN algorithm is devised for genomes with square instances having square-connected components. With this, the algorithm presented by Belenzo[8] was improved with respect to the number of translocations. The MINTRANSYN algorithm performs best for instances of the genome whose synteny graphs are 2-Regular, Wheel, or Star graph. For these instances, the MINTRANSYN algorithm's running time is $O(n^3)$, and the number of translocations is less than or equal to the number of vertices in the graph, or the number of chromosomes in the genome.

7. Recommendation for Future Works

The MINTRANSYN algorithm works only on square instances with square connected components. Future researchers may look at incorporating the algorithm towards approaching other instances of the genome. Other work could also include adding another level of prioritization so that the algorithm works on genome instances with fully-connected synteny graph. As of the moment, there are instances of genomes having fully connected synteny graphs where the algorithm's prioritization mechanism becomes exhaustive - this happens for big graphs where all candidate indices for k have the same *IndexCount*. As for the algorithm's time complexity, improvement could still be done so that the running time of $O(n^3)$ could still be reduced.

References

1. M. Ridley, *Genome: The Autobiography of a Species in 23 Chapters* (Harper Collins, New York, USA, 2006).

2. Lister Hill National Center for Biomedical Communications, *The Human Genome Project* (US National Library of Medicine, 8600 Rockville Pike, Bethesda, MD 20894, 2016).
3. V. Ferretti, J. H. Nadeau and D. Sankoff, *Original Synteny*, in *Combinatorial Pattern Matching: 7th Annual Symposium, CPM 96 Laguna Beach, California, June 10–12, 1996 Proceedings*, eds. D. Hirschberg and G. Myers (Springer Berlin Heidelberg, Berlin, Heidelberg, 1996), Berlin, Heidelberg, pp. 159–167.
4. B. Dasgupta, T. Jiang, S. Kannan, M. Li and E. Sweedyk, On the complexity and approximation of syntenic distance, *Discrete Applied Mathematics* **88**, 59 (1998).
5. D. Liben-Nowell, On the structure of syntenic distance, *Journal of Computational Biology* **8**, 53 (February 2001).
6. D. Liben-Nowell, Gossip is synteny: Incomplete gossip and the syntenic distance between genomes, *J. Algorithms* **43**, 264 (May 2002).
7. H.-J. Böckenhauer and D. Bongartz, *Algorithmic Aspects of Bioinformatics (Natural Computing Series)* (Springer-Verlag New York, Inc., Secaucus, NJ, USA, 2007).
8. C. Belenzo, C. S. Corpuz, H. Adorna, J. Clemente, R. A. Juayong and J. M. Yap, *Polynomial-time Algorithm for Translocation Syntenic Distance*, in *Theory and Practice of Computation*, (WORLD SCIENTIFIC, 2017), pp. 1–25.

Appendix A. The MinTranSyn Algorithm

Algorithm 7.1 The main Algorithm. It performs rounds of translocation between selected V_is and V_js until G1 is transformed to G2, as explained in this paper.

Input: Graphs G and G2, the corresponding synteny graphs of $\mathcal{G}_1$ and $\mathcal{G}_2$, respectively.

Output: $TranslocationCount$, the number of translocations performed to transform G to G2.

1: **procedure** MINTRANSYN(Graph G, Graph G_2)
2:    $int TranslocationCount = 0$
3:    list $IndexCount[rows][2]$
4:    list $Matches[rows][rows]$
5:    list $VertexCount[rows][2]$
6:    $VertexCount = ComputeVertexCount(G)$
7:    $IndexCount = ComputeIndexCount(G)$
8:    $Matches = MatchesCount(G)$
9:    **while** $G \neq G_2$ **do**
10:      $k = FindK(IndexCount)$
11:      $V_i = VertexMaxScore(G, VertexCount, IndexCount, k)$
12:      $V_j = $
   $VertexMaxMatch(G, VertexCount, IndexCount, Matches, V_i, k)$
13:      $V_i, V_j = Translocate(G, V_i, V_j)$
14:      $TranslocationCount = TranslocationCount + 1$
15:      $VertexCount = ComputeVertexCount(G)$
16:      $IndexCount = ComputeIndexCount(G)$
17:      $Matches = MatchesCount(G)$
18:    **end while**
19:    **if** $G == G_2$ **then**
20:      Return $TranslocationCount$
21:    **end if**
22: **end procedure**

Algorithm 7.2 Returns the length of Item I.

    Input: Item I, a vertex in the graph.

    Output: $len(I)$, the number of indices contained by vertex I.

1: **procedure** COUNTITEMS(Item I)
2:     Return $len(I)$
3: **end procedure**

Algorithm 7.3 Computes the number of Vertices in which each Index appears.

    Input: Graph G, the working synteny Graph.

    Output: $IndexCount$, an array that shows the number of vertices in which every index is present.

1: **procedure** COMPUTEINDEXCOUNT(Graph G)
2:     list $IndexCount[rows][2]$
3:     **for** each vertex V in G **do**
4:         **for** each j in V **do**
5:             $IndexCount[j][1] = IndexCount[j][1]$
6:         **end for**
7:     **end for**
8:     **for** each vertex V in G **do**
9:         **if** $CountItems(V) == 1$ and $IndexCount[V][1] == 1$ **then**
10:            $IndexCount[V][1] = 0$
11:         **end if**
12:     **end for**
13:     Return $IndexCount$
14: **end procedure**

Algorithm 7.4 Returns the Cardinality of the Intersection of Two Vertices V_i and V_j.

Input: Graph G, Vertex V_i, and Vertex V_j, the working synteny graph and vertices to be translocated in a translocation round.

Output: $IntersectionCount$, the number of indices present in both V_i and V_j.

1: **procedure** COMPUTEINTERSECTION(Graph G, Vertex V_i, Vertex V_j)
2:      int $IntersectionCount = 0$
3:      **for** each n in V_i **do**
4:          **if** n in $V_j == True$ **then**
5:              $IntersectionCount = IntersectionCount + 1$
6:          **end if**
7:      **end for**
8:      Return $IntersectionCount$
9: **end procedure**

Algorithm 7.5 Returns a 2D Array that contains the number of indices contained in each vertex in Graph G.

Input: Graph G, the working synteny graph.

Output: $VertexCount$, an array the shows the number of indices present in each vertex.

1: **procedure** COMPUTEVERTEXCOUNT(Graph G)
2:      list $VertexCount[rows][2]$
3:      int $i = -1$
4:      **for** each Vertex V in G **do**
5:          $i = i + 1$
6:          $VertexCount[i][0] = V$
7:          $VertexCount[i][1] = CountItems(V)$
8:      **end for**
9:      Return $VertexCount$
10: **end procedure**

Algorithm 7.6 Returns a 2D array that stores the number of common indices for each pair-wise combination of vertices in Graph G.

Input: Graph G, the working synteny graph.

Output: *Matches*, an array that shows the count of common indices for each pair-wise combination of vertices.

1: **procedure** COMPUTEMATCHES(Graph G)
2:      list $Matches[rows][rows]$
3:      int $i = -1$
4:      int $j = -1$
5:      **for** each V_i in G **do**
6:          $i = i + 1$
7:          **for** each V_j in G **do**
8:              $j = j + 1$
9:              **if** $V_i \neq V_j$ **then**
10:                 $Matches[i][j] = ComputeIntersection(G, V_i, V_j)$
11:                 $Matches[j][i] = Matches[i][j]$
12:             **end if**
13:         **end for**
14:     **end for**
15:     Return $Matches$
16: **end procedure**

Algorithm 7.7 Returns the index k that appears least among all connected vertices in Graph G.

Input: *IndexCount*, an array that shows the number of vertices in which every index is present.

Output: k, an index present in at least one of the vertices in Graph G that appears least among the vertices.

1: **procedure** FINDK(list $IndexCount[rows][2]$)
2:     int $k = 0$
3:     **while** $IndexCount[k][1] == 0$ **do**
4:         $k = k + 1$
5:     **end while**
6:     **for** int i from 0 to $rows$ **do**
7:         **if** $IndexCount[i][1]$ < $IndexCount[k][1]$ and $IndexCount[i][1] \neq 0$ **then**
8:             $k = i$
9:         **end if**
10:    **end for**
11:    Return k
12: **end procedure**

Algorithm 7.8 Performs the Translocation operation between Two Vertices V_i and V_j.

Input: Graph G, Vertex V_i, and Vertex V_j, the working synteny graph and vertices to be translocated in a translocation round.

Output: Vertex V_i, and Vertex V_j, the working vertices after a translocation round.

1: **procedure** TRANSLOCATE(Graph G, Vertex V_i, Vertex V_j, Index k)
2:     **if** k in $V_j == True$ **then**
3:         $V_j.pop(k)$
4:     **end if**
5:     **for** each index x in V_i **do**
6:         **if** $k \neq x$ **then**
7:             $V_i.pop(x)$
8:             $V_j.append(x)$
9:         **end if**
10:    **end for**
11:    Return V_i, V_j
12: **end procedure**

Algorithm 7.9 Returns a working vertex V_i which containts k and has the most number of connected edges and most number of indices.

Input: The working synteny graph G, the list $VertexCount$ that contains the number of indices in each vertex, the list $IndexCount$ that contains the number of vertices in which each index is present, and index k, the index that appears least among the vertices.

Output: V_i, one of the two vertices to be translocated.

1: **procedure** VERTEXMAXSCORE(Graph G, List $VertexCount[rows][2]$, List $IndexCount[rows][2]$, Index k)

2:     list $CandidateScore[IndexCount[k][1]][2]$

3:     int $CandidateCount = 0$

4:     **for** each Vertex V in G **do**

5:         **if** k in $V == True$ **then**

6:             $CandidateScore[CandidateCount][0] = V$

7:             $CandidateCount = CandidateCount + 1$

8:         **end if**

9:     **end for**

10:     **for** int j from 0 to $CandidateCount$ **do**

11:         $CandidateScore[j][1] = VertexCount[CandidateScore[j][0]][1] + IndexCount[CandidateScore[j][0]][1]$

12:     **end for**

13:     $V_i = CandidateScore[0][0]$

14:     $V_iScore = CandidateScore[0][1]$

15:     **for** int i from 0 to $CandidateCount$ **do**

16:         **if** $CandidateScore[i][1] > V_iScore$ **then**

17:             $V_i = CandidateScore[i][0]$

18:             $V_iScore = CandidateScore[i][1]$

19:         **end if**

20:     **end for**

21:     Return V_i

22: **end procedure**

Algorithm 7.10 Returns a round vertex V_j which may or may not contain k and has the most number of common indices with V_i.

Input: The working synteny graph G, the list $VertexCount$ that contains the number of indices in each vertex, the list $IndexCount$ that contains the number of vertices in which each index is present, the vertex V_i in which a selected V_j will be translocated with and index k, the index that appears least among the vertices.

Output: V_j, the vertex to be translocated with V_i.

1: **procedure** VERTEXMAXMATCH(Graph G, List $VertexCount[rows][2]$, List $IndexCount[rows][2]$, List $Matches[rows][rows]$, Vertex V_i, Index k)
2:     list $CandidateScore[IndexCount[k][1]][3]$
3:     int $CandidateCount = 0$
4:     int $ExistenceOfK = 0$
5:     **for** each Vertex V in G **do**
6:         **if** $V \neq V_i$ **then**
7:             $CandidateScore[CandidateCount][0] = V$
8:             $CandidateScore[CandidateCount][1] = ComputeIntersection(G, V_i, V)$
9:             **if** k in $V == True$ **then**
10:                 $CandidateScore[CandidateCount][2] = 1$
11:                 $ExistenceOfK = 1$
12:             **else**
13:                 $CandidateScore[CandidateCount][2] = 0$
14:             **end if**
15:             $CandidateCount = CandidateCount + 1$
16:         **end if**
17:     **end for**
18:     $V_j = null$
19:     $V_j Score = 0$
20:     **for** int i from 0 to $CandidateCount$ **do**
21:         **if** $ExistenceOfK == 1$ **then**
22:             **if** $CandidateScore[i][1] > V_j Score$ and $CandidateScore[i][2] == 1$ **then**
23:                 $V_j = CandidateScore[i][0]$
24:                 $V_j Score = CandidateScore[i][1]$
25:             **end if**
26:         **else**
27:             **if** $CandidateScore[i][1] > V_j Score$ **then**
28:                 $V_j = CandidateScore[i][0]$
29:                 $V_j Score = CandidateScore[i][1]$
30:             **end if**
31:         **end if**
32:     **end for**
33:     Return V_j
34: **end procedure**

An Oracle Design for Grover's Quantum Search Algorithm for Solving the Exact String Matching Problem

Jeffrey A. Aborot

Computer Software Division
Advanced Science and Technology Institute
Department of Science and Technology
Philippines
E-mail: jep@asti.dost.gov.ph

Grover's quantum search algorithm is a template for doing quantum search in unstructured search spaces. The details of the oracle in Grover's algorithm is abstracted for the purpose of analyzing the bound on the number of queries the algorithm must make in order to find the target element of the search space. In order for Grover's quantum search algorithm to be usable in a specific unstructured search problem, one must provide details on the inner workings of the oracle.

Specifically, we present a high-level and basic design of the oracle using the quantum computing model specific to the exact string matching problem. We describe our design using the quantum circuit model of computing and show that the gate complexity of the circuit is linear with respect to the product of the length of the pattern and the size of the alphabet. We have suggested a quantum memory structure for storage and retrieval of the input text. The quantum circuit we presented requires scratch qubits linear to the product of the length of the pattern and the size of the alphabet to reduce the size of the scratch register without exponential increase in the count of elementary gates required for the computation.

Keywords: Quantum computing; Quantum circuit model; Pattern matching; Grover's quantum search algorithm; Oracle.

1. Introduction

Grover's quantum algorithm for the unstructured search problem is one of the earliest discovered quantum algorithms[1], contemporary to Shor's quantum algorithm for prime factorization[2]. Given an unstructured search space we can classically perform a generate-and-test procedure on the indices of the elements of the search space. We pick an index from the search space and test if the element in that index corresponds to our target element. One can perform this procedure until the picked index corresponds to the target element. This procedure can be performed with or without replacement of the picked index. The distribution of the probabilities of picking each element in the unstructured search space can be expressed in quantum mechanical notation as

$$\frac{1}{\sqrt{N}} \sum_{i=0}^{N-1} |i\rangle$$

where N is the size of the unstructured search space and i is the index of each element in the search space. In this distribution, each element in the space has the same probability of getting picked when performing the generate-and-test procedure, which is $1/N$. Grover's discovery of the quantum mechanical technique *amplitude amplification* as part of his quantum search algorithm influences the probability distribution of the elements of the search space by increasing the probability of a target index and decreasing that of the others. Grover's quantum search algorithm makes use of an *oracle* in order to abstract the identification of the target element within the search space. An oracle is used in an algorithm when one wishes to set aside the details of a sub-procedure which will be specific to the domain area to which the algorithm will be applied. Algorithms which solve the same problem may be compared with each other in terms of the count of their calls to the oracle necessary to solve the problem, e.g. number of oracle calls of a classical unstructured search algorithm v. number of oracle calls of a quantum unstructured search algorithm. Algorithms assume an $\mathcal{O}(1)$ time complexity for an oracle. Application of an algorithm which uses an oracle to a specific problem will require specific implementation details of the oracle for it to be useful. The complexity of the oracle is expected to be polynomial (or better) with respect to the size of its input for the overall algorithm to be efficient with respect to the size of the problem input.

Grover's quantum unstructured search algorithm has been used in solving the exact pattern matching problem on strings [3-5]. In the exact pattern matching problem on strings, one is given an input string of length N denoted as the text T and another input string of length M denoted as the pattern P such that $M < N$. Both strings are defined over some alphabet Σ. The goal is to identify an index i of a substring in T which exactly matches P, i.e. $T_{i+j} = P_j$ for $0 \leq i < N - M$ and $0 \leq j < M$. All throughout the rest of this paper, let $T_{i,k} = T_i, T_{i+1}, \ldots, T_{i+k}$. For example, if $\Sigma = \{a, c, t, g\}$, $T = actg$ and $P = ct$ then the expected solution index in T will be the index 1, $T_{1,2} = P$. In Ref. 3 the computation of the oracle is translated to the task of identifying subsequences with Hamming distance equal to 0 with respect to an input sample sequence. In Ref. 4, a combination of probabilistic oracle and deterministic oracle is used to minimize the search space and then to validate the remaining elements. In Ref. 5 the computation of the oracle is translated to the execution of a set of query operators which identifies existence of specific symbols within each substring. These works substantiates the applicability of Grover's quantum unstructured search algorithm into the exact pattern matching problem on strings. However, no details on the lower level design of the oracle have been provided in these works. In all these works, the setting of the registers into states corresponding to substrings of the input text and the comparison of these substrings to the input pattern are simply assumed.

In this paper we provide a lower level design of the oracle for Grover's quantum unstructured search algorithm for the exact pattern matching problem on strings by presenting a quantum circuit which implements the comparison between the substrings of the input text and the input pattern.

Specifically, we make the following contributions.

(1) We describe how substrings of the input text can be stored and retrieved in a quantum mechanical setting (Section 2.1).
(2) We present a quantum circuit design which implements the comparison between two input strings with gate complexity in $\mathcal{O}(M \log(|\Sigma|))$ using 2-qubit and 1-qubit elementary gates (Section 2.2).

We then conclude in Section 3.

2. A quantum circuit for string matching oracle

We divide the operation of the oracle into two steps.

(1) The retrieval of each M-length substring of input string T given each index in T.
(2) The comparison of each M-length substring of T to the input string P.

Given an index i in T encoded as state of a register, $|i\rangle$, the oracle shifts the phase of the state of a register when the substring $T_{i,i+M-1}$ exactly matches P. This operation can be expressed as

$$|i\rangle \rightarrow (-1)^{f(i)}|i\rangle$$

such that

$$f(i) = \begin{cases} 1 & \text{if } T_{i,i+M-1} = P \\ 0 & \text{otherwise.} \end{cases}$$

A high-level description of the operation of the oracle for string matching is shown in Fig. 1.

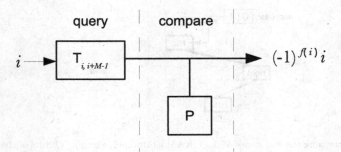

Fig. 1. A high-level description of the operation of the oracle. The operation of the oracle is divided into the query step and the comparison step.

2.1. *QRAM for substring storage and retrieval*

We query the M-length substrings of T using a *random access memory*. A random access memory is a computer memory module which allows for access of elements within the memory in a non-sequential manner. A *quantum random access memory* (QRAM) is a random access memory which utilizes input and output registers composed of qubits instead of classical bits. In Ref. 6, V. Giovannetti, S. Lloyd and L. Maccone presented a QRAM architecture which allows for accessing elements in $\mathcal{O}(\log(N))$ time steps. For example, an *address register* a and a *data register* d are set into the quantum superposition state $\sum_i \alpha_i |i\rangle_a |0\rangle_d$. The operation of the QRAM given the state of the address register is the transformation

$$\sum_i \alpha_i |i\rangle_a |0\rangle_d \to \sum_i \alpha_i |i\rangle_a |D_i\rangle_d$$

where D_i is the data stored at address i. The QRAM architecture proposed by Giovannetti et al. is a bifurcation graph of switches of height $\log(N)$. Each switch in the bifurcation is a *qutrit*, i.e a three-level quantum physical system, which has three possible states, namely, $|wait\rangle$, $|left\rangle$ and $|right\rangle$. An element of a QRAM is indexed from $00\ldots0$ to $11\ldots1$. Each element in the QRAM is accessed by tracing a route from the root node of the bifurcation graph down to its leaf nodes. To trace a route from the root node to the a leaf node, each qubit of the address register is sent through the bifurcation graph in sequence. For example, a QRAM which has size 8 and a 3-qubit address register a in state $|011\rangle$ will have the bifurcation graph in Fig. 2 after all the qubits of its address register have been sent from the root node down to its leaf nodes. When a qubit in state $|0\rangle$ reaches a switch in $|wait\rangle$ state, the switch's state is transformed from its current state into the

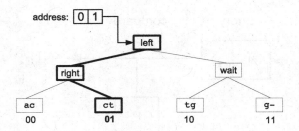

Fig. 2. Accessing the leaf nodes of the QRAM's bifurcation graph. Qubits of the address register are sent through the graph in succession until the leaf nodes are reached. The element at address 01 is reached by carving the trace *left* (0) → *right* (1).

state $|\text{left}\rangle$. Otherwise, the state of the switch is transformed into the state $|\text{right}\rangle$. A qubit which reaches a switch that is not in state $|\text{wait}\rangle$ is directed towards the state of the switch, which is either $|\text{left}\rangle$ or $|\text{right}\rangle$. Once a trace has been made from the root node to the target leaf node a *bus qubit* is sent through the trace to the leaf node where the target data resides. The bus qubit interacts with the memory cell in the leaf node in order to copy the target data. The bus qubit is sent back through the trace in order to decorrelate it from the address register. This decorrelation process happens by uncomputing, i.e. application of same unitary transformation, the state of each switch back to $|\text{wait}\rangle$ state as the bus qubit passes through each one of them. After uncomputing the state of the root node, the state of the bus qubit is swapped with the state of the data register. This makes the state of the address register and that of the data register correlated with each other. For example, in Fig. 3 the data in address 01 of the QRAM is made accessible via the state of the data register. If the state of the address register is a quantum superposition state, then the state of the data register after the query operation is a superposition of states which encode target data and which is also correlated with their corresponding states in the address register.

Specific to the exact pattern matching problem on strings, we will use Giovannetti et al.'s QRAM architecture and algorithm for storing and retrieving substrings of the input string T. The leaf nodes in the bifurcation graph of the QRAM will be the M-length substrings of the input string T. The address register of the QRAM is composed of $\log(N)$ qubits while its data register is composed of $M \log(|\Sigma|)$ qubits. The depth of the bifurcation graph of the QRAM will be $\log(N)$ and it will be composed of $2(N-1)$ qutrit switches. Only $\log(N)$ of the qutrit switches will be active

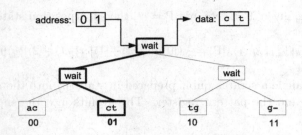

Fig. 3. Copying data from a leaf node of a QRAM's bifurcation graph to the data register. The bus qubit is sent back through the trace carved by the address qubits from the addressed leaf node to the root node. The bus qubit swaps its state with the state of the data register. The state of each switch along the trace are also reverted to the *wait* state as the bus qubit state passes through each of them.

during each query to the QRAM. By setting the address register and the data register of the QRAM into the superposition state

$$\sqrt{\frac{1}{N}} \sum_{i=0}^{N-1} |i\rangle_a |0\rangle_d \tag{1}$$

we expect the QRAM to perform the transformation

$$\sqrt{\frac{1}{N}} \sum_{i}^{N-1} |i\rangle_a |0\rangle_d \rightarrow \sqrt{\frac{1}{N}} \sum_{i=0}^{N-1} |i\rangle_a |T_{i,i+M-1}\rangle_d. \tag{2}$$

For example, given $\Sigma = \{a, c, t, g\}$, $T = actg$ and $P = ct$ the state of the address and data register of the QRAM will be

$$\frac{1}{2} \sum_{i=0}^{3} |i\rangle_a |T_{i,i+M-1}\rangle_d = \frac{1}{2} (|0\rangle|ac\rangle + |1\rangle|ct\rangle + |2\rangle|tg\rangle + |3\rangle|g-\rangle)$$

We use a filler symbol − to fill the rightmost positions in the state $|3\rangle|g-\rangle$. This keeps the count of the superpositioned states in Eq. 2 equal to N.

2.2. *Quantum circuit for symbol comparison*

Given the output state of the address register and data register of the QRAM, we entangle a *pattern register* prepared in the state $|P\rangle$. This results to the superposition state

$$\sqrt{\frac{1}{N}} \sum_{i=0}^{N-1} |i\rangle_a |T_{i,i+M-1}\rangle_d |P\rangle. \tag{3}$$

For example, given $T = actg$ and $P = ct$, the superposition state will be

$$\sqrt{\frac{1}{N}} \sum_{i=0}^{N-1} |i\rangle_a |T_{i,i+M-1}\rangle_d |P\rangle = \frac{1}{2} \left(|0\rangle |ac\rangle |ct\rangle + |1\rangle |ct\rangle |ct\rangle + |2\rangle |tg\rangle |ct\rangle + |3\rangle |g-\rangle |ct\rangle \right)$$

We also entangle a scratch qubit prepared in state $|0\rangle$ into the registers of the QRAM and the pattern register. This results into the superposition state

$$\sqrt{\frac{1}{N}} \sum_{i=0}^{N-1} |i\rangle_a |T_{i,i+M-1}\rangle_d |P\rangle |0\rangle \tag{4}$$

In our example, the resulting superposition state will be the state

$$\frac{1}{2} \left(|0\rangle |ac\rangle |ct\rangle |0\rangle + |1\rangle |ct\rangle |ct\rangle |0\rangle + |2\rangle |tg\rangle |ct\rangle |0\rangle + |3\rangle |g-\rangle |ct\rangle |0\rangle \right)$$

We will use the scratch qubit to record the result of our comparison between each substring and P. We put the scratch qubit into the state $|1\rangle$ if a substring exactly matches with P. In our example, the result of the comparison operation will be the superposition state

$$\frac{1}{2} \left(|0\rangle |ac\rangle |ct\rangle |0\rangle + |1\rangle |ct\rangle |ct\rangle |1\rangle + |2\rangle |tg\rangle |ct\rangle |0\rangle + |3\rangle |g-\rangle |ct\rangle |0\rangle \right)$$

Only the state of the scratch qubit entangled with the index 1 of T will be transformed from state $|0\rangle$ to $|1\rangle$ since $T_{1,2} = P$.

We perform comparison of symbols of substrings and P using binary encodings of symbols in Σ. For example, if we assume the following binary encoding for the symbols in Σ,

$$a \rightarrow 000 \quad c \rightarrow 001 \quad t \rightarrow 010 \quad g \rightarrow 011 \quad - \rightarrow 100$$

then the state of the registers can be written as

$$\frac{1}{2}(|0\rangle |000, 001\rangle |001, 010\rangle |0\rangle + |1\rangle |001, 010\rangle |001, 010\rangle |1\rangle$$
$$+ |2\rangle |010, 011\rangle |001, 010\rangle |0\rangle + |3\rangle |011, 100\rangle |001, 010\rangle |0\rangle)$$

We may keep the encoding of the state of the address register in decimal format since we will not be performing computation on it. An example quantum circuit for the comparison of two strings of the same length is shown in Fig. 5. The quantum circuit for the comparison of two strings will be be composed of CNOT gates, Toffoli gates and NOT gates shown in Fig. 4.

The quantum circuit for comparison of two strings will require two input quantum registers, each encoding one of the input strings. We let the data

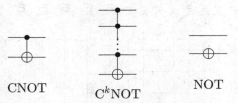

CNOT **C^kNOT** **NOT**

Fig. 4. Quantum gates composing the quantum circuit for string comparison. The CNOT gate flips the state of its target qubit if the state of its control qubit is $|1\rangle$. Similarly, the C^kNOT gate flips the state of its target qubit if the state of its k control qubits are both in state $|1\rangle$. The NOT gate simply flips the state of its target qubit.

register of a QRAM and the pattern register be the input registers to the quantum circuit. Each register will be composed of $M \log(|\Sigma|)$ qubits. For example, given our binary encoding for the symbols in Σ and the input string $P = ct$ and the substring $T_{0,1} = ac$, the input registers will be in the state

$$|d_{0,0}d_{0,1}d_{0,2}, d_{1,0}d_{1,1}d_{1,2}\rangle = |000, 001\rangle \tag{5}$$

and

$$|p_{0,0}p_{0,1}p_{0,2}, p_{1,0}p_{1,1}p_{1,2}\rangle = |001, 010\rangle. \tag{6}$$

The quantum circuit will also require $M \log(|\Sigma|)$ scratch qubits initialized in the state $|0\rangle$.

The first set of CNOT operators performs the comparison of the two input strings for each of their corresponding qubits such that

$$|s_{i,j}\rangle = |p_{i,j} \oplus d_{i,j}\rangle \tag{7}$$

for $0 \leq i < M, 0 \leq j < \log(|\Sigma|)$ where $|s_{i,j}\rangle$ is the state of the ij-th scratch qubit and M is the length of the input strings. For example, given the state of the registers in Eq'n. 5 and 6, the result of the computation of the first set of CNOT register in the circuit will be

$$|s_{0,0}\rangle = |0 \oplus 0\rangle = |0\rangle$$
$$|s_{0,1}\rangle = |0 \oplus 0\rangle = |0\rangle$$
$$|s_{0,2}\rangle = |0 \oplus 1\rangle = |1\rangle$$
$$|s_{1,0}\rangle = |0 \oplus 0\rangle = |0\rangle$$
$$|s_{1,1}\rangle = |0 \oplus 1\rangle = |1\rangle$$
$$|s_{1,2}\rangle = |1 \oplus 0\rangle = |1\rangle$$

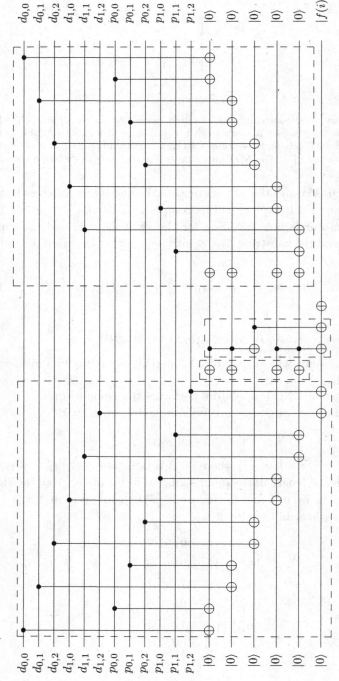

Fig. 5. A quantum circuit for comparing two strings of equal length. $d_{i,j}$ and $p_{i,j}$ correspond to the state of the qubits of two registers which encode the two input strings. In this example circuit, each symbol in the input strings is encoded using three qubits and the input strings have a length of two. The quantum circuit includes scratch bits with count equal to the length of the input strings multiplied by the number of qubits used to encode a single symbol. In this example circuit, 6 scratch qubits are required.

Corresponding qubits $d_{i,j}$ and $p_{i,j}$ which have the same state are evaluated into the state $|0\rangle$.

The succeeding set of NOT operators flips the state of the qubits of the scratch register. After the computation of these operators, scratch qubits which encode a match are put into the state $|1\rangle$ while those scratch qubits which encode a non-match are put into the state $|0\rangle$. In our example, the state of the scratch qubits are then transformed such that

$$|s_{0,0}\rangle = |1\rangle \quad |s_{0,1}\rangle = |1\rangle \quad |s_{0,2}\rangle = |0\rangle \quad |s_{1,0}\rangle = |1\rangle \quad |s_{1,1}\rangle = |0\rangle \quad |s_{1,2}\rangle = |0\rangle.$$

The next set of Toffoli and CNOT operators compute for the overall result of the comparison of the two input strings. If the two input strings matches exactly, the state of the last qubit will be transformed into the state $|0\rangle$. In our example, the computation of the Toffoli operators into the state of the qubits of the scratch register will result to the state

$$|s_{0,0}\rangle = |1\rangle \quad |s_{0,1}\rangle = |1\rangle \quad |s_{0,2}\rangle = |1\rangle \quad |s_{1,0}\rangle = |1\rangle \quad |s_{1,1}\rangle = |0\rangle \quad |s_{1,2}\rangle = |0\rangle.$$

The application of the single CNOT gate will transform the state of the scratch qubits such that

$$|s_{0,0}\rangle = |1\rangle \quad |s_{0,1}\rangle = |1\rangle \quad |s_{0,2}\rangle = |1\rangle \quad |s_{1,0}\rangle = |1\rangle \quad |s_{1,1}\rangle = |0\rangle \quad |s_{1,2}\rangle = |1\rangle.$$

Lastly, a single NOT operator is applied into the last scratch qubit. In our example, this flips the state of the qubit $s_{1,2}$. The resulting state of the scratch register will be

$$|s_{0,0}\rangle = |1\rangle \quad |s_{0,1}\rangle = |1\rangle \quad |s_{0,2}\rangle = |1\rangle \quad |s_{1,0}\rangle = |1\rangle \quad |s_{1,1}\rangle = |0\rangle \quad |s_{1,2}\rangle = |0\rangle.$$

The mirror half of the quantum circuit resets the state of the scratch qubits except for the last one. In our example, this set of CNOT operators transforms the state of the scratch register into the state

$$|s_{0,0}, s_{0,1}, s_{0,2}, s_{1,0}, s_{1,1}, s_{1,2}\rangle = |000000\rangle.$$

The state of the data register, pattern register and scratch register in our example will then be transformed into the final state

$$|000, 001\rangle|001, 010\rangle|000000\rangle.$$

The result of function $f(i)$ is encoded as the state of the last qubit in the scratch register, $|s_{M-1,\log(|\Sigma|-1)}\rangle$. In our example, the result of $f(0)$ for $T_{0,1} = ac$ and $P = ct$ is encoded as the state $|0\rangle$ and which corresponds to a non-exact match result. Executing the quantum circuit into $i = 1$ where $T_{1,2} = ct$ and $P = ct$ will transform the state of the last scratch qubit into the state $|1\rangle$.

The state of the registers after the execution of the quantum circuit for string comparison will be the superposition state

$$\sqrt{\frac{1}{N}} \sum_{i=0}^{N-1} |i\rangle_a |T_{i,i+M-1}\rangle |P\rangle_d |s_{M-1,\log(|\Sigma|)-1}\rangle \tag{8}$$

where we only included the state of the last qubit in the scratch register. To achieve the operation of the oracle for the exact string matching problem, we apply a Z operator into the last scratch qubit. This will result into the superposition state

$$\sqrt{\frac{1}{N}} \sum_{i=0}^{N-1} |i\rangle_a |T_{i,i+M-1}\rangle |P\rangle_d (-1)^{s_{M-1,\log(|\Sigma|)-1}} |s_{M-1,\log(|\Sigma|)-1}\rangle$$

$$= \sqrt{\frac{1}{N}} \sum_{i=0}^{N-1} |i\rangle_a |T_{i,i+M-1}\rangle |P\rangle_d (-1)^{f(i)} |s_{M-1,\log(|\Sigma|)-1}\rangle$$

$$= \sqrt{\frac{1}{N}} \sum_{i=0}^{N-1} (-1)^{f(i)} |i\rangle_a |T_{i,i+M-1}\rangle |P\rangle_d |s_{M-1,\log(|\Sigma|)-1}\rangle \tag{9}$$

We can then denote the transformation on the states of the registers resulting from the steps we defined in Section 2 as the superposition state

$$\sqrt{\frac{1}{N}} \sum_{i=0}^{N-1} (-1)^{f(i)} |i\rangle_a \tag{10}$$

where we exclude the states of the data register, pattern register and scratch register from Eq'n. 10. The resulting superposition state in Eq'n. 10 is then the same superposition state resulting from the oracle query in Grover's quantum search algorithm.

2.3. *Complexity*

The quantum circuit for the comparison of strings will require

- $2M \log(|\Sigma|)$ CNOT gates
- $M \log(|\Sigma|) - M + 1$ NOT gates
- M $C^{\log(|\Sigma|)-1}$NOT gates
- 1 C^{M-1}NOT gate

A single C^kNOT gate can be decomposed into $2(k-1)$ C^2NOT gates and 1 CNOT gates using $k-1$ additional scratch qubits. A single C^2NOT can be decomposed using 2 CNOT gates, 2 CV gates and 1 $CV^\dagger$ gate where

$V^2 = NOT$ gate[7]. The quantum circuit for string comparison will then be composed of

- $2M \log(|\Sigma|)$ CNOT gates
- $M \log(|\Sigma|) - M + 1$ NOT gates
- M $C^{\log(|\Sigma|)-1}$NOT gates $= 4M \log(|\Sigma|) - 7M$ CNOT gates $+ 4M \log(|\Sigma|) - 8$ CV gates $+ 2 \log(|\Sigma|) - 4$ $CV^\dagger$ gates
- 1 C^{M-1}NOT gate $= 4M - 7$ CNOT gates $+ 4M - 8$ CV gates $+ 2M - 4$ $CV^\dagger$ gates

Then, the quantum circuit for string comparison has gate complexity of $\mathcal{O}(M \log(|\Sigma|))$ where the quantum gates are 2-qubit and 1-qubit elementary gates[8].

3. Conclusion and further work

Grover's quantum search algorithm provides a template for quantum search on unstructured spaces. The oracle in Grover's quantum search algorithm abstracts away the details of the identification of solution elements within the search space. One needs to provide concrete design of the oracle in Grover's quantum search algorithm in order to fit the algorithm into specific unstructured search problems such as the exact string matching problem. We presented a high-level design of the oracle using the quantum circuit model of computing. We also suggested a quantum memory structure for storage and retrieval of the input text.

The quantum circuit we presented requires scratch qubits linear to the product of the length of the pattern and the size of the alphabet. We hope to reduce the size of the scratch register without exponential increase in the count of elementary gates required for the computation.

References

1. L. K. Grover, A fast quantum mechanical algorithm for database search, in *Proceedings, STOC 1996*, 1996.
2. P. W. Shor, Polynomial-Time Algorithms for Prime Factorization and Discrete Logarithms on a Quantum Computer *, *SIAM Journal on Computing* **26**, 1484 (1997).
3. L. C. Hollenberg, Fast quantum search algorithms in protein sequence comparisons: quantum bioinformatics., *Physical Review E* **62**, p. 4 (nov 2000).

4. H. Ramesh and V. Vinay, String matching in O(sqrt(n)+sqrt(m)) quantum time, *Journal of Discrete Algorithms* **1**, 103 (2003).

5. P. Mateus and Y. Omar, A Quantum Algorithm for Closest Pattern Matching, in *Quantum Information Processing: From Theory to Experiment*, eds. D. G. Angelakakis, M. Christandl, A. K. Ekert, A. Kay and S. Kulik (IOS Press, 2006) pp. 180–183.

6. V. Giovannetti, S. Lloyd and L. MacCone, Quantum random access memory, *Physical Review Letters* **100**, 1 (2008).

7. M. A. Nielsen and I. L. Chuang, *Quantum Computation and Quantum Information*, 1st edn. (Cambridge University Press, Cambridge, 2000).

8. A. Barenco, C. H. Bennett, R. Cleve, D. P. Divincenzo, N. Margolus, P. Shor, T. Sleator, J. A. Smolin and H. Weinfurter, Elementary gates for quantum computation, *Physical Review A* **52**, 3457 (1995).

PepSquad: A Tool for Finding Compact Structural Motifs from Peptides

Jym Paul A. Carandang, Jhoirene B. Clemente*,

John Erol M. Evangelista, and Henry N. Adorna

Algorithms of Complexity Lab, Department of Computer Science, University of the Philippines Diliman *E-mail: jbclemente@up.edu.ph*

Structural motifs are short segments of a protein 3D structure that may appear to be conserved in a group of functionally related set of proteins. Finding such structures are essential in the field of proteomics for drug discovery. In this paper, we present a tool for finding structural motifs from a given a set of peptides. The computational model of the problem is NP-hard. We provide a tool which is an implementation of a polynomial-time approximation scheme (PTAS) for identifying conserved regions of the peptide. The tool is able to find compact structural motifs efficiently and with a customizable performance guarantee.

Keywords: Structural Motif Finding, Polynomial-time Approximation Scheme.

1. Introduction

The ever-expanding database of amino acid sequences as well as the growing Protein Data Bank (PDB) of three-dimensional data of biological molecules have pushed the science beyond protein characterization to the study of the interplay between sequence, structure, and functions. Laboratory experiments, whilst still the gold standard, are unable to keep pace with the high-throughput developments in genomics and structural genomics. Thus, computational methods are required for such a study.

A structural motif is a segment present in a set of proteins that exhibits a high level of similarity. These substructures are known to be more conserved over the course of evolution[1] and are closely knit to protein function[2]. Thus, motifs provide valuable information in the study of the sequence-structure-function relationships. Majority of the approaches rely on well known databases of identified structural motifs, which is not capable of finding new structural motifs given a set of new peptides. This study, however, is focused on finding de novo structural motifs from a group of new peptides. The structural motif finding problem is a straightforward generalization of the motif finding problem in DNA and protein sequences. We are interested in a restricted variant called the compact structural motif finding problem, where we only consider structural motifs that can be enclosed in a ball with a specified radius. Notice that we fit our motif within a containing ball of radius, R. The assumption here is that our motif is compact and can be contained in a bounding sphere[3,4]. In[3], they showed that even with the restricted case, the problem of finding such segment is still NP-hard.

In this paper, we present the details of our implementation of Qian's Compact Motif Finding Algorithm in[3]. The algorithm is polynomial-time approximation scheme which provides a guarantee to the quality of the output solution. We modified the original algorithm which involves exhausting the discretized rotational space in 3D by using Kabsch algorithm in[5,6] for structural alignment. The implementation is available in a online repository which can be downloaded using the following link[a].

2. Preliminaries

Peptides are proteins which are composed of a short sequence of amino acids (or residues). The structure of a peptide is represented as a matrix composed of 3D coordinates for each atom. To further simplify the representation of proteins, we only consider the 3D coordinates of alpha carbons for each amino acid in the sequence.

Informally, we define the structural motif as a spatial pattern shared by subsets of the residues from different proteins. Here, we consider only the (R, C)-**compact motif** that is bounded by a sphere of radius R and contains no more than C non-motif residues. Formally, we use the following definition.

Definition 2.1. (R, C)-**Compact Motif Finding Problem**[3]
Given n protein structures $\mathcal{P}_1, \mathcal{P}_2, ..., \mathcal{P}_n$, the length of the motif, ℓ, the radius of a containing ball $R \in \mathbb{R}$, and the maximum allowable number of non-motif residue, C, find a consensus, $q = (q_1, q_2, ..., q_\ell)$; the (R, C)-compact motif u_i, $|u_i| = \ell$ that minimizes $\sum_{i-1}^{n} d(q, \tau_i(u_i))$ and its corresponding rigid transformation τ_i, $1 \leq i \leq n$.

The (R,C)-compact motif problem is shown to be NP-Hard in[3] due to its reduction from the local multiple alignment problem in sequences. The

---

[a]https://github.com/jbclemente/pepSquad.git

compactness of the motif given by parameter R in the input reduces the total number of feasible solutions that are subject to the minimization.

In order to evaluate how a collection of segments are similar to each other, we use the computaion of the $dRMSD$[3] which is the total pairwise dissimilarity of the RMSD between every pair of segments. The dRMSD is also used as our objective function. Given two substructures, $u = (u_1, u_2, ..., u_\ell)$ and $u = (v_1, v_2, ..., v_\ell)$, we define $dRMSD$ as $d(u, v) = \sum_{i=1}^{\ell} ||u_i - v_i||^2$, $||.||$ being the the euclidean distance.

In order to be able to compare protein molecules, we need to align them first. This is known as the structural alignment problem which aims to classify proteins via the similarity of their structures often by employing an objective function like the root mean square deviation (RMS). Approaches to this problem typically uses pairwise comparison between two molecules. These include the Monte Carlo-based DALI[7], incremental combinatorial extension (CE) methods[8], TMalign that employs dynamic programming[9], MATT[10], and CLeFAPS[11]. While fast, many of these algorithms employ heuristics and therefore the solution is not guaranteed to be optimal or even near optimal. In response to this, Qian, et. al. devised a polynomial-time approximation algorithm for pairwise structural alignment.

For this, we apply rigid transformations to the molecules in the 3D space and aim to find the best alignment between proteins. A rigid transformation, τ is a 6D vector $\tau = (t_x, t_y, t_z, r_1, r_2, r_3)$, $t_x, t_y, t_z \in \mathbb{R}$ (translation), and $r_1, r_2, r_3 \in [0, 2\pi]$ (rotation). For the translation part of the vector, t_x, t_y, t_z, it is easy to see that coinciding the centroids of the proteins will provide the best results. This is formalized by the following lemmas from[3]:

Lemma 2.1. *Given two sets of n points, $(a_1, a_2, ..., a_n)$ and $(b_1, b_2, ..., b_n)$, in 3D space, minimizing $\sum_i ||\rho(a_i) + T - b_i||^2$ with ρ being the rotation matrix and T, the translation vector, requires T to make the centroid of a_i and b_i coincide with each other.*

Lemma 2.2. *The optimal solution of (R, C)-compact motif has the centroids of $\tau(u_i)$ with the centroid of the consensus, q, for $1 \le i \le n$.*

Lemma 2 is a corollary of Lemma 1. Thus, the translation is simplified to be the rotation vector (r_1, r_2, r_3). One approach on finding the optimal rotation vector proposed by Qian, et.al. was to divide the range of $r_1, r_2, r_3 \in [0, 2\pi]$ to bins each of size ϵ and determine which of these bins minimizes our objective function[3].

3. Algorithm

Algorithm 3.1 is a polynomial-time approximation scheme presented by Qian et al.,[3]. Existence of such schemes allow us to have a parameter, in this case, $1 \le r \le n$ as an input and provides us an efficient approximation algorithm that has a guaranteed quality. As the value of the parameter r approaches n, the algorithm produces an approximate solution with quality as good as the optimal solution. As a trade off, a better quality solution requires a longer running time of the algorithm.

Algorithm 3.1 (R, C)-Compact Motif Finding Algorithm[3]

1: **procedure** MOTIFFINDING$(\mathcal{P}_1, \mathcal{P}_2, ...\mathcal{P}_n, \ell, C, r, R, \epsilon)$
2:     Fix $\mathcal{P}_1$
3:     **for all** $\mathcal{P}_i$ in $\{\mathcal{P}_2, \mathcal{P}_3, ...\mathcal{P}_n\}$ **do**
4:         Translate $\mathcal{P}_i$ to coincide its centroid with $\mathcal{P}_1$
5:     **end for**
6:     **for all** r length-ℓ (R, C)-compact motif $u_1, u_2, ..., u_r$, u_i is a substructure of some $\mathcal{P}_j$ **do**
7:         **for all** $r - 1$ transformations $\tau_1, \tau_2, ..., \tau_r$ from $\frac{\epsilon}{Rn\ell}$-net rotation space $\mathcal{T}$ **do**
8:             $u \leftarrow \frac{1}{r}(u_1 + \tau_2(u_2) + ... + \tau_r(u_r))$
9:             **for** i in $1...n$ **do**
10:                 Find (R, C)-compact motif of length ℓ, v_i of $\mathcal{P}_i$ and the optimal rigid transformation τ_i' that minimizes $d(u, \tau_i'(v_i))$
11:                 $c(u) \leftarrow \sum_{i=1}^{n} d(u, \tau_i'(v_i))$
12:             **end for**
13:         **end for**
14:     **end for**
15:     **return** u, v_i, τ_i' that minimizes $c(u)$
16: **end procedure**

Let us provide an intuition how the algorithm works. To start, lines 3-5 of the algorithm assures that for the center of mass of all proteins coincide. Given the parameter r at the start of the computation, the algorithm checks all possible r-combination of l-length residues of the given protein vectors $\mathcal{P}$. Given a collection of segments from line 6, the succeeding step is to get the optimal multiple structural alignment of the segments to form a representative segment u. Lines 9-11, provides a feasible solution which is a collection of v_i's for each $\mathcal{P}_i$. The collection of v_i's with the minimum total deviation computed by dRMSD is the output structural motif occurrences.

They have proven that Algorithm 3.1 will output a solution that is guaranteed to be no more than $(1 + \frac{1}{r})c_{opt} + O(\epsilon)$. They have also shown that it is a polynomial-time approximate algorithm that runs in $O(\frac{n^{4r-2}m^{5r+5}R^{3r-3}\ell^{cr+c+3r-2}}{\epsilon^{3r-3}})$ time. The proof of this theorem is found in [3].

3.1. *Kabsch Algorithm*

Qian's algorithm employed an iterative search to determine the best rotation that would minimize the RMSD between two peptides. How close the rotation will be from the optimal rotation depends on the how we set the parameter, ϵ. For our algorithm, we used Kabsch algorithm[5,6] to determine the optimal rotation between two peptides. Kabsch algorithm was formulated by Wolfgang Kabsch in 1976 to determine the optimal superposition of vectors via the use of linear and vector algebra. Similar to Qian's method, it starts by aligning the centroids of the proteins to the origin. Algorithm 3.2 illustrates Kabsch algorithm.

Algorithm 3.2 Kabsch algorithm[5,6]

1: **procedure** KABSCH($\mathcal{P}_1, \mathcal{P}_2$)
2:     Align the centroids of $\mathcal{P}_1$ and $\mathcal{P}_2$ to the origin.
3:     Calculate matrix $\mathbf{R}$ s.t. its elements, $r_{i,j} = \sum_n w_n \mathcal{P}_{2ni}\mathcal{P}_{1nj}$
4:     $\mathbf{A} = \mathbf{R}^T\mathbf{R}$
5:     Calculate eigenpairs, $(m_k, \boldsymbol{v_k})$, where m_k's are the eigenvalues and $\boldsymbol{v_k}$'s are the eigenvectors.
6:     Sort the eigenpairs s.t. $m_1 \geq m_2 \geq m_3$
7:     Set $\boldsymbol{v_3} = \boldsymbol{v_1} \times \boldsymbol{v_2}$
8:     Calculate $\boldsymbol{c_k} = \mathbf{R}\boldsymbol{v_k}$. Compute $\boldsymbol{b_1}$ and $\boldsymbol{b_2}$ by normalizing $\boldsymbol{c_1}$ and $\boldsymbol{c_2}$
9:     Set $\boldsymbol{b_3} = \boldsymbol{b_1} \times \boldsymbol{b_2}$
10:     $\mathbf{U} = u_{ij} = \sum_k b_{ki}a_{kj}$
11:     Compute $RMSD$
12:     **return** U
13: **end procedure**

3.2. *PepSquad Algorithm*

We now present Algorithm 3.3 that lists the steps of PepSquad. We adopt Qian's sampling strategy for our algorithm (line 6 onwards). This enable us to retain the same approximation ratio of $1 + \frac{1}{r}$. The main difference lies on the use of Kabsch algorithm to determine the optimal rotation of a protein with respect to another peptide(line 6 and line 12) instead of iterating on a set of bins.

Algorithm 3.3 PepSquad Algorithm

1: **procedure** PEPSQUAD($\mathcal{P}_1, \mathcal{P}_2, ... \mathcal{P}_n, \ell, C, r, R$)

2:     Fix $\mathcal{P}_1$

3:     **for all** $\mathcal{P}_i$ in $\{\mathcal{P}_2, \mathcal{P}_3, ... \mathcal{P}_n\}$ **do**

4:          Translate $\mathcal{P}_i$ to coincide its centroid with $\mathcal{P}_1$

5:     **end for**

6:     **for all** r length-ℓ (R, C)-compact motif $u_1, u_2, ..., u_r$, u_i is a substructure of some $\mathcal{P}_j$ **do**

7:          **for all** $u_i \in u_2, ..., u_r$ **do**

8:             $\tau_i = Kabsch(u_1, u_i)$

9:          **end for**

10:         $u \leftarrow \frac{1}{r}(u_1 + \tau_2(u_2) + ... + \tau_r(u_r))$

11:         **for** i in $1...n$ **do**

12:             Find (R, C)-compact motif of length ℓ, v_i of $\mathcal{P}_i$ and the optimal rigid transformation τ_i' that minimizes $d(u, \tau_i'(v_i))$ using Kabsch algorithm.

13:             $c(u) \leftarrow \sum_{i=1}^{n} d(u, \tau_i'(v_i))$

14:         **end for**

15:     **end for**

16:     **return** u, v_i, τ_i' that minimizes $c(u)$

17: **end procedure**

Based on the alignment of the alpha carbon atoms, we can reconstruct the alignment of the original protein by applying the same rotational matrices from Kabsch algorithm. In Fig. 1, we show an example result from PepSquad. The rotational matrices obtained from the alignments were use to obtain the alignment of the original backbone of the proteins. The side chains of the peptides were removed for simplicity of the illustration.

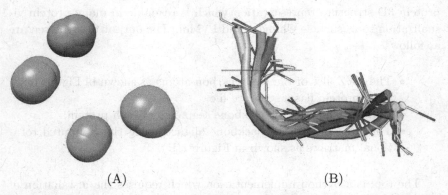

Fig. 1.   PepSquad Sample Results. (A) 4 Alpha carbon atom alignments with minimum dRMSD. (B) Backbone superposition of peptides from rotational matrices obtained from (A).

4. PepSquad Usage

The 3D input structure of proteins are represented in a standard file format called the PDB format. The file contains the atomic coordinates of a particular protein. It is used for structures in the Protein Data Bank maintains the collection of protein structures as a result of wet lab experiments. For simplicity, we accept as an input a directory location containing all the backbone of the proteins written in PDB format. Additional parameters must be specified as follows.

```
> python pepSquad.py <sourcedirectory>/* <l> <r> <R> <d>
```

- The parameter l is a non-zero positive natural number that specifies the length of the amino acid sequence.
- The parameter r is an integer ranging from 1 to n. As the parameter r approaches n, there is an improvement of the performance guarantee but is expected to require more time to run.
- The parameter R is a real number specifying the radius of the ball size used for evaluating the compactness of the substructure. The parameter R is measured in Angstrom.
- The parameter d is an integer strictly less than l which specifies the maximum allowable error.

The tool is a command line script that produces a command line description of the results. Moreover, predicted structural motif occurrences are also written in a simple XYZ format. The file format is also a standard protein 3D structure representation which is readable in many protein visualization tools such as Chimera and PyMol. The output files written are as follows.

- The XYZ files of the alpha carbon atoms as shown in Figure 1(A). Each protein has a separate file
- The XYZ files of the backbone segments of each protein.
- The XYZ files of the backbone aligned using the computed rotational matrices as shown in Figure 1(B).

The tool is a python implementation which requires the installation of Biopython. We only used the PDB module which allows us to manipulate standard protein files from the protein data bank.

Since we tried the tool using actual protein structures, we saw that there are also some limitations to the combinatorial model of the problem. The minimum total dRMSD of the alpha carbons may not necessarily get the best alignment of the whole protein. We show a particular instance in Fig. 2.

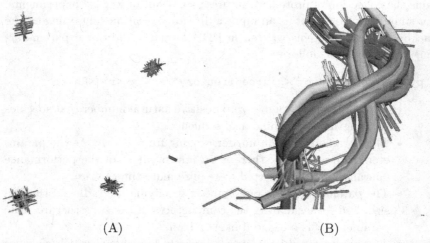

(A)   (B)

Fig. 2.   Example case where the alignment of alpha carbon atoms does not imply alignment of the protein structure. (A) 4 Alpha carbon atom alignments with minimum dRMSD (B) Backbone superposition of peptides from rotational matrices obtained from (A).

5. Conclusion and Future Works

In this paper, we present an implementation of the polynomial-time approximation scheme for finding de novo compact structural motifs from a set of proteins. The combinatorial model of the problem is hard but due to the existence of the PTAS we can provide good enough solutions. The performance guarantee can be specified by the user using the parameter r in the input. For future works, we would like to generalize the problem formulation, such that all backbone atoms are considered during the minimization. Moreover, the actual implementation can be further improved by incorporating parallelization. A GPU implementation of this algorithm is a prospect due to the nature of the algorithm and its numerous matrix operations.

6. Acknowledgments

This work is under the *Conus Structural Exogenomics* program funded by the Emerging Interdisciplinary Research (EIDR) program of University of the Philippines, Diliman.

References

1. Einat Sitbon and Shmuel Pietrokovski. Occurrence of protein structure elements in conserved sequence regions. *BMC structural biology*, 7(1):3, 2007.
2. Patrick Aloy, Enrique Querol, Francesc X Aviles, and Michael JE Sternberg. Automated structure-based prediction of functional sites in proteins: applications to assessing the validity of inheriting protein function from homology in genome annotation and to protein docking. *Journal of molecular biology*, 311(2):395–408, 2001.
3. Jianbo Qian, Shuai Cheng Li, Dongbo Bu, Ming Li, and Jinbo Xu. Finding compact structural motifs. In *CPM*, pages 142–149. Springer, 2007.
4. Lu He, Fabio Vandin, Gopal Pandurangan, and Chris Bailey-Kellogg. Ballast: a ball-based algorithm for structural motifs. *Journal of Computational Biology*, 20(2):137–151, 2013.
5. Wolfgang Kabsch. A solution for the best rotation to relate two sets of vectors. *Acta Crystallographica Section A: Crystal Physics, Diffraction, Theoretical and General Crystallography*, 32(5):922–923, 1976.
6. Wolfgang Kabsch. A discussion of the solution for the best rotation to relate two sets of vectors. *Acta Crystallographica Section A:*

Crystal Physics, Diffraction, Theoretical and General Crystallography, 34(5):827–828, 1978.

7. Liisa Holm and Chris Sander. Protein structure comparison by alignment of distance matrices. *Journal of molecular biology,* 233(1):123–138, 1993.

8. Ilya N Shindyalov and Philip E Bourne. Protein structure alignment by incremental combinatorial extension (ce) of the optimal path. *Protein engineering,* 11(9):739–747, 1998.

9. Yang Zhang and Jeffrey Skolnick. Tm-align: a protein structure alignment algorithm based on the tm-score. *Nucleic acids research,* 33(7):2302–2309, 2005.

10. Matthew Menke, Bonnie Berger, and Lenore Cowen. Matt: local flexibility aids protein multiple structure alignment. *PLoS computational biology,* 4(1):e10, 2008.

11. Sheng Wang. Clefaps: fast flexible alignment of protein structures based on conformational letters. *arXiv preprint arXiv:0903.0582,* 2009.

An Actor-Based Execution Model of an FRP Language for Small-Scale Embedded Systems

Takuo Watanabe

Department of Computer Science, Tokyo Institute of Technology
W8-75, 2-12-1 Ookayama, Meguroku Tokyo 152-8552, Japan
Email: takuo@acm.org

Functional reactive programming (FRP) is a programming paradigm for reactive systems based on declarative abstractions to express time-varying values. Previous works showed that FRP is beneficial to embedded systems. In this paper, we propose a new execution mechanism for an FRP language designed for resource constrained embedded systems. The mechanism is based on the Actor model, a concurrent computation model in which computation is achieved by actors communicating via asynchronous messages. We adopt actors for the run-time representation of time-varying values and event streams. With this representation, we can naturally integrate asynchronous execution mechanism in the runtime of the language.

Keywords: Functional Reactive Programming; Embedded Systems; Actor Model.

1. Introduction

Reactive systems are computational systems that respond to external events. Embedded systems are typical instances of reactive systems, in which changes in sensor values and switch states are examples of external events. The order of events in a reactive system is usually not predictable, as they arrive asynchronously. Thus, describing reactive behaviors in conventional sequential programming languages is not straightforward. In practice, *polling* and *callbacks* are commonly used techniques to handle asynchronous events. However, they usually split the control flow of a program into multiple small pieces and thus are obstacles to modularity.

Functional Reactive Programming (FRP)[1] is a programming paradigm for reactive systems based on the functional (declarative) abstractions of time-varying values and events. Such abstractions are essential in FRP because we often employ continuously changing data over time as the sources of external events. Environmental sensor values are examples of such data.

Time-varying values provide straightforward ways to express reactive behaviors. We can, of course, use them to represent discrete events.

FRP has been actively studied and recognized to be promising for various kinds of reactive systems including robots[2]. The application to robots suggests that FRP can be useful for other embedded systems. However, with a few exceptions, the majority of the FRP systems developed so far are Haskell-based, and therefore they require substantial runtime resources. Hence, it is virtually impossible to run such FRP systems on resource constrained platforms.

We designed and developed a series of FRP languages CFRP[3] and Emfrp[4] that target small-scale embedded systems. The term small-scale here means that the target platforms are not powerful enough to run conventional operating systems such as Linux. The basic design of CFRP follows those of common functional languages such as ML. For example, it supports first-class anonymous functions as usual. In contrast, Emfrp throws them away to suppress dynamic memory allocations used to implement function closures. In addition, Emfrp does not treat time-varying values as first-class data to guarantees that the amount of the runtime memory used by an Emfrp program is predictable. So Emfrp is more suitable for resource-constrained systems.

The runtime system of Emfrp is based on a push-based, synchronous evaluation of time-varying values. However, we sometimes need to realize asynchrony for efficient execution[5]. Since Emfrp is a simple language specialized for the description of reactive behaviors, interfaces to external devices (including the runtime system) rely on libraries (I/O code) written in C. One problem caused by this design is that if we wish to add an asynchronous execution mechanism to the runtime, it might be realized as an ad-hoc C code.

To address the issue, we propose an integration of the Actor model[6] in Emfrp runtime, which provides a high-level view of the internals of the I/O code as well as a high-level abstraction for inter-device communication. In this integration, actors provide not only the representation of time-varying values, but also an asynchronous interface to the internals of the runtime.

The rest of the paper is organized as follows. The next section briefly describes Emfrp using an example of a simple air-conditioner controller. In Section 3, we present our Actor-based execution model. The section also shows the implementation of delayed nodes as an application to an asynchronous computation. Then Section 4 concludes the paper.

2. Overview of Emfrp

Emfrp[4][a] is a purely functional programming language designed for resource constrained embedded systems. This section briefly describes the language with some examples.

2.1. *Design Considerations*

Designing abstraction mechanisms for time-varying values and events is the central topic of FRP language design. Most of existing FRP languages and libraries, such as Elm[5] or Yampa[2], treat time-varying values as first-class data that encapsulate time dependencies. Data types (or type constructors) for the purpose are either built-in (*e.g.*, Signal in Elm) or user-definable using type constructors such as arrows[7].

We adopt a different approach for Emfrp. We often represent a program in (functional) reactive style as a directed graph whose nodes and edges represent time-varying values and their dependencies respectively. The design of Emfrp directly reflects this representation. An Emfrp program consists of a fixed number of named *nodes* that express time-varying values. A node corresponds to a signal or a behavior in other languages.

Because Emfrp is mainly targeted at small-scale embedded systems, we designed the language to have the following characteristics to make the amount of runtime memory consumption predictable.

- Nodes (time-varying values) are not first-class value. We must, therefore, always specify nodes with their names.
- The language does not provide ways to alter the dependency relation between nodes at runtime. In other words, the graph representation of a program is static.
- Recursion is not allowed in function and type definitions.

2.2. *Example: Air-Conditioner Controller*

An Emfrp program consists of one or more *modules*. Figure 1 is an example Emfrp module for a simple air-conditioner controller. It reads data from two environmental sensors (temperature and humidity) and turns an air-conditioner on only during the discomfort index[b] calculated from the sensor values is more than or equal to 75, otherwise turns it off.

---

[a]https://github.com/sawaken/emfrp/
[b]a.k.a. temperature-humidity index. About 50% of people feel uncomfortable if it reaches 75.

```
 1 module ACController    # module name
 2 in   tmp : Float,      # temperature sensor
 3      hmd : Float        # humidity sensor
 4 out ac  : Bool          # air-conditioner
 5 use Std                 # standard library
 6
 7 # discomfort (temperature-humidity) index
 8 node di = 0.81 * tmp + 0.01 * hmd
 9           * (0.99 * tmp - 14.3) + 46.3
10
11 # air-conditioner switch
12 node ac = di >= 75.0
```

Fig. 1.   Emfrp Module for an Air-Conditioner Controller

A module definition contains a single module header followed by one or more type, function or node definitions used in the module. In Fig. 1, the module header (lines 1–5) defines the module name (ACController), then declares two input nodes (tmp and hmd) and one output node (ac), and specifies the library module (Std) used in this module.

The rest of the module (lines 7–12) consists of two node definitions. A node definition looks like

$$\textbf{node } [\textbf{init}[c]] \; n = e$$

where n is the node name and e is an expression that describes the (time-varying) value of the node. The optional **init**[c] specifies the constant c as the initial value of the node. Note that if e contains another node name m, we say that n depends on m. While the value of m changes over time, the value of n varies also.

Emfrp has three kinds of nodes: *input*, *output* and *internal*. Each input or output node has a connection to an external device, while an internal node has no such connection. The value of an input node always expresses the current value (or state) of the device connected, and the value of an output node acts on its device. Thus, an input node needs no node definition in the module. In contrast, other kinds of nodes require explicit definitions to determine their values.

In the example, tmp and hmd are input nodes connected to the sensors. Their values represent the current environmental data. The internal node di (lines 8–9) always expresses the latest discomfort index depending on tmp and hmd. The output node ac (line 12) serves as a time-varying Boolean value that controls the on/off status of the air-conditioner.

2.3. *Expressing History-Sensitive Behaviors*

In fact, the air-conditioner controller in Fig. 1 has a serious flaw. Let us consider a situation that the discomfort index drifts around the threshold (75.0). In such a case, the time-varying Boolean value of the output node ac may change at a fast rate, which results in quick changes of the on/off status of that are hazardous to the air-conditioner

```
11 # air-conditioner switch
12 node init[False] ac = di >= 75.0 + ho
13
14 # hysteresis offset
15 node ho = if ac@last then -0.5 else 0.5
```

Fig. 2. Improved Air-Conditioner Controller.

To avoid such situation, we add a history-sensitive behavior (hysteresis) to the controller by replacing lines 11–12 in Fig. 1 with Fig. 2. This patch adds a new internal node ho that represents a history-sensitive offset to the threshold. The node definition of ho has an expression ac@last, which refers to the value of ac at the "previous moment" — the value evaluated in the previous *iteration* (see Section 2.4).

The new program behaves as follows. While the air-conditioner is off, namely, ac is False, di must be more than or equal to 75.5 to turn it True. Once it becomes True, di must be less than 74.5 to turn it False. As a result, we can avoid the quick changes of the on/off status explained above.

The operator @last in Emfrp generalizes foldp in Elm. The latter only allows a node to refer to the previous value of itself, whereas the former provides access to those of arbitrary nodes. Owing to this simple operator and other features, Emfrp offers a flexible and intuitive way of describing reactive behaviors.

2.4. *Execution Model*

As described in Section 2.1, an Emfrp program can be represented as a directed graph whose nodes and edges correspond to time-varying values and

64

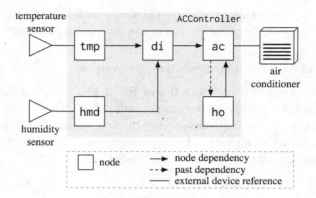

Fig. 3. Graph Representation of Fig. 2.

their dependencies respectively. Figure 3 shows the graph representation of Fig. 2, which consists of five nodes and five edges.

We categorize the edges (dependencies) into two kinds: *past* and *present*. A past edge from node m to n means that n has m@last in its definition. A present edge from node m to n, in contrast, means that n directly refers to m. In Figure 3, the dotted arrow line from ac to ho is the past edge. All other edges are present.

By removing the past edges from the graph representation of an arbitrary Emfrp program, we obtain a directed-acyclic graph (DAG). The topological sorting on the DAG gives a sequence of the nodes. For Figure 3, we have: tmp, hmd, ho, di, ac.

The execusion model of Emfrp is push-based[1]. The runtime system updates the values of the nodes by repeatedly evaluating the elements of the sequence. We call a single evaluation cycle an *iteration*. The order of updates (scheduling) in an iteration must obey the partial order determined by the above mentioned DAG.

The value of n@last is the value of n in the last iteration. At the first iteration, where no nodes have their previous values, n@last refers to the initial value c specified with **init**[c] in the definition of n. The definition of ac in the modified program (Fig. 2) has the initial value as ho refers to ac@last.

3. Integration of the Actor Model

This section briefly describes an integration of the Actor model in Emfrp. In this integration, each node is represented by an actor and a depen-

```
1 class Actor {
2 public:
3     virtual void send(Message *m);
4     virtual void receive(Message *m);
5     virtual void activate(Message *m) = 0;
6 }
```

Fig. 4.   C++ Class for Actors.

dency between two nodes is expressed as an actor reference. As a natural consequence, iterations are realized by message passing. The actor-based representation provides a higher-level abstraction for nodes in the I/O code of an Emfrp program.

3.1. *Representing Nodes as Actors*

We use C++ objects to represent actors. The class Actor (Fig. 4) provides the basic actor APIs. The method send puts a message in the system queue. When the message is scheduled to be received by an actor, receive and activate are invoked at the receiver in this order.

The compiler for the actor-integrated version of Emfrp is supposed to produce a collection of actor classes that represent the nodes in the original Emfrp program. Fig. 5 shows the definitions of actors that represent nodes tmp and di. The class Actor2 is a *join actor*[c] that requires two messages to invoke activate. Join actors represent nodes that depend on multiple nodes. We have Actor3, Actor4, . . . as well.

The compiler also generates a piece of code that instantiates actors in static area as follows.

```
ACNode ac();
HONode ho(&ac);
DINode di(&ac);
TMPNode tmp(&di);
HMDNode hmd(&di);
```

Since node dependencies are static in Emfrp, actor references are provided as arguments of constructors. A single iteration starts with messages to actors that represent the input nodes as follows.

```
tmp->send(Message::unitMessage(&sys_actor));
hmd->send(Message::unitMessage(&sys_actor));
```

---

[c]Similar notion to *join continuation*[6]

```
1  class TMPNode : public Actor {
2  public:
3      TMPNode(Actor2 *di, TMPSensor *tmp);
4      virtual ~TMPNode() {}
5      virtual void activate(Message *m);
6  private:
7      Actor2 *di;
8      TMPSensor *tmp;
9  }
10
11 void TMPNode::activate(Message *m) {
12     di->send1(
13         Message::floatMessage(tmp->read(),
14                               m->cust));
15 }
16
17 class DINode : public Actor2 {
18 public:
19     DINode(Actor *ac) ac(ac) { ... }
20     virtual ~DINode() {}
21     virtual void activate(Message *m);
22 private:
23     Actor *ac;
24 }
25
26 void DINode::activate(Message *mt,
27                       Message *mh) {
28     assert(mt->cust == mh->cust);
29     float t = mt->getFloat();
30     float h = mh->getFloat();
31     float di = 0.81 * t + 0.01 * h
32                * (0.99 * t - 14.3) + 46.3;
33     ac->send(
34         Message::floatMessage(di, mt->cust));
35 }
```

Fig. 5. Actors for Nodes tmp and di.

The iteration ends with messages to the actor sys_actor sent from the actors that represent the output nodes.

```
1  module ACController   # module name
2  in   tmp : Float,      # temperature sensor
3       hmd : Float       # humidity sensor
4       pulse10ms : Bool  # 10 msec interval timer
5  out ac  : Bool,        # air-conditioner
6      led : Bool         # LED
7  use Std                # standard library
8
9  # discomfort (temperature-humidity) index
10 node di = 0.81 * tmp + 0.01 * hmd
11            * (0.99 * tmp - 14.3) + 46.3
12
13 node init[0] timer =
14      if !pulse10ms@last && pulse10ms
15      then (timer@last + 1) % 600
16
17 # air-conditioner switch
18 node ac = if timer@last != timer && timer == 0
19              then di >= 75.0
20
21 # LED blinks at 1Hz
22 node led = (timer % 100) < 50;
```

Fig. 6.   Air-Conditioner Controller using a Timer.

3.2. *Example: Air-Conditioner Controller using a Timer*

Timers are crucial components of most embedded systems. Figure 6 shows another implementation of the air-conditioner controller that utilizes a timer. Figure 7 depicts its graph representation. In this implementation, the changes of the on/off status occur at most once per minute. The input node pulse10ms is connected to a hardware interval timer with 10 msec interval. The internal node timer constantly counts up on each rising edge of pulse10ms and resets to 0 every one minute. The value of ac may change only when timer becomes 0 and di $\geq$ 75. In addition, an LED blinks at 1Hz to indicate that the system is in operation.

A possible problem of this code is that, due to the push-based execution model of Emfrp, di, tmp and hmd are updated in every iteration regardless of their necessities. In fact, however, we can see from the definition of ac

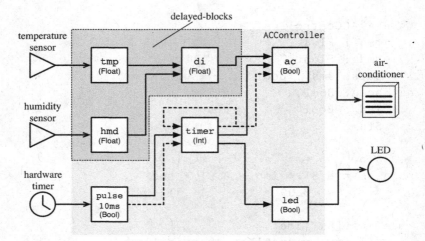

Fig. 7.   Graph Representation of Fig. 6.

(lines 18–19) that the value of di (hence tmp and hmd) is required only once per minute. The results of all other updates are just ignored. Such wasteful computation is unfavorable especially for small-scale embedded systems since it leads to higher power consumption.

3.3. *Delayed Blocks*

The problem described in the previous subsection can be resolved using a pull-based execution model. However, the execution of periodically updating nodes such as timer and LED require push-based model. Thus we need a mixture of both execution models.

We extend Emfrp with a simple mechanism called *delayed block*. Syntactically, a delayed block is an expression suffixed with @delay. Figure 8 shows an example use of a delayed block with which lines 17–19 of Fig. 6 should be replaced.

In Fig. 6, node ac depends on both timer and di. However, in Fig. 8, di is removed from the dependency of ac. So di is no longer in the dependency

```
17 # air-conditioner switch
18 node ac = if timer@last != timer && timer == 0
19             then ( di >= 75.0 )@delay
```

Fig. 8.   Delayed Block.

```
1  class DINode : public Actor2 { ... }
2
3  void DINode::activate(Message *mt,
4                        Message *mh) {
5      float t = mt->getFloat();
6      float h = mh->getFloat();
7      float di = 0.81 * t + 0.01 * h
8                 * (0.99 * t - 14.3) + 46.3;
9      mt->cust->send(
10         mkFloatMessage(di, mt->cust));
11 }
12
13 class ACNode : public Actor { ... }
14
15 void ACNode::activate(Message *m) {
16     if (m->prevInt() != m->getInt() &&
17         m->getInt() == 0) {
18         tmp->send(Message::unitMessage(
19                       &acDelayedBlock));
20         hmd->send(Message::unitMessage(
21                       &acDelayedBlock));
22     }
23 }
24
25 class ACDelayedBlock : public Actor { ...}
26
27 void ACDelayedBlock::activate(Message *m) {
28     m->cust->send(
29         Message::booleanMessage(
30             m->getFloat() > 75.0, m->cust));
31 }
```

Fig. 9.   Implementation of the Delayed Block.

of any output nodes. This means that di, hence tmp and hmd are removed from the program graph. The value of di is needed only when the condition of if statement of Fig. 8 holds. Thus, the compiler performs a simple dependency analysis and produces the code so that starting messages to tmp and hmd are sent when the condition holds (Lines 6–9 in Fig. 9).

The compiler now treats DINode as an output node. Thus the result will be passed to the actor acDelayedBlock, which plays a role of the continuation of the starting messages to tmp and hmd. As a result, the sensor values and the discomfort index value are calculated only if the condition regarding the timer is satisfied.

4. Conclusion

This paper briefly describes a simple idea of integrating the Actor model into Emfrp, a functional reactive programming language designed for resource constrained embedded systems. The integration provides a higher-level view of the internal representation of nodes, representations of time-varying values, as well as an actor-based inter-device communication mechanism.

The group of actors representing the nodes of an Emfrp program are viewed as the meta-level of the program. Thus it is possible to apply a variation of group-wide reflection[8] to the actor group to realize more drastic customization such as application-oriented evaluation (scheduling) polities or dynamic node reconfiguration.

We have just started this project. We need to work on the abstraction of the APIs and the integration of inter-device communication mechanism.

Acknowledgments

The author thanks the anonymous reviewers for their detailed comments on an earlier version of this paper. This work is supported in part by JSPS KAKENHI Grant No. 15K00089.

References

[1] E. Bainomugisha, A. L. Carreton, T. Van Cutsem, S. Mostinckx and W. De Meuter, A survey on reactive programming, *ACM Computing Surveys* **45** (2013).

[2] P. Hudak, A. Courtney, H. Nilsson and J. Peterson, Arrows, robots, and functional reactive programming, in *Advanced Functional Programming*, , Lecture Notes in Computer Science Vol. 2638 (Springer-Verlag, 2003) pp. 159–187.

[3] K. Suzuki, K. Nagayama, K. Sawada and T. Watanabe, CFRP: A functional reactive programming language for small-scale embedded systems, in *Theory and Practice of Computation (WCTP 2016)*, (World Scientific, Sep. 2016). to appear.

[4] K. Sawada and T. Watanabe, Emfrp: A functional reactive programming language for small-scale embedded systems, in *Modularity 2016 Constrained and Reactive Objects Workshop (CROW 2016)*, (ACM, Mar. 2016).

[5] E. Czaplicki and S. Chong, Asynchronous functional reactive programming for GUIs, in *34th ACM SIGPLAN Conference on Programming Language Design and Implementation (PLDI 2013)*, (ACM, 2013).

[6] G. Agha, *Actors: A Model of Concurrent Computation in Distributed Systems* (MIT Press, 1986).

[7] J. Hughes, Generalising monads to arrows, *Science of Computer Programming* **37**, 67 (2000).

[8] T. Watanabe, Towards a compositional reflective architecture for actor-based systems, in *Workshop on Programming based on Actors, Agents, and Decentralized Control (AGERE!@SPLASH 2013)*, (ACM, Oct. 2013).

A Clique Finding Algorithm for the Approximate Gene Cluster Discovery Problem

Geoffrey Solano[*,†], Guillaume Blin[‡], Mathieu Raffinot[‡], and Jaime Caro[*]

[*] *Algorithms and Complexity Lab, Department of Computer Science*
University of the Philippines Diliman, Philippines
[†] *Mathematics and Computing Sciences Unit*
Department Physical Sciences and Mathematics
University of the Philippines Manila, Philippines
[‡] *Universite de Bordeaux, CNRS, Bordeaux-INP, LaBRI, UMR 5800*
33405 Talence, France

Finding gene clusters in genomes is an essential process in establishing relationships among organisms. Gene clusters may express functional dependencies among genes and may give insight into expression of specific traits and perhaps even of diseases. The problem of finding gene clusters among several genomes is referred to as Gene Cluster Discovery and several models have already been formulated for its definition. One formulation of this problem is the Approximate Gene Cluster Discovery Problem (AGCDP), which is modeled as a combinatorial optimization problem in some works. In this study we show the formulation of an instance of AGCDP into the Minimum Weighted t-partite Clique Problem (MWtCP), which is the problem of finding a t-clique with minimum weight given a complete edge-weighted t-partite graph. This study also presents an algorithm that runs on $O(n^2)$ in the metric case of inputs which is related to another algorithm for MWtCP presented in another study. However, this version allows more edges to be considered in approximating the t-clique with minimum weight. We show that this algorithm has a 2-approximation performance guarantee for the metric case and 1 approximation performance guarantee for the ultrametric case.

Keywords: Approximation algorithm, Cliques, Metric case, Ultrametric case, Performance guarantee, Minimum weighted t-clique.

1. Introduction

Across different organisms, any given gene may have different functions as its activity influences, and is influenced by a number of other genes[12]. A gene in one species may be almost exactly similar to another gene in some other species at the sequence level. Identifying set of genes that are closely related to each other is an essential step in establishing relationships between organisms and help to infer evolutionarily conserved modules of co-expressed genes.[2,3,9]

Identifying gene clusters is also an essential step in establishing relationships between organisms as well as discovery of drug and treatments for diseases. The problem of identifying this set of genes is called *Gene Cluster Discovery*. This problem has been modelled several times, examples of which are presented in a number of studies[4,8,10], where genes are modelled as integers and genomes are either permutations or sequences defined over the set of all genes. Models in a particular study[4] also takes into account gene clusters with (max-gap clusters) and without gaps (exact clusters).

The focus of this work is on the model presented by Rahmann et. al.[10], where they define *Approximate Gene Cluster Discovery Problem (AGCDP)* as a combinatorial problem which identifies the set of genes that are kept "more or less" together across genome sequences. Probing the hardness of this problem was the focus of another study[5]. An Integer Linear Programming (ILP) formulation is also presented by Rahmann[10]. Several modifications of the model, specifically on the objective function, is also presented to take into account characteristics of real biological data. Among these includes, absence of gene cluster occurrence in some of the input genomes, identification of valid gene clusters, and use of certain reference genome.

Graphs have proven to be very useful tools in representing the structure of biological networks[6]. In one study[1], AGCDP was represented as a graph problem. In that study, it was defined how the set of inputs, i.e. gene and genome representations, were transformed into a specific graph called G_{ACGDP}, and it was also discussed how the problem is reduced to finding minimum weight $star(u)$ in such a graph. The scenarios of having and not having a given reference genome were both modelled in this paper. However, though the study attempted to describe AGCDP as a graph problem, the classification of the complexity of the problem as well as the proposition of approximation algorithms for the problem for the cases of both having and not having a reference gene were yet to be explored.

The aim of this particular study is to represent $AGCDP$ as a clique-finding problem in a graph, specifically, the problem of finding a t-clique with minimum weight given a complete edge-weighted t-partite graph, where $n = mt$ and there are m vertices per partition. This formulation was initially presented in a recent related study[11] as the Minimum Weight t-partite Clique Problem (MWtCP), and will be thoroughly discussed in this particular study. Finding maximum or minimum weighted cliques in graphs have been thoroughly studied in the past. With the discovery of its applications in various biological domains, such studies are expected to be pursued more extensively.

1.1. Basic Representations of Genes and Genomes

Necessary for our understanding of the succeeding sections are the following definitions and representations defined in the study of Rahmann et. al.[10].

(1) **Gene** A *gene* is represented by an integer $g \in \mathcal{Z}^0$. Special genes represented by the integer 0 are genes with non existing homologs, with which we are not interested of in this problem.

(2) **Gene Universe** The set of all unique genes is called the *gene universe* and is denoted by $\mathcal{U} = \{0, 1, 2, \ldots, N\}$.

(3) **Genome** For simplicity, the genome of a certain individual can be represented as a single sequence of genes from a chromosome. For instance, $g^i = (g_1^i, g_2^i, \ldots, g_{n_i}^i)$, where each g_j^i is the jth gene in the ith genome. In general, a set of genomes is represented by $\mathcal{G} = \{g^1, g^2, \ldots, g^t\}$ for some $t \in \mathcal{Z}^+$, where each g^i has length $n_i \in \mathcal{Z}^+$.

(4) **Linear Interval** A *linear interval* J^i in a genome $g^i = (g_1^i, g_2^i, \ldots, g_{n_i}^i)$ is an index set which can either be empty $J^i = \emptyset$ or $J^i = \{j, j+1, \ldots, k\}$, which can also be denoted as J_{j_i, k_i}^i where $1 \leq j_i \leq k_i \leq n_i$. A set of linear intervals from all genomes is denoted by J.

(5) **Gene Content** The *gene content* $G(J_{j,k}^i)$ of a linear interval $J_{j,k}^i$ in genome g^i is the set of unique genes contained in that interval.

(6) **Set Difference** The set difference between two distinct gene contents $G(J_{j_i, k_i}^i)$ and $G(J_{j_p, k_p}^p)$, $1 \leq i \leq t$, $1 \leq p \leq t$ and $i \neq p$, is defined as $G(J_{j_i, k_i}^i) \backslash G(J_{j_p, k_p}^p) = \{g | g \in G(J_{j_i, k_i}^i) \text{ and } g \notin G(J_{j_p, k_p}^p)\}$.

1.2. On the Approximate Gene Cluster Discovery Problem

Given the definitions listed above, the problem of discovering approximate gene clusters aims to find a gene set $X \subset \mathcal{U}$, where $0 \notin X$ and a set of linear intervals $J = J_{j_i, k_i}^i$ where the gene content $G(J_{j_i, k_i}^i)$ for each genome g^i is roughly equal to X. To define formally how close X is to the gene contents $G(J_{j_i, k_i}^i)$, the number of missing genes $|X \backslash G(J_{j_i, k_i}^i)|$ and additional genes $|G(J_{j_i, k_i}^i) \backslash X|$ are computed.

Let us formally define the Basic Approximate Gene Cluster Discovery Problem (AGCDP).

Definition 1.1 (AGCDP[10]). *Given the gene universe* $\mathcal{U} = \{0, 1, \ldots, N\}$, *set of genomes* $\mathcal{G} = \{g^1, g^2, \ldots, g^t\}$, *size range* $[D^-, D^+]$ *or positive constant* D, *and integer weights* w^- *and* w^+ *corresponding to cost of missing and additional genes in an interval, identify* $X \subset \mathcal{U}$, $0 \notin X$, $D^- \le |X| \le D^+$ *or* $|X| = D$ *and a set of linear intervals* $J = \{J^i_{j_i, k_i}\}$, $\forall\, i$ *such that the cost function*

$$cost(X, J) = \sum_{i=1}^{t} [(w^- \cdot |X \setminus G(J^i_{j_i, k_i})|) + (w^+ \cdot |G(J^i_{j_i, k_i}) \setminus X|)]$$

is **minimum**.

AGCDP is a double minimization problem. In order to identify the cost of X, we identify the set of linear intervals J which minimizes the value of the objective function $cost(X, J)$. The naive way of identifying the set X is to check the cost of all possible $X \subset \mathcal{U}$, which is $\binom{N}{D}$ if $|X| = D$, otherwise

$$\sum_{\forall d} d \binom{N}{d}, \text{ where } D^- \le d \le D^+$$

if we have $D^- \le |X| \le D^+$. Also note that we have to identify the set of linear intervals for each genome which minimizes the cost given X. Naively this can be done by checking all possible linear intervals in each genome. The total running of time the naive AGCDP solver is the number of $X \subset \mathcal{U}$ satisfying the constraint $|X| = D$, times the running time of identifying the best linear interval given X. Thus, naive AGCDP solver takes $O(N!(n^{2t}))$.

Further details of their integer linear programming formulation are presented the work of Rahmann[10]. In the case where there is no reference gene is involved, and thus the cost will be between two intervals, the cost function is defined as follows:

$$cost(u, v) = [(w^- \cdot |G(J^x_{j_x, k_x}) \setminus G(J^y_{j_y, k_y})|) + (w^+ \cdot |G(J^y_{j_y, k_y}) \setminus G(J^x_{j_x, k_x})|)]$$

1.3. *On the Minimum Weight t-Partite Clique Problem*

Necessary for our understanding of MWtCP are the following definitions[11]

A t-partite graph is a set of graph vertices decomposed into t disjoint sets, or partitions, such that no two graph vertices within the same set are adjacent. A complete t-partite graph is such a graph, wherein every pair of graph vertices in the t sets are adjacent[7].

Let $G = (V, E, w)$ be an edge-weighted, t-partite complete graph. Each part in V is denoted by $|U_i|$, such that $|U_i| = m$, for all $1 \le i \le t$. Since graph G is a complete t-partite graph, each pair of vertices from two distinct parts has an edge with a non-negative weight.

From the definition of graph G, the total number of vertices is $n = mt$, where there are m vertices per partition and each vertex v has $deg(v) = m(t - 1)$. Using the Handshaking Lemma, the total number of edges in graph G, is $|E| = m^2 \binom{t}{2}$.

Definition 1.2. Given a complete edge-weighted t-partite graph, the Minimum Weighted t-partite Clique Problem (MWtCP) is the problem of finding a t-clique with minimum weight

Every maximal clique in graph G is of size t, each of which has $\binom{t}{2}$ edges, and the total number of unique t-cliques in G is m^t. Each unique edge is a part of m^{t-2} cliques. Naively, we can check all t-cliques and determine which among them has the minimum total weight in $O(m^t)$.

The problem of MWtCP is called *metric* if all edge weights in G obeys the triangle inequality, i.e., for any $a, b, c, \in V$, $w(a, b) \leq w(b, c) + w(c, a)$. The problem of MWtCP is called *ultrametric* if all edge weights in G obeys the weight function w (i.e., for any $a, b, c, \in V', w(a, b) \leq max(w(b, c), w(c, a)))$.

2. MWtCP as a means of discovering approximate gene clusters

In this section, we show that the solution returned by MWtCP are approximate gene clusters.

Theorem 2.1. *G_{AGCDP} can be represented as a complete edge-weighted t-partite graph, where every partition has m vertices.*

Proof. Given the definition of AGCDP, we now construct a graph G_{AGCDP} in a manner similar to that described in a previous work[1], and show that it is a complete weighted t-partite graph, where every partition has m vertices. We define the vertex set, the edge set and finally the edge weights.

The Vertex Set of graph G_{AGCDP}

Given the set of genomes $\mathcal{G} = \{g^1, g^2, \ldots, g^t\}$, for some $t \in \mathcal{Z}^+$, where each g^i has length $n_i \in \mathcal{Z}^+$, we let each $n_i = p$. Furthermore, given a size range $[D^-, D^+]$ or positive constant D, where $1 \leq D \leq p$, if each gene unique within each genome g^i, then there will be possible m linear intervals for each genome g^i, where $m = p - D + 1$, namely, $J^i_{1,D}, J^i_{2,D+1}, \ldots, J^i_{p-D+1,p}$. For each linear interval $J_{j,k}^i$ of each genome g^i, the corresponding gene content $G(J_{j,k}^i)$ is then identified.

A vertex $v((J_{j,k}^i))$ in G_{AGCDP} is then mapped to each identified gene content $G(J_{j,k}^i)$. The vertex set of G_{AGCDP} is thus grouped into t partitions, with each partition corresponding to a genome g^i in the set of genomes $\mathcal{G} = \{g^1, g^2, \ldots, g^t\}$, and partition has m vertices corresponding to the gene content $G(J_{j,k}^i)$ of the m linear intervals in g^i.

We further note that this vertex set construction will hold whether gene clusters are modelled as either common intervals or max-gaps in either permutations or strings, since vertices represent gene contents of intervals. We have, the following observations, however, for each case:

- If gene clusters are modelled as common intervals in permutations:
  - nodes have same length and are unique per partition
- If gene clusters are modelled as common intervals in strings:
  - nodes do not have same length are not unique per partition
- If gene clusters are modelled as max-gaps in permutations:
  - nodes do not have same length are unique per partition
- If gene clusters are modelled as max-gaps in strings:
  - nodes do not have same length are not unique per partition

Thus, G_{AGCDP} will have have t partitions corresponding to the t genomes, where each partition has m vertices, where $m = p - D + 1$.

The Edge Set of graph G_{AGCDP}

An edge is defined for every pair of vertices $u, v, u \in U_x, v \in U_y, x \neq y$, where U_x and U_y are partitions in G_{AGCDP} corresponding to genomes g^x and g^y. This makes each of the m vertices in U_i adjacent to all other $m(t-1)$ vertices not in U_i, thus associating each gene content $G(J_{j,k}^i)$ of each linear interval in genome g^i to the gene contents of linear intervals in all other genomes.

Thus each of the m vertices in U_i adjacent to all other $m(t-1)$ vertices not in U_i, but not to the other $m - 1$ vertices in U_i.

The Weights of the Edge Set of graph G_{AGCDP}

If vertex u then is mapped to the gene content $G(J_{j_x,k_x}^x)$ in genome g^x and vertex v then is mapped to the gene content $G(J_{j_y,k_y}^y)$ in genome g^y, then the weight then of such edge $(u, v) =$

$$cost(u,v) = [(w^- \cdot |G(J_{j_x,k_x}^x) \setminus G(J_{j_y,k_y}^y)|) + (w^+ \cdot |G(J_{j_y,k_y}^y) \setminus G(J_{j_x,k_x}^x)|)]$$

Graph G_{AGCDP} is therefore a weighted complete t-partite graph.

□

Theorem 2.2. *The vertices of the minimum weight t-clique on G_{AGCDP} are approximate gene clusters.*

Proof. Since each vertex in a partition U_i corresponds to the different gene content $G(J^i_{j_i,k_i})$ of a linear interval $J^i_{j_i,k_i}$ in a genome g^i, and the weight between two vertices u and v, where $u \in U_p$ and $v \in U_q$ such that U_p and U_q are partitions in $V(G_{AGCDP})$ and $p \neq q$, is

$$cost(u,v) = [(w^- \cdot |G(J^x_{j_x,k_x}) \setminus G(J^y_{j_y,k_y})|) + (w^+ \cdot |G(J^y_{j_y,k_y}) \setminus G(J^x_{j_x,k_x})|)],$$

then searching for the minimum weight t-clique in G_{AGCDP} is therefore determining the set of t gene contents, each one of size D, each coming from a different genome across all genomes $\mathcal{G}$, which resemble each other the most.

Since approximate gene clusters have been defined by Rahmann[10] as the set of genes that are kept "more or less" together across genome sequences, then vertices of the minimum weight t-clique on G_{AGCDP} are approximate gene clusters.

□

3. An Approximation Algorithm for the Metric Case of MWtCP

It was shown[11] that MWtCP is APX-Hard. By definition, in the general case, it would not be possible for us to develop and algorithm that yields a constant-time approximation ratio. This opens up the question of whether the presence of restrictions on edge weights, such as the triangle inequality, would provide for more approximable results. In the same study, a 2-approximation algorithm we shall henceforth refer to as the Star Algorithm was presented for MWtCP in the metric case that runs in $O(n^2)$ and uses only $(t-1)$ out of the $\frac{t(t-1)}{2}$ edges of the t-clique in its approximation. Here we show an extension of such algorithm to $(2t-3)$ out of the $\frac{t(t-1)}{2}$ edges of the t-clique in the approximation.

3.1. Approximation using $(2t - 3)$ out of the $\frac{t(t-1)}{2}$ edges of the t-clique

For each $v_i \in V(G)$ and $\in$ partition U_i, Algorithm 3.1 searches for v_j such that $v_j = v_j \notin U_i$ weight(v_i, v_j) is minimum. It then proceeds as to search the remaining $t - 2$ partitions, selecting from each partition av_k such that weight(v_i, v_k) + weight(v_j, v_k) is minimum. The vertices v_i, v_j and all the $(t - 2)v_k$'s will then make up the solution clique of the algorithms. Thus, Algorithm 3.1 selects the $(t - 2)$ minimum weight triangles, wherein each triangle has edge v_i, v_j as one side, and the other two edges are incident to a vertex v_k from $(t - 2)$ partitions such that the total weights of the two edges is minimum.

This algorithm aims to provide a better approximation as it considers an additional $t - 2$ to that of $t - 1$ edges of the $\binom{t}{2}$ edges considered by Star Algorithm, since for each of the $(t - 2)v_k$'s an additional edge was considered. A comparison on edges considered by Start Algorithm and 3.1 is shown in Fig. 1 for $t = 5$. It is interesting to note that the portion of the t-clique being whose edges are not considered in the approximation actually form a $(t - 2)$-clique.

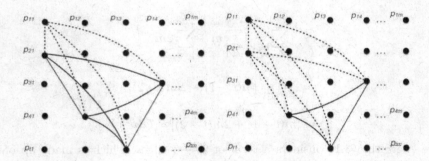

Fig. 1. A comparison on edges considered by the Star Algorithm [11] (left) and Algorithm 3.1(right) for $t = 5$. Dashed edges are those considered in the algorithm while the solid edges are not.

Theorem 3.1. *Algorithm 3.1 is a 2-approximation algorithm for MWtCP which runs in $O(n^2)$.*

Proof. Clearly Algorithm 3.1 takes

Algorithm 3.1 Minimum Weighted $t-2$ Triangles Algorithm for MWtCP

Input: A complete weighted t-partite graph $G = (V, E, w)$

for each vertex $v_i \in V$ where $1 \le i \le n$ **do**
    Find vertex j such that $weight[i, j]$ is minimum
    $cost(i) \leftarrow cost(i) + weight[i, j]$
    $clique(i) \leftarrow clique(i) + i + j$
    for each of the remaining $t - 2$ partitions **do**
        Find vertex k such that $weight[i, k] + weight[j, k]$ is minimum
        $cost(i) \leftarrow weight[i, k] + weight[j, k]$
        $clique(i) \leftarrow clique(i) + k$
    end for
end for
Find minimum $cost(i)$ each vertex $v_i \in V$ where $1 \le i \le n$
t-clique $\leftarrow t$ vertices in clique(i) with cost(i) with all the induced edges
return t-clique

Output: the minimum weighted t-Clique

$$\sum_{v \in V} [\sum_{p=1}^{t-1} m + \sum_{p=1}^{t-2} 2m]$$

$$= \sum_{v \in V} [m(t-1) + 2m(t-2)]$$

$$= n[m(t-1) + 2m(t-2)] = O(n^2)$$

Algorithm 3.1 considers a total of $2t - 3$ edges, which is made up of $(t - 2)$ triangles, each of which has a common edge (v_i, v_j), and the other two edges are incident to a vertex v_k from each of the $(t-2)$ partitions such that do not contain v_i and v_j. For the purposes our discussion we refer to this as $(t - 2)$-triangles. In doing so the algorithm uses the total weight of these $2n - 3$ edges of the $(t - 2)$-triangles to approximate the total weight of $\binom{t}{2}$ edges.

As in the proof used in the Star Algorithm[11], given a complete t-partite graph G consisting of positive edge weights, and each t-clique has e edges such that $e = \binom{t}{2}$, we let the Q be the t-clique of minimum weight, whose edges have the weights $w_1, w_2, w_3, ..., w_e$ and Q' be the t-clique of solution returned by Algorithm 3.1 whose edges have the weights $w_1', w_2', w_3', ..., w_e'$ such that

$$cost(Q) = \sum_{i=1}^{e} w_i \quad \text{and} \quad cost(Q') = \sum_{i=1}^{e} w_i'.$$

We note that $cost(Q) \leq cost(Q')$. We let Q^ς be the minimum weighted $(t-2)$-triangles. An instance where $t = 5$ is shown in Fig. 2, where Q^ς has dashed edges and the common edge among the triangles (i.e. (v_i, v_j) in the algorithm) is (v_1', v_t').

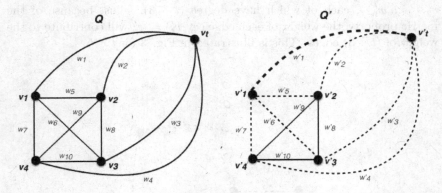

Fig. 2. The optimal t-clique Q and the solution Q' for graph G for Algorithm 3.1 for $t = 5$

Furthermore, for Q' we let v_t' be the hub of Q^ς and (v_t', v_1'), (v_t', v_2'), (v_t', v_3'), ... , (v_t', v_{t-1}') be the edges in Q^ς such that the weight of edge $(v_t', v_i') = w_i'$ for $1 \leq i < t$. But since Q^ς is composed of $(t-2)$ triangles, aside from having a $(t-1)$-star, there are $t-2$ additional edges with weights w_i' for $t \leq i < 2t-3$. These edges make up $(t-2)$-star with v_1 as the hub and $v_2, v_3, ..., v_{t-1}$ as leaves. Clearly,

$$
\begin{aligned}
cost(Q) &\leq cost(Q') \\
\sum_{i=1}^{e} w_i &\leq \sum_{i=1}^{e} w_i' &= \sum_{i=1}^{2t-3} w_i' + \sum_{i=2t-2}^{e} w_i' \\
\sum_{i=1}^{e} w_i &\leq \sum_{i=1}^{e} w_i' &= cost(Q^\varsigma) + \sum_{i=2t-2}^{e} w_i'
\end{aligned}
$$

We note that the cost of $Q^\varsigma = \sum_{i=1}^{2t-3} w_i'$, while the total cost of the remaining $\binom{t-2}{2}/2$ edges that are part of Q' but not part of Q^ς is $\sum\limits_{i=2t-2}^{e} w'_i$. We note that these $\binom{t-2}{2}$ edges form the third side of $(t-2)$ triangles. However, because of the metric property, for $1 \le p < q \le t - 1$

$$
\begin{aligned}
cost(v'_p, v'_q) &\le cost(v'_t, v'_p) + cost(v'_t, v'_q) \\
&\le w'_p + w'_q
\end{aligned}
$$

Such will be applied to w'_i, where $2t - 2 \le i \le e$. We further note that these $\binom{t-2}{2}$ edges that are part of $E(Q') \setminus E(Q^\varsigma)$ involve vertices $v'_2, v'_3, ..., v'_{t-1}$, each of which have degree $(t - 3)$. Thus, because of the metric property, the weight of each edge $(v'_p, v'_t) = w'_p$ will contribute to the weight of $(t - 3)$ edges. This is illustrated in Fig. 3 for $t = 5$.

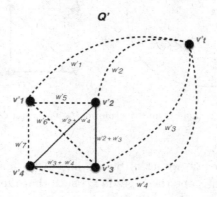

Fig. 3. The weights of the edges of Q^ς are used to provide upper bounds on the remaining edges of the solution Q' for $t = 5$

Hence,

$$
cost(Q' \setminus Q\varsigma) \le (t - 3) \cdot \sum_{i=2}^{t-1} w'_i
$$

This can therefore be used to provide bounds for the cost of Q'

$$cost(Q) \leq cost(Q')$$

$$\sum_{i=1}^{e} w_i \leq \sum_{i=1}^{2t-3} w_i' + \sum_{i=2t-2}^{e} w_i' \leq \sum_{i=1}^{2t-3} w_i' + (t-3) \cdot \sum_{i=2}^{t-1} w_i'$$

$$\sum_{i=1}^{e} w_i \leq \sum_{i=1}^{e} w_i' \leq cost(Q^\varsigma) + (t-3) \cdot \sum_{i=2}^{t-1} w_i'$$

Now to obtain a lower bound on $cost(Q)$. We note that, similar to the case in Star Algorithm, the $cost(Q^\varsigma) \leq$ the cost of any set of $(t-2)$–triangles in Q. So a good lower bound for Q is if $cost(Q^\varsigma)$ would be the same as cost of any set of $(t-2)$– triangles in Q. By assuming such uniform minimum cost, we multiply the weight per edge of Q^ς which is $\frac{1}{2t-3} \cdot cost(Q^\varsigma)$ and assign such weight to all the edges of Q.

Thus,

$$\frac{t(t-1)}{2} \cdot \frac{1}{2t-3} \cdot cost(Q^\varsigma) \leq cost(Q).$$

Therefore,

$$\frac{t(t-1)}{2} \cdot \frac{1}{2t-3} \cdot cost(Q^\varsigma) \leq cost(Q) \leq cost(Q') \leq cost(Q^\varsigma) + (t-3) \cdot \sum_{i=2}^{t-1} w_i'.$$

Based from the description of Q and Q', we obtain the values for *opt* and for *sol* which are:

$$
\begin{aligned}
sol \quad &= \quad \text{maximum } cost(Q') \\
&= \quad cost(Q^\varsigma) + \sum_{i=2t-2}^{e} w_i' \\
&= \quad \sum_{i=1}^{2t-3} w_i' + (t-3) \cdot \sum_{i=2}^{t-1} w_i' \\
opt \quad &= \quad \text{minimum } cost(Q) \\
&= \quad \frac{t(t-1)}{2} \cdot \frac{1}{2t-3} \cdot cost(Q^\varsigma).
\end{aligned}
$$

The computation for the approximation ratio c is as follows.

$$
\begin{aligned}
sol &\leq c \cdot opt, \\
sol/opt &\leq c,
\end{aligned}
$$

$$
\begin{aligned}
c &\geq \frac{cost(Q^\varsigma)+(t-3)\cdot\sum_{i=2}^{t-1} w_i'}{\frac{t(t-1)}{2}\cdot\frac{1}{2t-3}\cdot cost(Q^\varsigma)} \\
&\geq \frac{2(2t-3)}{t(t-1)} \cdot \frac{cost(Q^\varsigma)+(t-3)\cdot\sum_{i=2}^{t-1} w_i'}{cost(Q^\varsigma)}.
\end{aligned}
$$

We note that the weight per edge of Q^ς is $\frac{1}{2t-3}\cdot cost(Q^\varsigma)$, thus

$$
\begin{aligned}
&\geq \frac{2(2t-3)}{t(t-1)} \cdot \frac{cost(Q^\varsigma)+(t-3)\cdot(t-2)\cdot\frac{1}{2t-3}\cdot cost(Q^\varsigma)}{cost(Q^\varsigma)} \\
&\geq \frac{2t^2-6t+6}{t(t-1)} \\
&\geq 2 - \frac{4}{t} + \frac{2}{t(t-1)}.
\end{aligned}
$$

Therefore, Algorithm 3.1 is a 2-approximation algorithm for the metric MWtCP. $\qquad\square$

4. Varying the Strictness of the Metric Property

In the previous sections we have presented another algorithm that approximates the cost of $O(t^2)$ edges of a t-clique using $O(t)$ edges only in the metric case. In this section we observe how varying the strictness of applying the triangle inequality affects the resulting approximation ratio.

4.1. *Varying the strictness of the metricity through a given factor σ*

We introduce a variable σ as a means of tightening or relaxing the metric property.

4.1.1. *Applying the factor σ to Algorithm 3.1*

Theorem 4.1. *If for any $a,b,c,\in V$, $w(a,b) \leq \sigma(w(b,c) + w(c,a))$, then Algorithm 3.1 is a $(2\sigma - \frac{2\cdot(2\sigma-1)\cdot(2t-3)}{t\cdot(t-1)})$ -approximation algorithm for MWtCP .*

Proof. We note that the cost of $Q^\varsigma = \sum_{i=1}^{2t-3} w_i'$, while the total cost of the remaining $\binom{t-2}{2}/2$ edges that are part of Q' but not part of Q^ς is $\sum\limits_{i=2t-2}^{e} w'_i$.

We also note that these $\binom{t-2}{2}$ edges form the third side of $(t-2)$ triangles. However, because of the metric property, for $1 \le p < q \le t-1$

$$
\begin{aligned}
cost(v'_p, v'_q) &\le cost(v'_t, v'_p) + cost(v'_t, v'_q) \\
&\le w'_p + w'_q
\end{aligned}
$$

If for any $a, b, c, \in V$, $w(a,b) \le \sigma(w(b,c) + w(c,a))$, then

$$
\sum_{i=2t-2}^{e} w'_i = \sigma(t-3) \cdot \sum_{i=2}^{t-1} w'_i
$$

Then the computation for the approximation ratio c is as follows.

$$
\begin{aligned}
c \;\ge\;& \frac{cost(Q^\varsigma) + \sigma \cdot (t-3) \cdot \sum\limits_{i=2}^{t-1} w'_i}{\frac{t(t-1)}{2} \cdot \frac{1}{2t-3} \cdot cost(Q^\varsigma)} \\[2mm]
\ge\;& \frac{2(2t-3)}{t(t-1)} \cdot \frac{cost(Q^\varsigma) + \sigma \cdot (t-3) \cdot \sum\limits_{i=2}^{t-1} w'_i}{cost(Q^\varsigma)}
\end{aligned}
$$

We note that the weight per edge of Q^ς is $\frac{1}{2t-3} \cdot cost(Q^\varsigma)$, thus

$$
\begin{aligned}
\ge\;& \frac{2(2t-3)}{t(t-1)} \cdot \frac{cost(Q^\varsigma) + \sigma \cdot (t-3) \cdot (t-2) \cdot \frac{1}{2t-3} \cdot cost(Q^\varsigma)}{cost(Q^\varsigma)} \\[2mm]
\ge\;& \frac{2\sigma t^2 + 4t - 10\sigma t + 12\sigma - 6}{t(t-1)} \\[2mm]
\ge\;& 2\sigma - \frac{2 \cdot (2\sigma - 1) \cdot (2t-3)}{t \cdot (t-1)}
\end{aligned}
$$

Therefore, applying the property for any $a, b, c, \in V$, $w(a,b) \le \sigma(w(b,c) + w(c,a))$, will make Algorithm 3.1 a $(2\sigma - \frac{2 \cdot (2\sigma-1) \cdot (2t-3)}{t \cdot (t-1)})$ - approximation algorithm for MWtCP . $\qquad \square$

4.2. Approximation Ratios for Ultrametric Case for Algorithm 3.1

Theorem 4.2. *Algorithm 3.1 is a 1-approximation algorithm for ultrametric case of MWtCP.*

Proof. We note that for edges $(v_1, v_t), (v_2, v_t)...(v_{t-1}, v_t)$, $w(v_i, v_t) = w_i$.

Without loss of generality, for this case, we assume $(v_1, v_2) \leq (v_1, v_3) \leq ...(v_1, v_t) \leq (v_2, v_1) \leq ... \leq (v_{t-1}, v_t)$

thus, for $i < j, w(v_i, v_j) \leq max(w_i, w_j) = w_j$

In general, since all the internal edges will be predicted here are edges (v_i, v_j), where $1 \leq i \leq (t-3)$ and $(i+2) \leq j \leq (t-1)$ for a total of $\binom{t-1}{2} - (t-1) - 1$ edges.

Thus, $\sum\limits_{i=2t-2}^{e} w_i' = \sum\limits_{i=3}^{t-1} w_i' \cdot (i-2)$.

Therefore, for the approximation ratio is as follows:

$$
\begin{aligned}
opt &= \text{minimum } cost(Q) \\
&= \frac{t(t-1)}{2} \cdot \frac{1}{2t-3} \cdot cost(Q^\varsigma)
\end{aligned}
$$

$$
\begin{aligned}
sol &= \text{maximum } cost(Q') \\
&= cost(Q^\varsigma) + \sum\limits_{i=2t-2}^{e} w_i' \\
&= cost(Q^\varsigma) + \sum\limits_{i=3}^{t-1} w_i' \cdot (i-2)
\end{aligned}
$$

$$
\begin{aligned}
sol &\leq c \cdot opt, \\
sol/opt &\leq c,
\end{aligned}
$$

$$
\begin{aligned}
c &\geq \frac{cost(Q^\varsigma) + \sum\limits_{i=3}^{t-1} w_i' \cdot (i-2)}{\frac{t(t-1)}{2} \cdot \frac{1}{2t-3} \cdot cost(Q^\varsigma)} \\
&\geq \frac{2(2t-3)}{t(t-1)} \cdot \frac{cost(Q^\varsigma) + \sum\limits_{i=3}^{t-1} w_i' \cdot (i-2)}{cost(Q^\varsigma)}.
\end{aligned}
$$

We note that the weight per edge of Q^ς is $\frac{1}{2t-3} \cdot cost(Q^\varsigma)$, thus

$$
\begin{aligned}
&\geq \frac{2(2t-3)}{t(t-1)} \cdot \frac{cost(Q^\varsigma) + (\frac{t(t-1)}{2} - (2t-3)) \cdot \frac{1}{2t-3} \cdot cost(Q^\varsigma)}{cost(Q^\varsigma)} \\
&\geq \frac{t^2 - t}{t(t-1)} \\
&\geq 1 .
\end{aligned}
$$

Therefore, Algorithm 3.1 is a 1-approximation algorithm for the ultra-metric case of MWtCP. $\square$

5. Conclusion

Searching for gene clusters in genomes is an essential process in establishing relationship among organisms and providing insight into expression of specific traits, and even of diseases. One formulation of this problem is the Approximate Gene Cluster Discovery Problem (AGCDP) which is modelled as a combinatorial optimization problem in some works. In this study we have shown the formulation of AGCDP into the Minimum Weighted t-partite Clique Problem (MWtCP) which is the problem of finding a t-clique with minimum weight given a complete edge-weighted t-partite graph. A 2-approximation algorithms was presented which runs in $O(n^2)$ in the metric case of MWtCP by using more edges in the approximation than a previous study. It was also shown that this algorithm has a 2-approximation performance guarantee for the metric case and 1-approximation performance guarantee for the ultrametric case.

Acknowledgement

G. A. Solano is supported by the Engineering Research and Development for Technology (ERDT) Scholarship Program and the Commission of Higher Education Sandwich Program

References

1. J. A. Aborot, H. Adorna, J. B. Clemente, B. K. de Jesus and G. Solano. Search for a Star: Approximate Gene Cluster Discovery Problem (AGCDP) as a Graph Problem. Philippine Computing Journal, vol.7 no.2 (2012)
2. U. Alon. Biological networks: the tinkerer as an engineer. Science, 301:1866-1867 (2003)
3. A-L Barabasi and Z. N. Oltvai. Network biology: Understanding the cell's functional organization. Nature Reviews Genetics, 5:101-113, (2004)
4. A. Bergeron, S. Corteel, M. Raffinot, The Algorithmic of Gene Teams, Workshop on Algorithms in Bioinformatics (WABI), Vol. 2452 of LNCS, pp. 464476, (2002)
5. G. Cabunducan, J. Clemente, R. Relator, H. Adorna, Probing the Hardness of the Approximate Gene Cluster Discovery Problem (AGCDP), Third Workshop on Computing: Theory and Practice, WCTP 2013, (2013)

6. C. Cotta, M.A. Langston, P. Moscato. Combinatorial and algorithmic issues for microarray analysis. In Handbook of Approximation Algorithms and Metaheuristics, Gonzalez TF, ed. Chapman and Hall CRC, Boca Raton, FL, pp.74.71-74.14. (2007)

7. F. Harary, and I. C. Ross. A Procedure for Clique Detection Using the Group Matrix. Sociometry, vol. 20, pp. 205-215. (1957)

8. R. Hoberman, D. Durand. The Incompatible Desiderata of Gene Cluster Properties, In: McLysaght A, Huson DH, editors. Comparative Genomics: RECOMB 2005 International Workshop, Vol. 3678 of LNCS, pp. 73–87, (2005)

9. Z. N. Oltvai and A.-L. Barabasi. Systems biology. Life's complexity pyramid. Science, 298:763-764 (2002)

10. S. Rahmann, G. Klau, Integer Linear Programming Techniques for Discovering Approximate Gene Clusters, Bioinformatics Algorithms, Techniques and Applications, Wiley-Interscience, (2008)

11. G. Solano, G. Blin, M. Raffinot, J. Clemente. On the Approximability of Minimum Weight t-partite Clique Problem, Unpublished (2017)

12. L.F. Wu, T.R. Hughes, A.P. Davierwala, M.D. Robinson, R. Stoughton, and S.J. Altschuler. Large-scale prediction of saccharomyces cerevisiae gene function using overlapping transcriptional clusters. Nature Genetics, 31(3):255-265 (2002)

A Restart Strategy with Time Delay in Distributed Minimax Optimization

Kenta Hanada, Takayuki Wada, and Yasumasa Fujisaki

Graduate School of Information Science and Technology, Osaka University,
Suita, Osaka 565-0871, Japan
{k-hanada, t-wada, fujisaki}@ist.osaka-u.ac.jp

A restart strategy with time delay is proposed to a multi-agent consensus algorithm for an approximated distributed minimax optimization. The restart strategy controls a step length of a subgradient method and resets a local clock under certain criteria in the algorithm. A synchronization protocol with time delay is introduced in the algorithm to execute the restart strategy simultaneously. A numerical example illustrates that the proposed algorithm works well particularly in high approximation ratios.

Keywords: Distributed algorithms, Minimax optimization, Subgradient method, Restart strategy, Time delay.

1. Introduction

Distributed optimization is widely studied since many real world applications can be modeled as the distributed optimization[1-3]. The objective of the distributed optimization is to minimize the sum of the local objective functions among the agents. Consensus based distributed algorithms have been proposed to solve the distributed optimization and their convergence properties have been analyzed in a decade[4-8]. In these algorithms, agents have their decision variable and try to achieve a consensus in accordance with a given global objective by exchanging only their decision variable with their neighbors.

In this study, we deal with *distributed minimax optimization* via a consensus based distributed algorithm. The objective of the distributed minimax optimization is to minimize the maximum value of the local objective functions among the agents. This notion is suitable for considering a robustness of entire systems. One difficulty to get the optimal solution of the minimax optimization in a decentralized manner is that the agents must exchange not only their decision variable but also their value of the objective function in principle, since all of the agents have to evaluate the maximum value over the functions. It is an undesirable action in terms of a privacy issue. In Ref. 9, an equivalent reformulation of the original minimax optimization is considered and a penalty method based algorithm for the reformulation is proposed. However, this algorithm still has a privacy issue because the agents have to exchange an estimated optimal value in addition to their decision variable. On the other hand, in Ref. 10, the authors of the present paper propose an approximated problem of the original minimax optimization to deal with the drawback. Since this approximated problem is reduced to the distributed optimization whose objective function is defined by the sum of local ones, we can apply many algorithms to solve it.

Since we can choose an arbitrary approximation ratio in the approximated problem, we may be able to obtain a good approximated solution. However, a gradient of local functions with a high approximation ratio are very steep even in neighboring solutions from the optimal one. This fact causes a solution oscillation and a slow convergence to the optimal. We therefore introduce a novel step size with a *restart strategy* in order to reduce this phenomenon. The restart strategy is studied in order to speed up searchings in algorithms, and is achieved huge success especially in satisfiability problems[11,12]. An algorithm with the restart strategy for the distributed minimax optimization is first introduced by the authors of the present paper in Ref. 13. In this algorithm, a local tick counter will be reset in order to speed up the convergence if certain conditions are satisfied. Since an asynchronous protocol is used in the algorithm, the agents broadcast a reset signal when a certain agent detects that firing conditions are satisfied, which is not necessary for a synchronous protocol.

In this paper, we incorporate a synchronous protocol with time delay to a consensus based distributed optimization algorithm. The novel protocol requires only local communication among the agents and no broadcasting is required. A numerical example illustrates that the proposed algorithm works well particularly in high approximation ratios.

2. Distributed Minimax Optimization

In this paper, we consider a distributed minimax optimization over a multi-agent system. The distributed minimax optimization is defined by

$$f^* = \min_{x \in X} \max_{i \in V} f_i(x), \tag{1}$$

where $f^* \in \mathbb{R}$ is the optimal value, $x \in \mathbb{R}^m$ is a global (common) decision variable, $X \subseteq \mathbb{R}^m$ is a constraint set on x, $V = \{1, \dots, N\}$ is a set of agents, and $f_i : \mathbb{R}^m \to \mathbb{R}$ is a local objective function at each agent $i \in V$. We assume that the function f_i is convex and subdifferentiable with respect to x for all $i \in V$, it is known to only agent i, and it takes a non-negative value for any x, i.e.,

$$f_i(x) \geq 0 \qquad (2)$$

for all $x \in X$ and $i \in V$. The last assumption for f_i is critical to construct an approximated problem of (1). We also assume that the constraint set X is compact and convex, X is known to all agents, and the optimal solution set $X^* = \{x \in X \,|\, \max_{i \in V} f_i(x) = f^*\}$ is non-empty.

In order to get f^*, all of the agents must evaluate $\max_{i \in V} f_i(x)$, and thus the agents must exchange their values of the objective functions f_i in principle. It is undesirable action in terms of a privacy issue in the context of distributed optimization.

We therefore introduce an optimization

$$\bar{f}_p^* = \min_{x \in X} \sum_{i=1}^N \bar{f}_i(x), \qquad \bar{f}_i(x) = (f_i(x))^p, \qquad (3)$$

as an approximation of (1) [10]. Here $p \in \mathbb{N}$ is a fixed number which we call the approximation ratio. In fact, we see that

$$(\bar{f}_p^*)^{1/p} \to f^* \quad \text{as} \quad p \to \infty,$$

which comes from a well-known fact about p-norm. That is,

$$\|y\|_\infty \leq \|y\|_p \leq N^{1/p} \|y\|_\infty$$

holds true for any vector $y = [y_i] \in \mathbb{R}^N$ and any $p \geq 1$, where the norms are defined by

$$\|y\|_p = \left(\sum_{i=1}^N |y_i|^p \right)^{1/p}, \qquad \|y\|_\infty = \max_{1 \leq i \leq N} |y_i|.$$

We remark that the optimization (3) is the form of a standard distributed minimization [4,5] whose objective function is the sum of local functions. Notice here that the function $\bar{f}_i$ is convex for any p and for any convex function f_i which takes non-negative value [14]. We therefore see that we can apply any existing distributed algorithms, e.g., the methods developed in Ref. 4,5, to the approximated problem (3) under some assumptions.

3. Multi-agent Consensus Algorithm with Restart Strategy

3.1. *Multi-agent Consensus Algorithm*

In this section, we consider a multi-agent consensus algorithm with restart strategy for the approximated distributed minimax optimization (3).

Let $G = (V, E)$ be a graph, where $E \subseteq V \times V$ is the set of edges. We assume that the graph G is undirected and connected. Let us define the set of neighboring agents of agent i as $\mathcal{N}_i = \{j \in V | (i, j) \in E\}$. We assume that agent i can communicate with only neighboring agents. Since the graph G is undirected, agent j can also communicate with agent i if agent j is in $\mathcal{N}_i$ $(i \in \mathcal{N}_j)$. Let $D \in \mathbb{N}$ be the diameter of graph G, that is, D is the largest distance between any pair of agents, where the distance is the number of edges in the shortest path between agent i and j.

To find the optimal solution of the problem (3), we use a standard updating rule of a synchronous protocol[5]

$$v_i[k] = \sum_{j=1}^{N} a_{ij} x_j[k] \tag{4}$$

$$x_i[k + 1] = P_X \left(v_i[k] - r[k] g_i(x_i[k]) \right), \tag{5}$$

where $k \in \mathbb{N}$ is the k-th tick of the synchronous counter, $x_i[k] \in \mathbb{R}^m$ is an estimated optimal solution of (3) which is held by agent i at the k-th tick, P_X is the Euclidean projection on the set X, $r[k] \in \mathbb{R}$ is a step size, $g_i(x_i[k])$ is the subgradient of $\bar{f}_i$ at the $x_i[k]$, and $a_{ij} \in \mathbb{R}$ is the weight of agent i. If agent i gets the information from a neighboring agent j, a_{ij} is positive. Otherwise, $a_{ij} = 0$. We assume that the weight matrix $A = [a_{ij}]$ satisfies $a_{ij} \geq 0$, $\sum_{i=1}^{N} a_{ij} = 1$, and $\sum_{j=1}^{N} a_{ij} = 1$, e.g., A is a doubly stochastic matrix.

For this updating rule, we employ the diminishing step size

$$r[k] = \frac{1}{k}. \tag{6}$$

It is known that each $x_i[k]$ converges to the optimal solution of (3) by the updating rule (4) and (5)[5].

One important issue on the above updating rule is convergence speed. In our context, a large p is preferable for a good approximation. However, according to (3), the larger p is, the much larger (or smaller) a value of the subgradient is at a certain x. This may invoke a slow convergence even though it has a convergence property. We therefore introduce not (6) but another step size in order to reduce this phenomenon.

3.2. *Restart Strategy with Time Delay*

In this section, we incorporate a restart strategy with time delay into the multi-agent consensus algorithm in order to speed up the convergence.

In the existing algorithm employing an asynchronous protocol with the restart strategy[13], if at least one agent satisfies certain criteria, that agent sends a signal to all the other agents at the same time in order to reset their local counter. This broadcasting is not needed if we use a synchronous protocol.

We then propose the restart strategy with time delay in a synchronous protocol. First of all, the step size for the restart strategy is defined as

$$r[k] = \frac{1}{\alpha[k]} \cdot \frac{1}{c[k]}, \tag{7}$$

where $\alpha[k] \in \mathbb{R}$ is a non-decreasing function whose initial value is a positive parameter $\alpha[1] \in \mathbb{R}$ and $c[k]$ is the number of ticks from the latest reset to a current tick whose initial value is $c[1] = 1$. We should note that $\alpha[k]$ and $c[k]$ must be a common number among the agents due to a convergence guarantee[5].

The agents have to know the common number to execute the restart strategy simultaneously. We therefore introduce $k_i'[k]$ to know the candidate firing tick of the restart strategy. If $k_i'[k]$ converges to the same number for all $i \in V$ and $k = k_i'[k]$, then the agents execute the restart strategy. We use the following minimum consensus algorithm

$$k_i'[k+1] = \min_{j \in \mathcal{N}_i \cup \{i\}} k_j'[k]. \tag{8}$$

A detail of the overall updating procedure for agent i is as follows.

Step 1 (Initialize the settings) Agent i initializes D, p, $\alpha[1]$, $\alpha_{ub} \in \mathbb{R}$, $\beta \in \mathbb{R}$, $\epsilon \in \mathbb{R}$, $\tau \in \mathbb{N}$, $c[1] = 1$, $k = 1$, $k_i'[1] = +\infty$, and $x_i[1]$.

Step 2 (Exchange and update the information) Agent i exchanges the decision variable $x_i[k]$ and the candidate firing tick $k_i'[k]$ with her neighbors. She updates her decision variable $x_i[k]$ to $x_i[k+1]$ according to (4) and (5) with the step size (7). She also updates $k_i'[k]$ to $k_i'[k+1]$ according to (8).

Step 3 (Check the conditions) If $k_i'[k+1] = +\infty$, agent i checks the firing conditions

$$\|v_i[k]\| \geq \epsilon, \qquad c[k] \geq \tau, \qquad \alpha[k] \leq \alpha_{ub}, \tag{9}$$

where $\|\cdot\|$ is the the Euclidean norm. If all conditions are satisfied, she selects the candidate firing tick $k_i'[k+1] = k + D$.

Step 4 (Execute the restart strategy) If $k_i'[k+1] = k$, agent i executes the restart strategy, that is, she updates the parameter

$$\alpha[k+1] = p\,(\alpha[k] + \beta)^{p-1},$$

and resets the tick counter

$$c[k+1] = 1.$$

She also updates $k_i'[k+1] = +\infty$. Otherwise, $\alpha[k+1] = \alpha[k]$ and $c[k+1] = c[k] + 1$.

Step 5 $k \leftarrow k+1$ and go back to **Step 2**.

In **Step 1**, the agents initialize the problem settings. Although the diameter D of given graph G is the global information, a protocol is proposed in order to obtain D by using only local communication among the agents in Ref. 15. Thus, we assume that D is already known to the agents. The approximation ratio p is chosen as a large number ($p \geq 2$). The parameters $\alpha[1]$, α_{ub}, β, ϵ and τ are positive.

In **Step 2**, the agents exchange and update the decision variable and the candidate firing tick $k_i'[k]$, respectively.

In **Step 3**, the agents check the firing conditions (9) whether the restart strategy is needed or not. Note that $v_i[k]$ is the weighted local average of the neighbors of agent i obtained by (4). If agent i recognizes that the conditions (9) are all satisfied, then agent i selects the firing tick $k_i'[k+1]$.

In **Step 4**, the agents execute the restart strategy if the candidate firing tick $k_i'[k+1]$ is equal to k. The procedure iterates **Step 2** through **Step 5**.

The following theorem is to ensure that the candidate firing tick k_i' converges to the same number among the agents with finite ticks.

Theorem 3.1. *Suppose that* $k_i'[k] = +\infty$ *for all* $i \in V$ *and at least one agent selects* $k + D$ *as* $k_i'[k+1]$ *at* **Step 3** *in k-th tick. Then,* $k_i'[k+D+1] = k + D$ *is satisfied for all* $i \in V$.

Proof. Suppose that the current tick is k and agent i first recognizes that all conditions (9) are satisfied at **Step 3**. Then, $k_i'[k+1] = k + D$. Agent $j(\neq i)$ who has $k_j'[t+1] = +\infty$ at t-th tick, where t is greater than k, can change the value $k_i'[t+1]$ if $k_i'[t+1]$ is still $+\infty$ and the conditions (9) are all satisfied. Since agent j always selects $k_j'[t+1] = t + D$ at **Step 3** in t-th tick, the inequality $k + D < k_j'[t+1]$ always holds for any $j \in V$ and $t > k$. Thus, we see that agent j keeps $k + D$ as k_j' regardless of the former number of k_j' once she receives $k + D$ from her neighbors. Suppose that there exists agent l such that $k_l'[k + D + 1] \neq k + D$. This means that the number of edges in the shortest path from agent i to l is greater than D, which contradicts that the diameter of given graph G is D. $\square$

We should notice that the candidate firing tick k_i' turns back to $+\infty$ for all agents, that is, k_i' takes the initial value again after the agents executed the restart strategy in **Step 4**. Thus, the agents can start again to check the firing conditions and execute the restart strategy repeatedly.

We now state the convergence property of this algorithm.

Theorem 3.2. *For $p \geq 2$ and $\alpha[1] \geq 1$, the algorithm with restart strategy converges to some point in optimal solution set X^*.*

Proof. First of all, in order to prove the convergence of the updating rule (4) and (5) with the step size (7), (7) must be the same for all agents at each k-th tick according to Ref. 5. Since the restart strategy with time delay guarantees that $\alpha[k]$ and $c[k]$ are updated at the same time for all agents, the step size (7) can be the same at any k.

We will prove that the restart strategy is executed at most finite times, i.e., $\alpha[k]$ is updated at most finite times. We assume that the restart strategy is executed at k-th tick. For any k, since $p \geq 2$, $\alpha[k] \geq \alpha[1] \geq 1$, and β is the positive number, we obtain

$$\alpha[k] - \alpha[k-1] = p \left(\alpha[k-1] + \beta \right)^{p-1} - \alpha[k-1]$$
$$\geq p\alpha^{p-1}[k-1] + p\beta^{p-1} - \alpha[k-1].$$

Furthermore, since $p \geq 2$ and $\alpha[1] \geq 1$,

$$p\alpha^{p-1}[k-1] \geq \alpha[k-1],$$

holds for any k. Thus we have

$$\alpha[k] - \alpha[k-1] \geq p\beta^{p-1}.$$

We therefore see that $\alpha[k]$ can reach the constant α_{ub} within the finite number of iterations. If $\alpha[k]$ reaches some constant value $\alpha' \in \mathbb{R}$ within the finite number of iterations, the step size (7) can be expressed as

$$r[k] = \frac{1}{\alpha'} \cdot \frac{1}{c[k]},$$

for all $i \in V$ when k is sufficiently large. We see that the algorithm with the above step size converges to some point in optimal set X^* via the above updating rule according to Ref. 5. $\square$

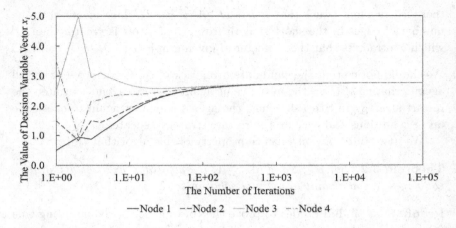

Fig. 1.   Behavior of the multi-agent system without the restart strategy when $p = 2$.

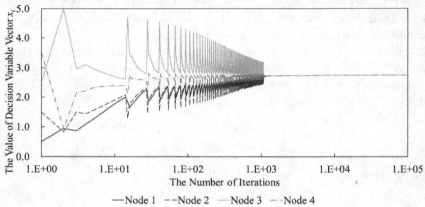

Fig. 2.   Behavior of the multi-agent system with the restart strategy when $p = 2$.

4. A Numerical Example

Let us consider a multi-agent system having four agents ($V = \{1, 2, 3, 4\}$) whose objective functions are

$$f_1(x) = \frac{1}{3}x, \quad f_2(x) = \frac{2}{3}x, \quad f_3(x) = -x + 5, \quad f_4(x) = \frac{1}{4}(x-1)^2,$$

where $x \in \mathbb{R}$ is a scalar ($m = 1$).   The set X is defined as $X = \{x \in \mathbb{R} | 0 \le x \le 5\}$.   Note that the optimal solution for this instance in (1) is 3.00.   The set of edges of network is defined as $E =$

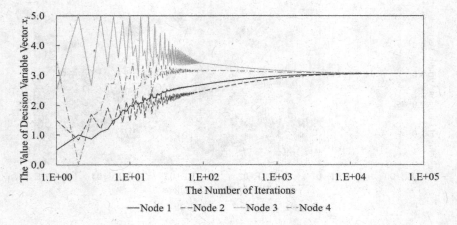

Fig. 3.   Behavior of the multi-agent system without the restart strategy when $p = 8$.

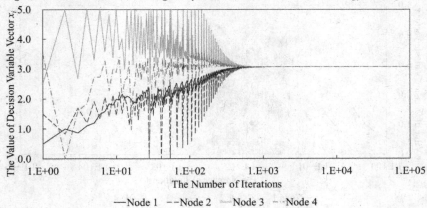

Fig. 4.   Behavior of the multi-agent system with the restart strategy when $p = 8$.

$\{(1, 2), (2, 3), (3, 4), (1, 4)\}$, that is, the system is a ring topology. The weight matrix A for the synchronous algorithm is selected as

$$A = \begin{bmatrix} 1.00 & 0.20 & 0.00 & 0.10 \\ 0.20 & 0.60 & 0.20 & 0.00 \\ 0.00 & 0.20 & 0.50 & 0.30 \\ 0.10 & 0.00 & 0.30 & 0.60 \end{bmatrix}. \tag{10}$$

We choose parameters as $\epsilon = 0.01$, $\alpha[1] = 1.00$, $\alpha_{ub} = 5.00$, $\beta = 0.05$ and $\tau = 10$ respectively.

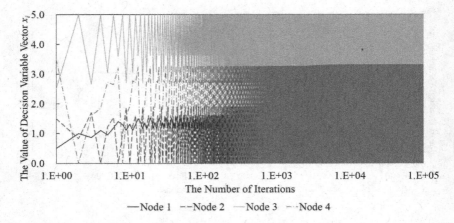

Fig. 5. Behavior of the multi-agent system without the restart strategy when $p = 128$.

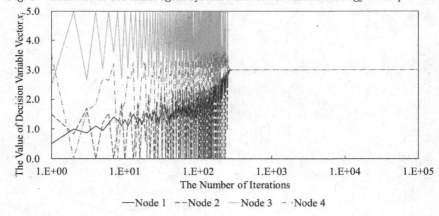

Fig. 6. Behavior of the multi-agent system with the restart strategy when $p = 128$.

We implemented the algorithm by Java and experiments run on a Java 1.8.0_74 runtime environment. Then, we performed $100,000$ iterations, where the initial condition was chosen as

$$x_1[1] = 0.5, \qquad x_2[1] = 1.5, \qquad x_3[1] = 2.5, \qquad x_4[1] = 3.5.$$

Figures 1, 3, and 5 show that the result of $p = 2$, 8, and 128 without the restart strategy. Figures 2, 4, and 6 show that the result of $p = 2$, 8, and 128 with the restart strategy. Note that the optimal solution for the instance in (3) ($p = 2$, 8, and 128) is 2.77, 3.07, and 3.01, respectively.

Wee see that all of the algorithms converge to near optimal except Fig. 5 ($p = 128$). Our proposed algorithm shows the faster convergence speed than the other algorithm.

5. Concluding Remarks

In this paper, we proposed a restart strategy with time delay to a multi-agent consensus algorithm in an approximated distributed minimax optimization. Since we introduce a synchronization protocol to execute the restart strategy with time delay, the algorithm uses only local communication among the agents. A numerical example illustrated that the proposed algorithm works well particularly in high approximation ratios.

Acknowledgments

This research was supported by JST CREST Grant Number JPMJCR15K2, Japan.

References

1. D. P. Palomar and M. Chiang, Alternative distributed algorithms for network utility maximization: Framework and applications, *IEEE Transactions on Automatic Control* **52**, 2254 (2007).
2. J. F. C. Mota, J. M. F. Xavier, P. M. Q. Aguiar and M. Püschel, Distributed optimization with local domains: Applications in mpc and network flows, *IEEE Transactions on Automatic Control* **60**, 2004 (2015).
3. C. Li, X. Yu, W. Yu, T. Huang and Z. W. Liu, Distributed event-triggered scheme for economic dispatch in smart grids, *IEEE Transactions on Industrial Informatics* **12**, 1775 (2016).
4. A. Nedic and A. Ozdaglar, Distributed subgradient methods for multi-agent optimization, *IEEE Transactions on Automatic Control* **54**, 48 (2009).
5. A. Nedic, A. Ozdaglar and P. A. Parrilo, Constrained consensus and optimization in multi-agent networks, *IEEE Transactions on Automatic Control* **55**, 922 (2010).
6. M. Zhu and S. Martinez, On distributed convex optimization under inequality and equality constraints, *IEEE Transactions on Automatic Control* **57**, 151 (2012).
7. I. Masubuchi, T. Wada, R. Morita, T. Asai, Y. Ohta and Y. Fujisaki, Distributed multi-agent optimization based on a constrained subgra-

dient method, *SICE Journal of Control, Measurement, and System Integration* **8**, 234 (2015).

8. I. Masubuchi, T. Wada, T. Asai, L. T. H. Nguyen, Y. Ohta and Y. Fujisaki, Distributed multi-agent optimization based on an exact penalty method with equality and inequality constraints, *SICE Journal of Control, Measurement, and System Integration* **9**, 179 (2016).

9. K. Srivastava, A. Nedić and D. Stipanović, Distributed min-max optimization in networks, *Proceedings of the 17th International Conference on Digital Signal Processing*, (Corfu, Greece, 2011).

10. K. Hanada, R. Morita, T. Wada and Y. Fujisaki, Simple Synchronous and Asynchronous Algorithms for Distributed Minimax Optimization, *SICE Journal of Control, Measurement, and System Integration* **10**, 557 (2017).

11. M. Luby, A. Sinclair and D. Zuckerman, Optimal speedup of las vegas algorithms, *Information Processing Letters* **47**, 173 (1993).

12. C. P. Gomes, B. Selman and H. Kautz, Boosting combinatorial search through randomization, *Proceedings of the Fifteenth National/Tenth Conference on Artificial Intelligence/Innovative Applications of Artificial Intelligence*, (Madison, USA, 1998).

13. K. Hanada, T. Wada and Y. Fujisaki, An asynchronous gossip algorithm with restart strategy in distributed minimax optimization, in *Proceedings of IFAC World Congress 2017* (Toulouse, France, 2017).

14. R. T. Rockafellar, *Convex analysis* (Princeton University Press, Princeton, N. J., 1970).

15. K. Hirayama, T. Matsui and M. Yokoo, Adaptive price update in distributed lagrangian relaxation protocol, in *Proceedings of the 8th International Joint Conference on Autonomous Agents and Multiagent Systems*, (Budapest, Hungary, 2009).

Untyped Call-by-Value Calculus with First-Class Continuations and Environments

Yuta Aoyagi and Shin-ya Nishizaki

Tokyo Institute of Technology,
Tokyo, 152-8552, Japan
E-mail:nisizaki@cs.titech.ac.jp

In programming languages, first-class object is an entity whch can be passed to a function as an actual parameter and returned from the function as a return value. You can classify and compare the programming languages from the point of view of first-class object. A continuation means a rest of computation at some point in a program, which corresponds to a call stack in a programming language processor. An environment is a mapping of variable names to bound values. In the framework of the lambda calculus, the first-class continuation was studied by Felleisen and the first-class environment has been studied by us.

In this paper, we propose a call-by-value lambda calculus with first-class continuations and environment. Its operational semantics is formalized as a small-step semantics using evaluation contexts. Then, we show the soundness property of the operational semantics with respect to the call-by-value lambda calculus with first-class continuations and records.

Keywords: Lambda Calculus; Call-by-Value Evaluation; First-Class Continuation; First-Class Environment.

1. Introduction

A *first-class entity,* or first-class object is an entity that can be passed to a function and returned from a function as a resulting value. For example, an integer is a first-class entity in many programming language like C. However, in C programming language, a pointer to a function is first-class but a funtion itself is not. In functional programming languages such as Scheme and Haskell, a function is first-class.

An *environment* is a notion of the programming language semantics that represents a mapping of variable names to bound values. In the lambda calculs, the environment is formulated as a substitution. For example, consider a lambda-term $\lambda x.\lambda y.(x + x + y)$.

If you give actual parameters 1 and 2, then we have

$$(\lambda x.\lambda y.(x+x+y))\, 1\, 2 \to (\lambda y.(x+x+y)[x{:=}1])\, 2 \to (x+x+y)[x{:=}1,\, y{:=}2].$$

The last term can be considered a term $(x + x + y)$ to which a substitution $[x{:=}1,\, y{:=}2]$ of 1 and 2 for x and y, respectively. The substition $[x{:=}1,\, y{:=}2]$ can be interpreted as an environment which assigns 1 and 2 to the variables x and y, respectively. In the $\lambda\sigma$-calculus[1] proposed by Abadi et al., an environment is formalized as a substitution not defined in the meta-level but in the object-level. In the lambda calculus, the substituion operation is formulated in the meta-level, but in the $\lambda\sigma$-calculus, it is formalized as the reduction as an object-level operation. Nishizaki[9][7][11][10] studied the first-class environment in the framework of the lambda calculus and the $\lambda\sigma$-calculus. In his calculus, he formalized the first-class environment by handling the lambda terms and the substitution uniformly.

A *continuation* is a notion of the semantics and the programming language processor, that represents a rest of computation at some point in time. A call-stack of a runtime system of a programming language can be considered as a continuation. If you utilize first-class continuations, you can save an image of the call-stack at some point and recover the saved image later. In programming language Scheme, you can implement global jumps, exception handling, and coroutines[2] using the first-class continuation.

In the lambda calculus, the continuation is formalized as an *evaluation context*, which is a device for pointing a sub-term which to be reduced. Consider the following reduction sequence of an arithmetic expression.

$$\underline{(1+2)} * (3+4) \to 3 * \underline{(3+4)} \to \underline{3*7} \to 21.$$

In the first expression $(1+2)*(3+4)$, $1+2$ is the subterm to be reduced. In the above sequence, the underline points to the subterm to be reduced. The underline can be represented as an evaluation context $E[\ ]$ such as

$$E[\ ] = [\ ] * (3+4),$$

which is a expresion with a hole $[\ ]$. The reduction is written as

$$E[1+2] \to E[3].$$

Plotkin[12] introduced the notion of evaluation context in order to represent the evaluation strategy of the lambda calculus. Felleisen et al.[3][4] formalize the first-class continuation using the evaluation context. Nishizaki[8] studied first-class continuation from the viewpoint of Girard's linear logic.

In this paper, we study the lambda calclus with both first-class environments and continuations. First, we define the lambda calculus λ_{CE}

with first-class environments and continuations. Second, we introduce the lambda calculus λ_{CRec} with records and first-class continuations. Third, we give a translation of λ_{CE} into λ_{CRec}. Forth, we show the translation preserves the reduction sequence, which assures the soundness of the λ_{CE}.

2. Lambda Calculus with First-class Continuations and Environments

In this section, we propose a lambda calculus with first-class continuations and environments. The first-class continuations are introduced in the style of Felleisen[3][4], using the $\mathcal{C}$ operator. The first-class environments are formulated in the style of Nishizaki[9], in which id returns the current environment and $(M \circ N)$ provides evaluation of M under an environment N. The former corresponds to (the-environment) and the latter to $(\text{eval } 'M \ N)$, in several implementations of Scheme[6].

We presuppose a set of $\mathbf{Var}_{\text{CEnv}}$ of *variables*. We usually denote variables by letters like x, y, z.

Definition 2.1 (Terms, Values, and Evaluation Contexts of λ_{CE}).
Terms $M, N, \ldots$, values $V, W, \ldots$, and evaluation contexts $E[\ ], E'[\ ], \ldots$ of λ_{CE} are defined inductively by the following grammar.

$$
\begin{aligned}
M ::= \ & x \\
| \ & (\lambda x.M) \\
| \ & (MN) \\
| \ & id \\
| \ & (M/x) \cdot N \\
| \ & (M \circ N) \\
| \ & \mathcal{C}(M) \\
| \ & \mathfrak{A}(E[\ ])
\end{aligned}
$$

$$
V ::= x \ | \ (\lambda x.M) \ | \ (\lambda x.M) \circ W \ | \ id \ | \ (V/x) \cdot W
$$

$$E[\ ] ::= [\ ]$$
$$|\ (E[\ ]\ N)$$
$$|\ (V\ E[\ ])$$
$$|\ (E[\ ]/x) \cdot N$$
$$|\ (V/x) \cdot E[\ ]$$
$$|\ (E[\ ] \circ V)$$
$$|\ (N \circ E[\ ])$$

The continuation operator $\mathcal{K}$, which corresponds to the call-with-current-continuation of programming language Scheme, can be defined using the operator $\mathcal{C}$ as follows.

$$\mathcal{K}(M) \stackrel{def}{=} \mathcal{C}(\lambda k.k(M\ k))$$

The operator $\mathfrak{A}$ is a variation of the abort operator $\mathcal{A}$ in the Felleisen's style[4,5]:

$$\mathfrak{A}(E[\ ]) = \lambda k.\mathcal{A}(E[k]).$$

If an evaluation context $E[\ ]$ contains the term $\mathfrak{A}(E[\ ])$, the hole $[\ ]$ appears in the term $\mathfrak{A}(E[\ ])$ is not considered as the hole of $E[\ ]$, in other words, the hole in $\mathfrak{A}(E[\ ])$ is closed.

Informally, $\mathfrak{A}(E[\ ])$ takes an actual parameter V; if its application to the parameter is evaluated, the current continuation $E'[\ ]$ is replaced by $E[\ ]$ and the parameter V is evaluated under the continuation $E[\ ]$:

$$E'[(\mathfrak{A}(E[\ ])\ V)] \rightarrow E[V]$$

We introduce a subset of the evaluation contexts as follows.

Definition 2.2 (Restricted Evaluation Context). *We define a subset of the evaluation contexts, called restricted evaluation contexts, by the following grammar.*

$$F[\ ] ::= [\ ]$$
$$|\ (F[\ ]\ N)$$
$$|\ (V\ F[\ ])$$
$$|\ (F[\ ]/x) \cdot N$$
$$|\ (V/x) \cdot F[\ ]$$
$$|\ (N \circ F[\ ])$$

Definition 2.3 (Call-by-value Reduction of λ_{CE}). *The call-by-value evaluation $\to$ of λ_{CE} is a binary relation between terms, defied by the following rules.*

$$E[((\lambda x.M)\ V)] \to E[M \circ ((V/x) \cdot id)] \qquad \textbf{\textit{Beta}}$$

$$E[((\lambda x.M) \circ W)\ V)] \to E[M \circ ((V/x) \cdot W)] \qquad \textbf{\textit{BetaClos}}$$

$$E[x \circ ((V/x) \cdot W)] \to E[V] \qquad \textbf{\textit{VarRef}}$$

$$E[y \circ ((V/x) \cdot W)] \to E[y \circ W] \qquad \textbf{\textit{VarSkip}}$$

$$E[(M\ N) \circ W] \to E[(x \circ W)(V \circ W)] \qquad \textbf{\textit{AppComp}}$$

$$E[((M/x) \cdot N) \circ W] \to E[(((M \circ W)/x) \cdot (N \circ W))] \qquad \textbf{\textit{ExtnComp}}$$

$$E[\mathfrak{A}(E[\ ]) \circ W] \to E[\mathfrak{A}(E[\ ] \circ W)] \qquad \textbf{\textit{AbortComp}}$$

$$E[(V \circ W) \circ W'] \to E[V \circ (W \circ W')] \qquad \textbf{\textit{CompAssoc}}$$

$$E[id \circ W] \to E[W] \qquad \textbf{\textit{IdL}}$$

$$E[V \circ id] \to E[V] \qquad \textbf{\textit{IdR}}$$

$$F[\mathcal{C}(M)] \to M(\mathfrak{A}(F[\ ])) \qquad \textbf{\textit{Cont}}$$

$$F[(\mathfrak{A}(E[\ ])\ V)] \to E[V] \qquad \textbf{\textit{Abort}}$$

3. Lambda Calculus with Records and First-class Continuations

In this section, we introduce a lambda calculus with records and first-class continuations. In the previous paper[9], the simply-typed lambda calculus with records is used as a target of the translation of the simply-typed lambda calculus with first-class continuations, in order to prove the strong normalizability. The calculus introduced in this section is its extended version. The first-class environments will be interpreted as the records in this translation in the following section.

We presuppose an infinite set $\textbf{Var}_{CRec}$ Of *variables* and a set **Const** of *constants*. We will usually denote variables by letters like u, v, w and constants by $c, d, \ldots$.. The variable symbols in the calculus λ_{CE} are considered as constants of λ_{CRec}.

Definition 3.1 (Term of λ_{CRec}). *Terms M of λ_{CRec} are defined inductively by the following grammar.*

$$
\begin{aligned}
M ::=\ & v \\
& |\ c \\
& |\ (\lambda v.M) \\
& |\ (MN) \\
& |\ \mathcal{C}(M) \\
& |\ \mathcal{A}(M) \\
& |\ \boldsymbol{upd}(L, M, N) \\
& |\ \boldsymbol{lookup}(M, N)
\end{aligned}
$$

Definition 3.2 (Values of λ_{CRec}). *A set of values **Val** is defined by the following grammar.*

$$
\begin{aligned}
V ::=\ & v \\
& |\ c \\
& |\ (\lambda v.M) \\
& |\ (xV) \\
& |\ \boldsymbol{upd}(V_1, V_2, V_3) \\
& |\ \boldsymbol{lookup}(V, U)
\end{aligned}
$$

where U is not a value of form $\boldsymbol{upd}(U', V', W')$.

Definition 3.3 (Evaluation context of λ_{CRec}). *An evaluation context $E[\ ]$ is defined inductively by the following grammar.*

$$
\begin{aligned}
E[\ ] ::=\ & [\ ] \\
& |\ (E[\ ]\ M) \\
& |\ (V\ E[\ ]) \\
& |\ \boldsymbol{upd}(E[\ ], M, N) \\
& |\ \boldsymbol{upd}(V, E[\ ], N) \\
& |\ \boldsymbol{upd}(V_1, V_2, E[\ ]) \\
& |\ \boldsymbol{lookup}(E[\ ], N) \\
& |\ \boldsymbol{lookup}(V, E[\ ])
\end{aligned}
$$

Definition 3.4 (Call-by-Value Reduction of λ_{CRec}).
The Call-by-Value Reduction *of λ_{CRec} is a binary relation $\rightarrow$ defined by the following rules.*

$$E[((\lambda v.M)V)] \rightarrow E[M[v := V]]$$
$$E[\textbf{\textit{lookup}}(c, \textbf{\textit{upd}}(c, V_2, V_3))] \rightarrow E[V_2]$$
$$E[\textbf{\textit{lookup}}(c, \textbf{\textit{upd}}(d, V_2, V_3))] \rightarrow E[\textbf{\textit{lookup}}(c, V_3)]$$
$$E[\mathcal{C}(M)] \rightarrow M(\lambda k.\mathcal{A}(E[k]))$$
$$E[\mathcal{A}(M)] \rightarrow M$$

4. Translation of λ_{CE} into λ_{CRec}

Definition 4.1 (Translation of terms and evaluation contexts).
For a term M of λ_{CE} and a value r of λ_{CRec}, its translation $[\![M]\!](r)$ is defined inductively by the following equations.

Simultaneously, a translation $E^{(r)}[\,]$ of an environment contexts $E[\,]$ of λ_{CE} into those of λ_{CRec} for a term r of λ_{CRec}, and a translation $r^{E[\,]}$ of a term r of λ_{CRec} for an evaluation context $E[\,]$ of λ_{CRec}, are also defined by the following equations.

$$[\![x]\!](r) = \textbf{\textit{lkp}}(x, r),$$
$$[\![\lambda x.M]\!](r) = \lambda v.[\![M]\!](\textbf{\textit{upd}}(x, v, r)),$$
$$[\![(MN)]\!](r) = ([\![M]\!](r)\,[\![N]\!](r)),$$
$$[\![id]\!](r) = r,$$
$$[\![(M \circ W)]\!](r) = [\![M]\!](w)([\![W]\!](r)),$$
$$\text{where } W \text{ is a value,}$$
$$[\![(M \circ N)]\!](r) = (\lambda w.[\![M]\!](w))([\![N]\!](r)),$$
$$\text{where } N \text{ is not a value,}$$
$$[\![(M/x) \cdot N]\!](r) = \textbf{\textit{upd}}(x, [\![M]\!](r), [\![N]\!](r)),$$
$$[\![\mathcal{C}(M)]\!](r) = \mathcal{C}([\![M]\!](r)),$$
$$[\![\mathfrak{A}(E[\,])]\!](r) = \lambda v.\mathcal{A}(E^{(r)}[v])$$

If $E[\,]$ is $[\,]$,

$$\begin{cases} E^{(r)}[\,] = [\,] \\ r^{E[\,]} = r \end{cases}$$

If $E[\,]$ is $(E'[\,]\ N)$,

$$\begin{cases} E^{(r)}[\,] = (E'^{(r)}[\,]\ \ [\![N]\!](r)), \\ r^{E[\,]} \quad = r^{E'[\,]} \end{cases}$$

If $E[\,]$ is $(V\ E'[\,])$,

$$\begin{cases} E^{(r)}[\,] = ([\![V]\!](r)\ \ E'^{(r)}[\,]), \\ r^{E[\,]} \quad = r^{E'[\,]} \end{cases}$$

If $E[\,]$ is $(E'[\,]/x)\cdot N$,

$$\begin{cases} E^{(r)}[\,] = \boldsymbol{upd}(x, E'^{(r)}[\,], [\![N]\!](r)), \\ r^{E[\,]} \quad = r^{E'[\,]} \end{cases}$$

If $E[\,]$ is $(V/x)\cdot E'[\,]$,

$$\begin{cases} E^{(r)}[\,] = \boldsymbol{upd}(x, [\![V]\!](r), E'^{(r)}[\,]), \\ r^{E[\,]} \quad = r^{E'[\,]} \end{cases}$$

If $E[\,]$ is $(E'[\,]\circ V)$,

$$\begin{cases} E^{(r)}[\,] = E'^{[\![V]\!](r)}[\,], \\ r^{E[\,]} \quad = [\![V]\!](r^{E'[\,]}) \end{cases}$$

If $E[\,]$ is $(N\circ E'[\,])$,

$$\begin{cases} E^{(r)}[\,] = (\lambda w.[\![N]\!](w))(E'^{(r)}[\,]), \\ r^{E[\,]} \quad = r^{E'[\,]} \end{cases}$$

Proposition 4.1. *If both V and r are values, $[\![V]\!](r)$ is a value.*

Proof. This is proved by induction on the value V.
Case $V = x$. We have $[\![x]\!](r) = \mathsf{lkp}(x, r)$. If r is not of form of environment extension, then $\mathsf{lkp}(x, r)$ is **lookup**(x, r). If r is an environment extionsion $(V/x)\cdot W$, then

$$\mathsf{lkp}(x, (V/x)\cdot W) = V,$$

which is a value.

If r is an environment extention $(V/y)\cdot W$ where $x \neq y$, then

$$\mathsf{lkp}(x, (V/y)\cdot W) = \mathsf{lkp}(x, W).$$

If you apply such a procedure using **VarSkip** repeatedly, then you have either some value V' by **VarRef** or some value of form $\mathsf{lkp}(x, W')$ for some value W' which is not an environment extentions, which is also a value.
Case $V = \lambda x.M$ or $(\lambda x.M)\circ V$. In both cases, $[\![V]\!](r)$ is a lambda abstraction, that is, a value.

Case $V = id$. We have

$$[\![V]\!](r) = [\![id]\!](r) = r,$$

which is a value.

Case $V = (V/x) \cdot W$. We have

$$[\![V]\!](r) = \mathbf{upd}(x, [\![V]\!](r), [\![W]\!](r)),$$

by the induction hypothsis, both $[\![V]\!](r)$ and $[\![W]\!](r)$ are values. Hence, $[\![V]\!]r$ is a value.

End of Proof.

The following property will be used later.

Proposition 4.2. *If M is not a value, then neither is $E[M]$.*

We can prove its contrapositive

If $E[M]$ is a value, then M is a value

easily by induction on the evaluation context $E[\ ]$.

The notion of the restricted evaluation context was introduced for the following property:

Proposition 4.3. *For a restricted evaluation context, $r^{F[]} = r$.*

The following property is the fundamental lemma for showing the soundness theorem.

Lemma 4.1. *For a term M which is not a value, $[\![E[M]]\!](r) = E^{(r)}[[\![M]\!](r^{E[\ ]})]$.*

Proof. We prove this lemma by induction on the structure of $E[\ ]$.

Case $E[\ ] = [\ ]$.

$$[\![E[M]]\!](r) = [\![M]\!](r)$$
$$= E^{(r)}[[\![M]\!](r^{E[\ ]})].$$

Case $E[\ ] = (E'[\ ]\ N)$.

$$[\![E[M]]\!](r)$$
$$= [\![(E'[M]\ N)]\!](r)$$
$$= ([\![E'[M]]\!](r)\ [\![N]\!](r))$$
$$= (E'^{(r)}[[\![M]\!](r^{E'[\ ]})]\ [\![N]\!](r))$$
$$\quad \text{by the induction hypothesis}$$
$$= E^{(r)}[[\![M]\!](r^{E[\ ]})]$$

Case $E[\ ] = (V\ E'[\ ])$.

$$\begin{aligned}
[\![E[M]]\!](r) &= [\![(V\ E'[M])]\!](r) \\
&= ([\![V]\!](r)\ [\![E'[M]]\!](r)) \\
&= ([\![V]\!](r)\ E'^{(r)}[\![M]\!](r^{E'[\ ]})]) \\
&\quad \text{by the induction hypothesis,} \\
&= E[[\![M]\!](r^{E[\ ]})]
\end{aligned}$$

Case $E[\ ] = (E[\ ]/x) \cdot N$.

$$\begin{aligned}
[\![E[M]]\!](r) &= [\![(E'[M]/x) \cdot N]\!](r) \\
&= \mathbf{upd}(x, [\![E'[M]]\!](r), [\![N]\!](r)) \\
&= \mathbf{upd}(x, E'^{(r)}[\![M]\!](r^{E'[\ ]}), [\![N]\!](r)) \\
&\quad \text{by the induction hypothesis,} \\
&= E^{(r)}[\![M]\!](r^{E[\ ]})]
\end{aligned}$$

Case $E[\ ] = (V/x) \cdot E'[\ ]$.

$$\begin{aligned}
[\]\!] &= [\![E'[M] \circ V]\!](r) \\
&= [\![E'[M]]\!]([\![V]\!](r)) \\
&= E'^{([\![V]\!](r))}[\![M]\!](([\![V]\!](r))^{E'[\ ]})]
\end{aligned}$$

by the induction hypothesis,

$$= E^{(r)}[[\![M]\!](r^{E[\ ]})]$$

Case $E[\ ] = (E'[\ ] \circ V)$.

$$\begin{aligned}
[\![E[M]]\!](r) &= [\![E'[M] \circ V]\!](r) \\
&= [\![E'[M]]\!]([\![V]\!](r)) \\
&= E'^{([\![V]\!](r))}[\![M]\!]([\![V]\!](r))^{E'[\ ]}]
\end{aligned}$$

Case $E[\ ] = (N \circ E[\ ])$.

$$\begin{aligned}
[\![E[M]]\!](r) &= [\![(N \circ E'[M])]\!](r) \\
&= (\lambda w.[\![N]\!](w))([\![E'[M]]\!](r)) \\
&\quad \text{since } E'[M] \text{ is not a value,} \\
&= (\lambda w.[\![N]\!](w))(E'^{(r)}[\![M]\!](r^{E'[\ ]})]) \\
&\quad \text{by the induction hypothesis,} \\
&= E^{(r)}[[\![M]\!](r^{E'[\ ]})]
\end{aligned}$$

End of Proof.

The following theorem shows soundenss of the call-by-value reduction of λ_{CE} with respect to that of λ_{CRec}.

Theorem 4.1. *If $E[M] \to E[M']$ then*

$$[\![E[M]]\!](r) \stackrel{*}{\to} [\![E[M']]\!](r).$$

Proof. We make case analysis on a rule deriving $E[M] \to E[M']$.
Case of Cont: $F[\mathcal{C}(M)] \to M(\mathfrak{A}(F[\ ]))$.

$$
\begin{aligned}
[\![F[\mathcal{C}(M)]]\!](r) &= F^r\big[[\![\mathcal{C}(M)]\!](r^{F[\ ]})\big], \\
&= F^r\big[\mathcal{C}([\![M]\!](r^{F[\ ]}))\big], \\
&\to ([\![M]\!](r^{F[\ ]}))(\lambda k.\mathcal{A}(F^{(r)}[k])),
\end{aligned}
$$

On the other hand,

$$
\begin{aligned}
[\![M(\mathfrak{A}(F[\ ]))]\!](r) &= ([\![M]\!](r)\ [\![\mathfrak{A}(F[\ ])]\!](r)) \\
&= ([\![M]\!](r)\ (\lambda k.\mathcal{A}(F^{(r)}[k])))
\end{aligned}
$$

Since $r^{F[\ ]} = r$, it holds that

$$[\![F[\mathcal{C}(M)]]\!](r) \to [\![M(\mathfrak{A}(F[\ ]))]\!](r).$$

Case of Abort. Suppose that

$$F[\mathfrak{A}(E[\ ])] \to E[V].$$

Then,

$$
\begin{aligned}
&[\![F[\mathfrak{A}(E[\ ])]\ V)]\!] \\
&= F^{(r)}[[\![\mathfrak{A}(E[\ ])\ V]\!](r^{F[\ ]})] \\
&= F^{(r)}[[\![\mathfrak{A}(E[\ ])\ V]\!](r)] && \text{since } r^{F[\ ]} = r \\
&= F^{(r)}\Big[([\![\mathfrak{A}(E[\ ])]\!](r)\ [\![V]\!](r))\Big] \\
&= F^{(r)}\Big[((\lambda v.\mathcal{A}(E^r[v]))\ [\![V]\!](r))\Big] \\
&\to F^{(r)}\big[(\mathcal{A}(E^r[[\![V]\!](r)]))\big] \\
&\to E^r[[\![V]\!](r)] \\
&= [\![E[V]]\!](r).
\end{aligned}
$$

Case of BetaClos: $E\big[(((\lambda x.M) \circ W)\ V)\big] \to E[M \circ ((V/x) \cdot W)]$.

$$
\begin{aligned}
&\Big[\!\big[E[(((\lambda x.M) \circ W)\ V)]\big]\!\Big](r) \\
&= E^{(r)}\Big[[\![(((\lambda x.M) \circ W)\ V)]\!](r^{E[\ ]})\Big] \\
&= E^{(r)}\Big[\Big([\![((\lambda x.M) \circ W)]\!](r^{E[\ ]})\ [\![V]\!](r^{E[\ ]})\Big)\Big] \\
&= E^{(r)}\Big[\Big([\![\lambda x.M]\!]([\![W]\!](r^{E[\ ]})\ [\![V]\!](r^{E[\ ]})\Big)\Big] \\
&= E^{(r)}\Big[\Big((\lambda v.[\![M]\!](\mathbf{upd}(x,v,[\![W]\!](r^{E[\ ]}))))\ [\![V]\!](r^{E[\ ]})\Big)\Big] \\
&\to E^{(r)}\Big[[\![M]\!]\Big(\mathbf{upd}(x,[\![V]\!](r^{E[\ ]}),[\![W]\!](r^{E[\ ]}))\Big)\Big]
\end{aligned}
$$

On the other hand, we have

$$
\begin{aligned}
&[\![E[M \circ ((V/x) \cdot W)]]\!](r) \\
&= E^{(r)}\Big[[\![M \circ ((V/x) \cdot W)]\!](r^{E[\ ]})\Big] \\
&= E^{(r)}\Big[[\![M]\!]\big(\mathbf{upd}(x,[\![V]\!](r^{E[\ ]}),[\![W]\!](r^{E[\ ]}))\big)\Big].
\end{aligned}
$$

Hence,

$$
[\![E[(((\lambda x.M) \circ W)\ V)]]\!](r) \to [\![E[M \circ ((V/x) \cdot W)]]\!](r).
$$

Case of Beta: $E\big[((\lambda x.M)\ V)\big] \to E[M \circ ((V/x) \cdot id)]$.

$$
\begin{aligned}
&\Big[\!\big[E[((\lambda x.M)\ V)]\big]\!\Big](r) \\
&= E^{(r)}\Big[[\![((\lambda x.M)\ V)]\!](r^{E[\ ]})\Big] \\
&= E^{(r)}\Big[\Big([\![\lambda x.M]\!](r^{E[\ ]})\ [\![V]\!](r^{E[\ ]})\Big)\Big] \\
&= E^{(r)}\Big[\Big((\lambda v.[\![M]\!](\mathbf{upd}(x,v,r^{E[\ ]})))\ [\![V]\!](r^{E[\ ]})\Big)\Big] \\
&\to E^{(r)}\Big[[\![M]\!]\Big(\mathbf{upd}(x,[\![V]\!](r^{E[\ ]}),r^{E[\ ]})\Big)\Big]
\end{aligned}
$$

On the other hand, we have

$$\big[E[M \circ ((V/x) \cdot id)]\big](r)$$
$$= E^{(r)}\Big[\big[M \circ ((V/x) \cdot id)\big](r^{E[\ ]})\Big]$$
$$= E^{(r)}\Big[[M]\big(\mathbf{upd}(x, [V](r^{E[\ ]}), r^{E[\ ]})\big)\Big].$$

Hence,

$$\big[E[((\lambda x.M)\ V)]\big](r) \to \big[E[M \circ ((V/x) \cdot id)]\big](r).$$

Case of VarRef: $E[x \circ ((V/x) \cdot W)] \to E[V]$.

$$\big[E[x \circ ((V/x) \cdot W)]\big](r)$$
$$= E^{(r)}\big[[x \circ ((V/x) \cdot W)](r^{E[\ ]})\big]$$
$$= E^{(r)}\big[[x]\big([(V/x) \cdot W](r^{E[\ ]})\big)\big]$$
$$= E^{(r)}\big[[x]\big(\mathbf{upd}(x, [V](r^{E[\ ]}), [W](r^{E[\ ]}))\big)\big]$$
$$= E^{(r)}\big[\mathbf{lookup}(x, \mathbf{upd}(x, [V](r^{E[\ ]}), [W](r^{E[\ ]}))\big]$$
$$\to E^{(r)}\big[[V](r^{E[\ ]})\big]$$
$$= \big[E[V]\big](r)$$

Case of VarSkip: $E[y \circ ((V/x) \cdot W)] \to E[y \circ W]$.

$$\big[E[y \circ ((V/x) \cdot W)]\big](r)$$
$$= E^{(r)}\big[[y]\big([(V/x) \cdot W](r^{E[\ ]})\big)\big]$$
$$= E^{(r)}\big[[y]\big(\mathbf{upd}(x, [V](r^{E[\ ]}), [W](r^{E[\ ]}))\big)\big]$$
$$= E^{(r)}\big[\mathbf{lookup}(y, \mathbf{upd}(x, [V](r^{E[\ ]}), [W](r^{E[\ ]})))\big]$$
$$\to E^{(r)}\big[\mathbf{lookup}(y, [W](r^{E[\ ]}))\big]$$

On the other hand,

$$\big[E[y \circ W]\big](r)$$
$$= E^{(r)}\big[[y \circ W](r^{E[\ ]})\big]$$
$$= E^{(r)}\big[[y]\big([W](r^{E[\ ]})\big)\big]$$
$$= E^{(r)}\big[\mathbf{lookup}(y, [W](r^{E[\ ]}))\big].$$

Hence,

$$\big[E[y \circ ((V/x) \cdot W)]\big](r) \to \big[E[y \circ W]\big](r).$$

Case of AppComp: $E[(MN) \circ W] \to E[(M \circ W)(N \circ W)]$.

$$
\begin{aligned}
&[\![E[(MN) \circ W]]\!](r) \\
&= E^{(r)} \big[[\![(MN) \circ W]\!](r^{E[\,]}) \big] \\
&= E^{(r)} \Big[[\![(MN)]\!]([\![W]\!](r^{E[\,]})) \Big] \\
&= E^{(r)} \Big[([\![M]\!]([\![W]\!](r^{E[\,]}))\ [\![N]\!]([\![W]\!](r^{E[\,]}))) \Big] \\
&= E^{(r)} \Big[([\![M \circ W]\!](r^{E[\,]})\ [\![N \circ W]\!](r^{E[\,]})) \Big] \\
&= E^{(r)} \big[[\![((M \circ W)\ (N \circ W))]\!](r^{E[\,]}) \big] \\
&= \big[E[((M \circ W)\ (N \circ W))] \big](r)
\end{aligned}
$$

Case of ExtnComp: $E[((M/x) \cdot N) \circ W] \to E[((M \circ W)/x) \cdot (N \circ W)]$.

$$
\begin{aligned}
&[\![E[((M/x) \cdot N) \circ W]]\!] \\
&= E^{(r)} \big[[\![((M/x) \cdot N) \circ W]\!](r^{E[\,]}) \big] \\
&= E^{(r)} \big[[\![((M/x) \cdot N)]\!]([\![W]\!](r^{E[\,]})) \big] \\
&= E^{(r)} \Big[\mathbf{upd}(x, [\![M]\!]([\![W]\!](r^{E[\,]})), [\![N]\!]([\![W]\!](r^{E[\,]}))) \Big] \\
&= E^{(r)} \Big[\mathbf{upd}(x, [\![M \circ W]\!](r^{E[\,]}), [\![N \circ W]\!](r^{E[\,]})) \Big] \\
&= E^{(r)} \big[[\![((M \circ W)/x) \cdot (N \circ W)]\!](r^{E[\,]}) \big] \\
&= \big[E[((M \circ W)/x) \cdot (N \circ W)] \big](r).
\end{aligned}
$$

Case of AbortComp: $F[\mathfrak{A}(E[\,]) \circ W] \to F[\mathfrak{A}(E[\,] \circ W)]$.

$$
\begin{aligned}
&\big[F[\mathfrak{A}(E[\,]) \circ W] \big](r) \\
&= F^{(r)} \Big[\big[\mathfrak{A}(E[\,]) \circ Q \big](r^{F[\,]}) \Big] \\
&= F^{(r)} \Big[\big[\mathfrak{A}(E[\,]) \big]([\![W]\!](r^{F[\,]})) \Big] \\
&= F^{(r)} \Big[\lambda v. \mathcal{A}(E^{([\![W]\!](r^{F[\,]}))}[v]) \Big]
\end{aligned}
$$

On the other hand,

$$
\begin{aligned}
&\big[F[\mathfrak{A}(E[\ ] \circ W)]\big](r)\\
&= F^{(r)}\Big[\big[\mathfrak{A}(E[\ ] \circ W)\big](r^{F[\ ]})\Big]\\
&= F^{(r)}\Big[\lambda v.\mathcal{A}((E[v] \circ W)^{r^{F[\ ]}})\Big]\\
&= F^{(r)}\Big[\lambda v.\mathcal{A}((E^{[\![W]\!](r^{F[\ ]})}[v])\Big]
\end{aligned}
$$

since $(E[\ ] \circ W)^{(r^{F[\ ]})} = E[\ ]^{[\![W]\!](r^{F[\ ]})}$. Hence,

$$
\big[F[\mathfrak{A}(E[\ ]) \circ W]\big](r) = \big[F[\mathfrak{A}(E[\ ] \circ W)]\big](r).
$$

Case of CompAssoc: $E[(M \circ V) \circ W] \to E[M \circ (V \circ W)]$.

$$
\begin{aligned}
&[\![E[(M \circ V) \circ W]]\!](r)\\
&= E^{(r)}\big[[\![(M \circ V) \circ W]\!](r^{E[\ ]})\big]\\
&= E^{(r)}\big[[\![M \circ V]\!]([\![W]\!](r^{E[\ ]}))\big]\\
&= E^{(r)}\big[[\![M]\!]([\![V]\!]([\![W]\!](r^{E[\ ]})))\big]\\
&= E^{(r)}\big[[\![M]\!]([\![V \circ W]\!](r^{E[\ ]}))\big]\\
&= E^{(r)}\big[[\![M \circ (V \circ W)]\!](r^{E[\ ]})\big]\\
&= [\![E[M \circ (V \circ W)]]\!](r).
\end{aligned}
$$

Case of IdL: $E[id \circ W] \to E[W]$.

$$
\begin{aligned}
&[\![E[id \circ W]]\!](r)\\
&= E^{(r)}\big[[\![id \circ W]\!](r^{E[\ ]})\big]\\
&= E^{(r)}\Big[[\![id]\!]([\![W]\!](r^{E[\ ]}))\Big]\\
&= E^{(r)}\Big[[\![W]\!](r^{E[\ ]})\Big]\\
&= [\![E[W]]\!](r).
\end{aligned}
$$

Case of IdR: $E[M \circ id] \to E[M]$.

$$
\begin{aligned}
&\big[E[M \circ id]\big](r)\\
&= E^{(r)}\big[[\![M \circ id]\!](r^{E[\ ]})\big]\\
&= E^{(r)}\big[[\![M]\!]([\![id]\!](r^{E[\ ]}))\big]\\
&= E^{(r)}\big[[\![M]\!](r^{E[\ ]})\big]\\
&= \big[E[M]\big](r).
\end{aligned}
$$

End of Proof.

5. Conclusion

We studied coexistence of the first-class continuations and environments in the framework of the lambda calculus, in which we succeed improving Felleisen's abort operator $\mathcal{A}$. We give a translation of the calculus λ_{CE} into the record calculus λ_{CRec} with first-class continuations, which preserves the reduction relations.

We focus on the call-by-value evaluation strategy in this paper; the call-by-name evaluation strategy in the calculus with first-class continuations and environments should be studied as the future study of this research.

References

1. M. Abadi, L. Cardelli, P.-L. Curien, and J.-J. Lévy. Explicit substitutions. *Journal of Functional Programming*, 1(4):375–416, October 1991.
2. M. Wand C. T. Haynes, D. P. Friedman. Continuations and coroutines. In *Proceedings of the 1984 ACM Symposium on LISP and Functional Programming*, pages 293–298, 1984.
3. M. Felleisen, D. P. Friedman, E. Kohlbecker, and B. Duba. Reasoning with continuations. In *Proceedings of the Symposium on Logic in Computer Science*. IEEE Computer Society Press, 1986.
4. M. Felleisen, D. P. Friedman, E. Kohlbecker, and B. Duba. A syntactic theory of sequential control. *Theoretical Computer Science*, 1987.
5. T. G. Griffin. A formulae-as-types notion of control. In *Conference Record of the Seventeenth Annual ACM Symposium on Principles of Programming Languages*, 1990.
6. O. Laumann. *Reference Manual for the Elk Extension Language Interpreter*, 1990.
7. S. Nishizaki. ML with first-class environments and its type inference algorith. In *Lecture Notes in Computer Science*, volume 792, pages 95–116. Springer-Verlag Berlin Heidelberg, 1994.
8. S. Nishizaki. Programs with continuations and linear logic. 21(2):165–190, 1994.
9. S. Nishizaki. Simply typed lambda calculus with first-class environments. *Publications of Research Institute for Mathematical Sciences Kyoto University*, 30(6):1055–1121, 1995.
10. S. Nishizaki. Second-order type theory for first-class environment. *AIP Conference Proceedings*, 1839(1):020143, 2017.
11. S. Nishizaki and Mizuki Fujii. Strong reduction for typed lambda cal-

culus with first-class environments. In *Lecture Notes in Computer Science*, volume 7473, pages 632–639. Springer-Verlag Berlin Heidelberg, 2012.

12. G. Plotkin. Call-by-name, call-by-value, and the λ-calculus. *Theoretical Computer Science*, 1:125–159, 1975.

118

Towards Improvements of Bounded Realizability Checking

Masaya Shimakawa[*], Shigeki Hagihara[†] and Naoki Yonezaki[‡]

[*] *Tokyo Institute of Technology, 2-12-1 Ookayama, Meguro-ku, Tokyo 152-8552 Japan.*

[†] *Tohoku University of Community Service and Science, 3-5-1 Iimoriyama, Sakata, Yamagata 998-8580, Japan.*

[‡] *Tokyo Denki University, 2-1200 Muzai Gakuendai, Inzai-shi, Chiba 270-1382 Japan. Email: masaya@fmx.cs.titech.ac.jp[*], hagihava@koeki-u.ac.jp[†], yonezaki@mail.dendai.ac.jp[‡]*

Many fatal accidents involving safety-critical reactive systems occur in unexpected situations that were not considered during the development of the specification. However, realizability verification of reactive system typically involves complex and intricate analyses. To avoid this difficulty, Schewe et al. (2007) introduced the notion of bounded realizability that requires the existence of a model of size k that satisfies the given specification. Further to our works on bounded realizability checking that we have reported previously, we have put forward ideas on how this method might be improved in this paper. Specifically, we discuss bounded nonemptiness checking for Universal Co-Büchi Tree automata (UCT), based on simulation relations or state equivalences of UCT. Our method constructs a universal co-Büchi tree automata (UCT) that accepts models of a system (environment) that satisfy (do not satisfy) the specifications in all cases. Then, we check bounded nonemptiness for the automaton. We reduce bounded nonemptiness checking to a SAT problem, and solved the problem using a fast SAT solver. Through experiments, we demonstrated that our method can check problems at a lower cost in many cases. Based on simulation relations or state equivalences of UCT, we have shown the proposed approach has improved the SAT-based bounded nonemptiness checking process for UCT more efficient than those presented in our previous work, in terms of checking bounded realizability.

Keywords: Realizability; Specification; Verification; Bounded Checking.

1. Introduction

Many safety-critical systems, such as those that control nuclear power plants or air traffic control systems, are considered reactive systems. Reactive systems interact with their environment and respond to requests from an environment in a timely manner. In designing a system of this kind, the specifications should be verified. If a specification has a flaw, such as inappropriate case-splitting, the developed system may show unintended behavior. Realizability[1,2] is a fundamental concept of specification verification, which is defined according to whether the specification has a system model that can respond in a timely manner to any request at any time. Realizability verification can detect flaws in a specification that are otherwise very difficult to identify. A system model can be synthesized from a realizable specification[1]. However, realizability verification typically involves complex and intricate analyses. Therefore, it can only be applied at a limited scale.

Schewe et al. introduced the bounded property of realizability in Refs. 3 and 4, and presented a method based on satisfiability modulo theories (SMTs) in Ref. 4 [a]. They restricted the size of witnesses (i.e., models of correct systems) or counterexamples (i.e., models of oppositional environments) to a given k. The advantage of bounded (un-)realizability checking is the ability to efficiently check for the existence of a small witness (counterexample). In our experience, many practical unrealizable specifications have a small counterexample, which this approach can detect at low cost.

In Ref. 5, we presented a more efficient method for bounded realizability using a fast satisfiability (SAT) solver. Our method constructs a universal co-Büchi tree automaton (UCT) that accepts models of a system (environment) that satisfy (do not satisfy) the specifications in all cases. Then, we check bounded nonemptiness for the automaton. We reduce bounded nonemptiness checking to a SAT problem, and solved the problem using a fast SAT solver. Through experiments, we demonstrated that our method can check problems at a lower cost in many cases.

In this work, we present ideas on how to improve our method of conducting bounded realizability. Specifically, we discuss bounded nonemptiness checking for UCT, based on simulation relations or state equivalences of UCT.

The remainder of this paper is organized as follows. In Section 2, we introduce the concepts of reactive systems, specifications, realizability, and bounded realizability. Moreover, we describe a procedure for bounded realizability checking. In Section 3, we introduce the SAT-based method of bounded nonemptiness checking for UCT (Ref. 5). In Section 4, we present ideas on how to improve our nonemptiness checking method for UCT. We present conclusions and recommendations for future work in Section 5.

---

[a]The method is also used for distributed systems

2. Preliminaries

In this section, we introduce the concepts of reactive systems, specifications, realizability, and bounded realizability. We also describe a procedure for bounded realizability checking.

2.1. *Reactive Systems and Environments*

A reactive system responds appropriately to requests from the environment in a timely manner.

Definition 2.1. A reactive system is a reaction function $f : (2^X)^* \to 2^Y$, where X is a set of events caused by the environment, and Y is a set of events caused by the system. An environment is a reaction function $g : (2^Y)^+ \to 2^X$.

We refer to events caused by the environment as 'input events,' and to those caused by the system as 'output events.' The reaction function f(resp., g) relates sequences of sets of previously occurring input events (resp., output events) to a set of current output events (resp., input events).

2.2. *Reactive System Specifications*

The timing of input and output events is an essential element of reactive systems. LTL is a suitable language for describing the timing of events. In this paper, we use LTL to describe the specifications of reactive systems. In LTL, in addition to Boolean operators, we can use temporal operators **X** and **U**. We treat input events and output events as atomic propositions.

Formulas in LTL are inductively defined as follows:

- Atomic propositions (i.e., input events and output events) are formulas.
- $\psi_1 \wedge \psi_2$, $\neg\psi_1$, $\mathbf{X}\psi_1$, $\psi_1 \mathbf{U} \psi_2$ are formulas if ψ_1 and ψ_2 are formulas.

The notation $\mathbf{X}\psi_1$ means that 'ψ_1 holds the next time,' while $\psi_1 \mathbf{U} \psi_2$ means that 'ψ_1 always holds until ψ_2 holds.' The notations $\psi_1 \vee \psi_2$, $\psi_1 \to \psi_2$, $\psi_1 \leftrightarrow \psi_2$ and $\top$ are abbreviations for $\neg(\neg\psi_1 \wedge \neg\psi_2)$, $\neg(\psi_1 \wedge \neg\psi_2)$, $\neg(\psi_1 \wedge \neg\psi_2) \wedge \neg(\neg\psi_1 \wedge \psi_2)$ and $\neg\bot$, respectively, where $\bot$ is an atomic proposition representing 'falsity.'

A behavior is an infinite sequence of sets of events. Let i be an index such that $i \geq 0$. The i-th set of a behavior σ is denoted by $\sigma[i]$. The i-th suffix of a behavior σ is denoted by $\sigma[i \ldots]$. When a behavior σ satisfies a formula ψ, we write $\sigma \models \psi$, and inductively define this relation as follows:

- $\sigma \models p$ iff $p \in \sigma[0]$, where $p \in X \cup Y$.
- $\sigma \not\models \perp$
- $\sigma \models \psi_1 \wedge \psi_2$ iff $\sigma \models \psi_1$ and $\sigma \models \psi_2$
- $\sigma \models \neg\psi_1$ iff $\sigma \not\models \psi_1$
- $\sigma \models \mathbf{X}\psi_1$ iff $\sigma[1\ldots] \models \psi_1$
- $\sigma \models \psi_1\mathbf{U}\psi_2$ iff $\exists j \geq 0.((\sigma[j\ldots] \models \psi_2)$ and $\forall k(0 \leq k < j. \sigma[k\ldots] \models \psi_1))$

2.3. *Realizability*

It is important for reactive system specifications to satisfy realizability. Realizability requires the existence of a reactive system such that for any input event with any timing, the system produces output events such that the specification holds.

Definition 2.2. A specification *Spec* is *realizable* if there exists a reactive system f such that $f \models_{sys} Spec$, where $f \models_{sys} Spec$ is defined as $\forall a_0, a_1, a_2, \ldots \in 2^X.((f(\epsilon) \cup a_0)(f(a_0) \cup a_1)(f(a_0a_1) \cup a_2)\ldots \models_{bhv} Spec)$.

We also define unrealizability in the same manner.

Definition 2.3. A specification *Spec* is *unrealizable* if there exists an environment g such that $g \models_{env} \neg Spec$, where $g \models_{env} \neg Spec$ is defined as $\forall b_0, b_1, \ldots \in 2^Y.(b_0 \cup g(b_0))(b_1 \cup g(b_0b_1))\ldots \models_{bhv} \neg Spec$.

Note that a specification *Spec* is not realizable if and only if *Spec* is unrealizable, when the specification is described in LTL (or ω-regular expression, finite automata for ω-word).

2.4. *Bounded Realizability*

In bounded (un-)realizability, we restrict the size of the witness or counterexample to some k; that is, we consider only witnesses or counterexamples that are represented by a transition machine of size k.

Transition machine is a tuple $T = (\Sigma, D, S, s_I, \eta, o)$ where Σ is an alphabet, D is a finite set of directions, S is a finite set of states, s_I is an initial state, $\eta : S \times D \to S$ is a transition function, and $o : S \to \Sigma$ is a labeling function. We define $\zeta : D^* \to S$ as follows: $\zeta(\epsilon) = s_I$, $\zeta(x \cdot c) = \eta(\zeta(x), c)$, where $x \in D^*, c \in D$. The size $|T|$ of T is defined as $|T| = |S|$. A transition machine $T = (2^Y, 2^X, S, s_I, \eta, o)$ represents a reactive system f_T such that for all $\bar{a} \in (2^X)^*$, $f_T(\bar{a}) = o(\zeta(\bar{a}))$. In addition, a transition machine $T = (2^X, 2^Y, S, s_I, \eta, o)$ represents an environment g_T such that for all $\bar{b} \in (2^Y)^+$, $g_T(\bar{b}) = o(\zeta(\bar{b}))$.

Definition 2.4. Let *Spec* be a specification; $k \in \mathbb{N}$. *Spec* is k-realizable if there exists a transition machine T such that $f_T \models_{sys} Spec$ and $|T| = k$. *Spec* is k-unrealizable if there exists T such that $g_T \models_{env} \neg Spec$ and $|T| = k$.

Note that in a bounded setting, the fact that a specification *Spec* is not k-realizable does not imply that *Spec* is k-unrealizable. By definition, it is obvious that if *Spec* is k-realizable, *Spec* is also realizable. Moreover, in the case that *Spec* is described in LTL (or ω-regular expression, finite automata for ω-word), if *Spec* is realizable, *Spec* is k-realizable for some k.

2.5. *Procedure for Bounded Realizability Checking*

This subsection outlines a procedure for checking bounded realizability using ω-automata, which is presented in Ref. 4. Bounded unrealizability can also be checked in the same way.

(1) We obtain a universal co-Büchi word automaton $\mathcal{A}_{bhv}$ such that $L(\mathcal{A}_{bhv}) = \{\sigma \mid \sigma \models_{bhv} Spec\}$.
(2) From $\mathcal{A}_{bhv}$, we construct a universal co-Büchi tree automaton $\mathcal{A}_{sys}$ such that $L(\mathcal{A}_{sys}) = \{T \mid f_T \models_{sys} Spec\}$.
(3) We check whether there exists a transition system T of size k such that $T \in L(\mathcal{A}_{sys})$, i.e. k-*nonempty*. If it is k-nonempty, we conclude that *Spec* is k-realizable. Otherwise, we conclude that *Spec* is not k-realizable.

In Ref. 4, an SMT-based method of bounded nonemptiness checking for a universal co-Büchi tree automaton (UCT) is also given.[b] In a previous work(Ref. 5), we presented a SAT-based method of bounded nonemptiness checking of UCT, where we reduce bounded nonemptiness checking for UCT to a SAT problem, and solve the problem using a fast SAT solver. Our method is more efficient in many cases[5].

3. SAT-based Bounded Nonemptiness Checking for UCT

In this section, we introduce a SAT-based method of bounded nonemptiness checking for UCT, presented in Ref. 5.

---

[b]the method is also used for distributed systems.

3.1. *Universal co-Büchi Tree Automata(UCT)*

Here, we define the syntax and semantics for UCT.

Syntax : The UCT is a tuple $\mathcal{A} = (\Sigma, D, Q, q_I, \delta, F)$ where Σ is an alphabet, D is a finite set of directions, Q is a finite set of locations, q_I is an initial location, $\delta \subseteq Q \times \Sigma \times D \times Q$ is a transition relation, and $F \subseteq Q$ is a set of accepting locations.

Semantics for Transition Machines : Using run graph, we define the semantics of UCT for transition machines. For a UCT $\mathcal{A} = (\Sigma, D, Q, q_I, \delta, F)$ and a transition machine $T = (\Sigma, D, S, s_i, \eta, o)$, the run graph $G = (V, v_I, E, C)$ is defined as follows: $V := Q \times S$ (the set of nodes), $v_I := (q_I, s_I)$ (the initial node), $E := \{((q, s), (q', s')) \mid (q, o(s), c, q') \in \delta, s' = \eta(s, c)\}$ (the set of edges), and $C := \{(q, s) \mid q \in F, s \in S\}$ (the set of accepting nodes). We say $\mathcal{A}$ accepts T, if for all paths from the initial node in the run graph for $\mathcal{A}$ and T, the number of occurrences of accepting nodes in the path is finite.

3.2. *Characterization of Transition Machines of Size k Accepted by UCT*

Here, we characterize transition machines of size k that are accepted by UCT.

The number of accepting nodes in a run graph is bounded. From this, the following result is derived.[c]

Lemma 3.1. *If for all paths $\tilde{v}$ in a run graph G from a node v, the number of occurrences of accepting nodes in $\tilde{v}$ is finite, then for all paths $\tilde{v}$ from v in G, accepting nodes occur at most $|C|$ times in $\tilde{v}$.*

The property that "for all paths $\tilde{v}$ from v, the number of occurrences of accepting nodes is at most j"(denoted by $AtMost(v, j)$) is characterized as follows: For $v \in V \setminus C$ (for $v \in C$), $AtMost(v, j)$ holds if and only if for all successors $v' \in vE$, $AtMost(v', j)$ holds ($AtMost(v', j-1)$ holds), where $vE = \{v' \mid (v, v') \in E\}$. In addition, for all $v \in C$, $AtMost(v, 0)$ does not hold. Based on this idea, the following result is derived:

Theorem 3.1 (Refs. 6, 7 and 5). *Let $G = (V, v_I, E, C)$ be a run graph and $d \in \mathbb{N}$. For all paths $\tilde{v}$ from v_I in G, accepting nodes occur at most d*

---

[c]If the number of occurrences of accepting nodes in a path exceeds $|C|$, then there exists an accepting node v_c that occurs at least twice, which implies the existence of a path on which the accepting node v_c occurs infinitely often.

times if and only if there exists a sequence $V_0, V_1, \ldots, V_d$ *of sets of nodes such that the following are true:*

1. *The following condition (denoted by* $Init(V_0)$*) holds:*

$v \in V_0 \iff$ *(if* $v \in V \setminus C$ *then* $\forall v' \in vE.\ v' \in V_0$ *else* $\bot$*)*

2. *For all* $0 \leq j < d$*, the following condition (denoted by* $Trans(V_j, V_{j+1})$*) holds:*

$v \in V_{j+1} \iff$ *(if* $v \in V \setminus C$ *then* $\forall v' \in vE.\ v' \in V_{j+1}$ *else* $\forall v' \in vE.\ v' \in V_j$*)*

3. $v_I \in V_d$ *holds (denoted by* $Final(V_d)$*).*

From the above theorem, the following is derived.

Theorem 3.2 (Ref. 5). *Let* $\mathcal{A} = (\Sigma, D, Q, q_I, \delta, F)$ *be a UCT and* $k \in \mathbb{N}$*. For all* $d \in \mathbb{N}$*, (2) implies (1), and for* $d \geq k \cdot |F|$*, (1) implies (2), where (1) and (2) are as follows:*
(1) There exists a transition machine of size k *that is accepted by* $\mathcal{A}$*.*
(2) There exists a transition machine T *of size* k *such that for some sequence* $V_0, V_1, \ldots, V_d$ *of sets of nodes of the run graph* G *for* $\mathcal{A}$ *and* T*,* $Init(V_0) \wedge \bigwedge_{0 \leq j < d} Trans(V_j, V_{j+1}) \wedge Final(V_d)$ *holds.*

3.3. *SAT Encoding*

We present a reduction to a SAT problem based on Theorem 3.2. That is, for a UCT $\mathcal{A}$ and k, we give a construction of a Boolean formula $\|[acc(\mathcal{A}, k, d)]\|$ such that condition (2) of Theorem 3.2 holds iff $\|[acc(\mathcal{A}, k, d)]\|$ is satisfiable.

Variables: We use the following variables (assuming $\Sigma = 2^Y$), to represent a transition machine of size k (where $S = \{1, 2, \ldots k\}$), and $V_0, V_1, \ldots, V_d$. (a)y_i for $y \in Y$, $1 \leq i \leq k$, which indicate whether $y \in o(i)$ holds; (b) $tr_{(i,c,i')}$ for $1 \leq i \leq k$, $c \in D$, $1 \leq i' \leq k$, which indicate whether $\eta(i, c) = i'$ holds; and (c)$v_{(q,i)}^j$ for $q \in Q, 1 \leq i \leq k, 0 \leq j \leq d$, which indicate whether $(q, i) \in V_j$ holds.

Constraints: To represent "be a transition machine correctly," we prepare the following formula:

$\|[det(k)]\| := \bigwedge_{1 \leq i \leq k, c \in D} \bigvee_{1 \leq i' \leq k} tr_{(i,c,i')} \wedge \bigwedge_{1 \leq i \leq k, c \in D} \bigwedge_{1 \leq i' \leq k, i'' \neq i'} (tr_{(i,c,i')} \rightarrow \neg tr_{(i,c,i'')})$.

We define the formulaa $\|[Init(\mathcal{A}, k)]\|_0$, $\|[Trans(\mathcal{A}, k)]\|_{j,j+1}$ and $\|[Final(\mathcal{A}, k)]\|_d$, which indicate that $Init(V_0)$, $Trans(V_i, V_{i+1})$ and $Final(V_d)$ hold, respectively. The definitions are in Table 1, where $\|[b]\|_i$ is the formula $\bigwedge_{y \in b} y_i \wedge \bigwedge_{y \notin b} \neg y_i$, indicating that the label of state i is b.

Table 1. The definition of $|[Init(\mathcal{A},k)]|_0$, $|[Trans(\mathcal{A},k)]|_{j,j+1}$ and $|[Final(\mathcal{A},k)]|_d$

$|[Init(\mathcal{A},k)]|_0$	$\bigwedge_{q\in Q\setminus F, 1\le i\le k}\Big(v^0_{(q,i)}\leftrightarrow$ $\bigwedge_{(q,b,c,q')\in\delta, 1\le i'\le k}((|[b]|_i\wedge tr_{(i,c,i')})\rightarrow v^0_{(q',i')})\Big)\wedge$ $\bigwedge_{q\in F, 1\le i\le k}\Big(\neg v^0_{(q,i)}\Big)$
$|[Trans(\mathcal{A},k)]|_{j,j+1}$	$\bigwedge_{q\in Q\setminus F, 1\le i\le k}\Big(v^{j+1}_{(q,i)}\leftrightarrow$ $\bigwedge_{(q,b,c,q')\in\delta, 1\le i'\le k}((|[b]|_i\wedge tr_{(i,c,i')})\rightarrow v^{j+1}_{(q',i')})\Big)\wedge$ $\bigwedge_{q\in F, 1\le i\le k}\Big(v^{j+1}_{(q,i)}\leftrightarrow$ $\bigwedge_{(q,b,c,q')\in\delta, 1\le i'\le k}((|[b]|_i\wedge tr_{(i,c,i')})\rightarrow v^{j}_{(q',i')})\Big)$
$|[Final(\mathcal{A},k)]|_d$	$v^d_{(q_I,0)}$

We define the formula $|[acc(\mathcal{A},k,d)]|$ by $|[acc(\mathcal{A},k,d)]| := |[det(k)]|\wedge$ $|[Init(\mathcal{A},k)]|_0 \wedge \bigwedge_{0\le j<d}|[Trans(\mathcal{A},k)]|_{j,j+1} \wedge |[Final(\mathcal{A},k)]|_d$.

Theorem 3.3 (Ref. 5). *Let $\mathcal{A} = (2^Y, D, Q, q_I, \delta, F)$ and $k\in\mathbb{N}$. For all $d\in\mathbb{N}$, (2) implies (1), and for $d \ge k\cdot|F|$, (1) implies (2), where (1) and (2) are as follows:*
(1) There exists a transition machine of size k that is accepted by $\mathcal{A}$.
(2) $|[acc(\mathcal{A},k,d)]|$ is satisfiable.

4. Improvement of Bounded Realizability Checking

In this section, we present ideas on how to improve the bounded nonemptiness checking for UCT introduced in the previous section.

4.1. *Improvement by Using a Simulation Relation of UCT*

Here, we suggest improving the process by using a simulation relation of UCT.

The simulation relation of UCT $\mathcal{A} = (\Sigma, D, Q, q_I, \delta, F)$ is defined as follows. The simulation relation(denoted by $\preceq$) is the maximum relation $R \subseteq Q\times Q$ satisfying the following conditions: $(q_1, q_2)\in R$ implies

S1: $(q_1,q_2)\in\mathcal{F}(R)$,
   where $\mathcal{F}(R) := \{(q'_1,q'_2) \mid \forall b\in\Sigma.\forall c\in D.\forall q''_1\in Q.((q'_1,b,c,q''_1)\in\delta\implies \exists q''_2\in Q.((q'_2,b,c,q''_2)\in\delta \text{ and } (q''_1,q''_2)\in R))\}$, and
S2: $q_1\in F \implies q_2\in F$.

Let $\mathcal{A} = (\Sigma, D, Q, q_I, \delta, F)$ be a UCT, let $T = (\Sigma, D, S, s_i, \eta, o)$ be a transition machine, and let $G = (V, v_I, E, C)$ be the run graph of $\mathcal{A}$ and T.

We assume $q_1 \preceq q_2$ $(q_1, q_2 \in Q)$ and $s \in S$. By the definition of the simulation relation, for all paths $(q_1, s)(q_1^1, s^1)(q_1^2, s^2) \ldots$ from (q_1, s) in the run graph G, there exists a path $(q_2, s)(q_2^1, s^1)(q_2^2, s^2) \ldots$ in G s.t. $q_1^i \preceq q_2^i$ for any i (this implies $q_1^i \in F \implies q_2^i \in F$ and $(q_1^i, s^i) \in C \implies (q_2^i, s^i) \in C$). Then $\forall j. AtMost((q_2, s), j) \implies AtMost((q_1, s), j)$ holds.

Therefore, if $q_1 \preceq q_2$ and $s \in S$, then the following holds:

$$\forall j < d.((q_2, s), j) \in V_j \implies ((q_1, s), j) \in V_j.$$

The formulas $v_{(q_2,i)}^j \to v_{(q_1,i)}^j$ can be added in the SAT encoding. Because SAT solvers can utilize these formulas as new information, more effective checking can be expected.

4.2. Improvement by Using a State Equivalence of UCT

Here, we suggest improving the process by using a state equivalence of UCT.

In UCT $\mathcal{A} = (\Sigma, D, Q, q_I, \delta, F)$, if locations $q_1, q_2 \in Q$ satisfy the following two conditions (denoted by $q_1 \equiv q_2$), then the two locations q_1 and q_2 can be equated and merged (in the stage of constructing the UCT).

E1: $\delta(q_1) = \delta(q_2)$, where $\delta(q) = \{(b, c, q') \mid (q, b, c, q') \in \delta\}$, and
E2: $q_1 \in F \iff q_2 \in F$.

In this paper, we consider a relation that consists of only condition E1 (denoted by $q_1 \equiv_t q_2$). UCT cannot be simplified using the relation $\equiv_t$. (The relation $\equiv_t$ cannot be used to improve efficiency while constructing the UCT.) However, it can be used during bounded nonemptiness checking of UCT.

Let $\mathcal{A} = (\Sigma, D, Q, q_I, \delta, F)$ be a UCT, let $T = (\Sigma, D, S, s_i, \eta, o)$ be a transition machine, and let $G = (V, v_I, E, C)$ be the run graph of $\mathcal{A}$ and T. We assume that $\mathcal{A}$ be simplified using $\equiv$.

We assume $q_1 \equiv_t q_2$, $q_1 \in F$, $q_2 \notin F$ and $s \in S$. Based on the definition of the run graph, $\forall j. AtMost(v_1, j + 1) \iff AtMost(v_2, j)$ holds.

Therefore, if $q_1 \equiv_t q_2$, $q_1 \in F$, $q_2 \notin F$ and $s \in S$, then the following holds:

$$\forall j < d.((q_1, s), j + 1) \in V_{j+1} \iff ((q_2, s), j) \in V_j.$$

The variables $v_{(q_1,i)}^{j+1}$ and $v_{(q_2,i)}^j$ can be merged by SAT encoding. Because we can decrease the number of variables in the formulas, more effective checking can be expected.

4.3. *Improvement by Using a Pre-simulation Relation of UCT*

Here, we discuss improvements based on use of a pre-simulation relation.

We define the relation $\sim$ as follows: $q_1 \sim q_2$ iff $q_1 \preceq q_2$ and $q_2 \preceq q_1$. In UCT $\mathcal{A} = (\Sigma, D, Q, q_I, \delta, F)$, if $q_1 \sim q_2$ $(q_1, q_2 \in Q)$, then the two locations q_1 and q_2 can be equated and merged (in the stage of constructing the UCT).

Here, we consider a pre-simulation relation, which is weakened based on the ideas presented in the previous subsection.

The pre-simulation relation $\preceq_{pre} \subseteq Q \times Q$ of UCT is defined as follows: $(q_1, q_2) \in \preceq_{pre}$ iff

P1: $(q_1, q_2) \in \mathcal{F}(\preceq)$

In this relation, condition S2 is avoided in the initial step. We define the relation $\sim_{pre}$ as follows: $q_1 \sim_{pre} q_2$ iff $q_1 \preceq_{pre} q_2$ and $q_2 \preceq_{pre} q_1$.

While UCT cannot be simplified using the relation $\sim_{pre}$, the relation $\sim_{pre}$ can be used to improve efficiency in the stage of bounded nonemptiness checking of UCT, as is the case with the concepts presented in the previous subsection.

Let $\mathcal{A} = (\Sigma, D, Q, q_I, \delta, F)$ be a UCT, let $T = (\Sigma, D, S, s_i, \eta, o)$ be a transition machine, and let $G = (V, v_I, E, C)$ be the run graph of $\mathcal{A}$ and T. We assume that $\mathcal{A}$ be simplified using $\sim$.

We assume $q_1 \sim_{pre} q_2$, $q_1 \in F, q_2 \notin F$ and $s \in S$. By the definition of the run graph and the pre-simulation relation, $\forall j.AtMost(v_1, j+1) \Longleftrightarrow AtMost(v_2, j)$ holds.

Therefore, if $q_1 \sim_{pre} q_2$, $q_1 \in F, q_2 \notin F$ and $s \in S$, then the following holds:

$$\forall j < d.((q_1, s), j+1) \in V_{j+1} \Longleftrightarrow ((q_2, s), j) \in V_j.$$

The variables $v_{(q_1,i)}^{j+1}$ and $v_{(q_2,i)}^{j}$ can be merged in SAT encoding. Because $\equiv_t \subseteq \sim_{pre}$, more effective checking can be done compared to the ideas presented in the previous subsection.

5. Conclusion and Future Work

We assessed ways to improve the SAT-based bounded nonemptiness checking process for UCT presented in a previous work, to identify methods that can check bounded realizability more efficiently. The new methods are based on simulation relations or state equivalences of UCT.

In the future, we will develop a tool that implements these methods, and demonstrate its effectiveness in experiments.

References

1. A. Pnueli and R. Rosner, On the synthesis of a reactive module, in *Proc. 16th ACM SIGPLAN-SIGACT Symposium on Principles of Programming Languages*, (ACM, 1989).
2. M. Abadi, L. Lamport and P. Wolper, Realizable and unrealizable specifications of reactive systems., in *Proc. 16th International Colloquium on Automata, Languages, and Programming*, LNCS Vol. 372 (Springer, 1989).
3. S. Schewe and B. Finkbeiner, Bounded synthesis, in *Proc. 5th International Symposium on Automated Technology for Verification and Analysis*, LNCS Vol. 4762 (Springer, 2007).
4. B. Finkbeiner and S. Schewe, SMT-based synthesis of distributed systems, in *Proc. Second Workshop on Automated Formal Methods*, (ACM, 2007).
5. M. Shimakawa, S. Hagihara and N. Yonezaki, Reducing bounded realizability analysis to reachability checking, in *Proc. 9th International Workshop on Reachability Problems*, LNCS Vol. 9328 (Springer, 2015).
6. M. Shimakawa, S. Hagihara and N. Yonezaki, SAT-based Bounded Strong Satisfiability Checking of Reactive System Specifications, in *Proc. International Conference on Information and Communication Technology - EurAsia Conference 2013 (ICT-EurAsia 2013)*, LNCS Vol. 7804 (Springer, 2013).
7. M. Shimakawa, S. Hagihara and N. Yonezaki, Bounded strong satisfiability checking of reactive system specifications, *IEICE Trans. Inf. & Syst.* **E97-D**, 1746 (2014).

On Testing the Usability of Diabetes Bridge: A Mobile Application to Manage Health Care for People with Diabetes

Maria Caira P. Altea *, Romel Jordan E. Apostol †

BS Computer Science, University of the Philippines,
* E-mail: mpaltea@up.edu.ph
† E-mail: reapostol1@up.edu.ph

Iris Thiele Isip-Tan

Medical Informatics Unit, UP College of Medicine
Email: icisiptan@up.edu.ph

Rommel P. Feria‡, Ma. Rowena C. Solamo§, Ligaya Leah Figueroa¶

Department of Computer Science, University of the Philippines
‡ Email: rpferia@up.edu.ph
§ Email: rcsolamo@up.edu.ph
¶ Email: llfigueroa@up.edu.ph

For the past few years, there is a significant increase in the number of mobile health (mHealth) applications specifically for diabetes. These applications are mostly for self - management. However, most of these applications have the same features but it lack the part of educating patients and the involvement of medical professionals in the development process of an application. Diabetes Bridge aims to propose solutions to these problems.

Diabetes Bridge is a mobile health application intended to better facilitate care coordination for people with diabetes. This application was developed with the coordination of a healthcare professional. Some features of the application includes preparing for the consultation with listing down important questions, knowing what to do before going to laboratory tests, and educating patients with the common questions that diabetic people asked to their doctors.

The usability of Diabetes Bridge was evaluated by people with diabetes and a health practitioner using Mobile Application Rating Scale (MARS) as an evaluation tool to assess the mobile health application in four categories. A total of thirty (30) people participated in the testing. The participants perceived the application to be useful and that it was well - made for people with diabetes. The application's simplicity and ease of use receive a good feedback from the testers. Improvements can be made in the visuals of the application to make it more appealing for all age groups and not only for the older people. It is very useful in preparation with the patient's consultation, laboratory requests and results and educating the patient about his diseases.

Diabetes Bridge is positively received by diabetic people as a good mobile health application.

Keywords: Diabetes; Mobile applications; Mobile health.

1. Introduction

The continuous advancement of mobile phones in the world brought up the emergence of mobile applications. These mobile applications have different goals and purposes in which they have targeted different audiences. For the past few years, there is a significant increase in the number of mobile health (mHealth) applications especially for the management of diabetes. On July 2009, there were only sixty (60) diabetes mobile applications for Apple's App store alone.[1] This number increases in the past years that have passed. In fact, from July to September 2015, there are 2840 mobile applications for 26 diseases on different application stores. Out of this 2840 applications, there are 34.50% or almost 1000 diabetes mobile health applications.[2] Most of these are commercial mobile applications which have no study accessing them. With this, many questions arise if these mobile applications will be effective as a healthcare management application for people with diabetes. As there are only few studies that account to mobile health applications, medical practitioners have huge concern in the effectiveness and safety of most of these mobile health applications.[3] Also, there is a great number of unregulated mobile health applications. These are applications that have no medical professional involvement in the development of an application specifically in the design.[4] With this, a strict regulation of mobile health applications is required to ensure the reliability of the content of these applications.

Diabetes Bridge proposed a solution to these problems as the researchers coordinated the design and development with a health professional who has expertise on diabetes. This application intended to better facilitate care coordination for people with diabetes.

2. Review of the State of the Art

Most mobile applications that deal with health, specifically, diabetes, are considered and intended to be a self - management application. There are a lot of existing mobile health applications, specifically for diabetes. Because of this, different group of researchers have conducted studies to compare and contrast existing applications. Of all the existing features of a diabetes self - management, what is lacking but very important is education.[1] For the patient, education is necessary to be able to manage his illness correctly and to avoid making mistakes that may worsen his condition. Most applications support tasks such as tracking of physical activity, insulin dosage, and/or diet medication. However, aside from these features, it lacks the complexity of data entry, integration of health records and usability issues that is caused by different target audience. Applications should be able to improve the usability of applications depending on their target audience and it should have an emphasis to how an application can be useful for a patient.[5] Mobile health applications should not be only useful for the patient but also for the doctors and caregivers. There are studies that produced self - efficacy but it would be better if these results can be integrated to the health care system.[6]

A particular group that mobile health applications should be intended for are the elders. There are many older people that have diabetes. With this, a study was conducted that take in consideration diabetes patients with age 50 years or older. Most applications have the same functionalities; however, the resulting problem was usability and these applications showed signs that they are developed but not intended for the right target group. The researchers stated that doctors and patients should be involved in the process of developing such applications.[7] These reviews contribute to factors considered in the implementation of Diabetes Bridge, whose effectivity will be determined by how patients with diabetes perceive it through an evaluative and usability testing.

3. Diabetes Bridge

Diabetes Bridge is a mobile health application which aims to improve the health care between the doctor, caregiver, and the patient. It is an application for healthcare management that focuses on keeping consultation notes, laboratory requests, and laboratory results of the patient. It will remind the patient if the schedule of his consultation/laboratory test/laboratory test result is approaching. Also, the application will remind the patient what he needs to prepare for his scheduled appointment. For the laboratory test request, it will remind the patient what to prepare before his upcoming laboratory test. While for consultation, the patient can prepare questions that he needs to ask to his doctor-in-charge. With this, the patient will not be able to forget the questions he needs and wants to ask.

3.1. *Software Architecture*

The software architecture of the application can be described by four-tier architecture (layered architecture) which includes four (4) layers, namely presentation layer, business layer, persistence layer, and data layer. It was designed that each layers will form an abstraction.[8] The presentation layer handles all the views of the application. It display the information it received from the lower layer. The business layer perform the business logic of the application. It includes all the functions that will implement the features of the application. While the persistence layer of the application communicate with the databases. It retrieve, and store data from/to the databases. Finally, the data layer includes the two databases used in the application. It's where the data from the application are stored.

The application has a simple user interface. By having a simple user interface, it will increase the usability of the application. The application was created so that it will be easy-to-use for different age groups especially for middle and old age group. The researchers did not use complex functionalities that will lessen the usability of the application. This is followed and implemented because even if a mobile health application has good functionalities that support care management, but has poor usability, the patient will not be able to use the application well.[9] Most mobile health applications focused on tracking of the user's activity that needs regular input from the patient. In a recent study, it says that one barrier for continued use of mobile health applications is that it takes a lot of time and effort.[10] This is what Diabetes Bridge wants to solve; to ensure that Diabetes Bridge will be an effective healthcare management application, the researchers coordinated with a health professionals for the functionality of the application. Based on the suggestions given by the health professional, the following are the main modules of the mobile health (mHealth) - Diabetes Bridge:

(1) *Appointments (Home) Module*: The application will keep track of all the appointments of the patient to his doctor-in-charge and other specialists. The appointments comprise all the consultation, blood pressure and blood glucose reading log, laboratory request, and laboratory result entries of the patient. This module will summarize all the appointments that is grouped by date.
(2) *Consultations Module*: The consultation will include the questions the patient will ask to his doctor, and things that the doctor and the patient converse upon during their consultation.
(3) *Laboratory Module*: The application keeps track of all the laboratory

requests/results given to the patient.

(4) *Application Information Module*: The information module consists of different information pages about the mobile application. It displays all the information about the application, and frequently asked questions about diabetes.

4. Discussion

The development of the application followed the initial software architecture laid out. As time goes by, the software architecture changed based on the solution of all the issues encountered by the researchers. The application was created as an iOS mobile application since it will synchronize to Health application found in iPhone devices. But since Health application is only available to iPhone devices, synchronization of health data will only be implemented in iPhone devices.

Following the up-to-date designs of iOS mobile applications, the researchers implemented a tab bar view which will make an easy navigation of application's views. Based on previous researches and consultations with health practitioner, there are four (4) main modules in the application, namely Appointments (Home) module, Consultation module, Laboratory module, and Application Information module. The testing of the mobile application will focus on the features of these main modules of Diabetes Bridge.

4.1. *Testing*

The testing objective is to measure the usability of Diabetes Bridge for people with diabetes, and other people included in the care management for the disease diabetes.

(1) *Tester Profiling*: Diabetes Bridge is created for the use of people with diabetes. For the testing, a total of twenty nine (29) diabetic people and one (1) health practitioner participated in the testing of the mobile application. Twenty five (25) diabetic people have type 2 diabetes, three (3) diabetic people has type 1 diabetes, and the other one (1) diabetic people has type MODY diabetes. The people who participated in the testing have an iPhone or iPad device. Twenty (20) people used iPhone devices to test the application, while the other ten (10) people used iPad devices to test the application.

(2) *Methodology*: The testing was conducted by face-to-face interview, and online survey. For online survey, the form was created using Google

Forms and will be circulated in an online groups of people with diabetes, and will be posted in Endocrine Witch page, an information Facebook page about the disease diabetes handled by an endocrinologist. The following procedure were asked to do for the online survey:

(a) Using their iOS device (iPhone/iPad), the participants will download Diabetes Bridge from iOS App Store.
(b) The participants will open the google form and were asked to read until the section 2 (instructions for testing) of the form.
(c) The participants will test the features of the four (4) main modules of the application. The features essential for the testing are included in the section 2 of the google form survey.
(d) After testing the application, the participants can now evaluate the application by answering the rest of the google form survey.

For face-to-face interview, the researchers directly communicates with the participants of the testing. The researchers facilitated the testing by explaining systematically the procedure to the participant. The participant were asked to test the usability of the application while the researchers are observing the interaction of the participant with the application. The following steps are followed for face-to-face interview:

(a) Describe Diabetes Bridge to participant
(b) Give and explain the instructions on how to test the features of the application
(c) Guide the participant on testing the application
(d) After testing, the researchers ask the participant to evaluate the application.
(e) Lastly, the researchers will ask the participant some questions about their comments about the application

For both face-to-face interview, and online survey, the participants will answer the same set of questions.

(3) *Testing Instrument:* The application will be evaluated using the tool Mobile Application Rating Scale (MARS). The Mobile Application Rating Scale is an application quality assessment tool beyond star rating for health mobile applications. By using this evaluation tool, the mobile application will be evaluated based on four categories. The engagement, functionality, aesthetics, and information category. For each of the categories, there will be questions that will be rated from one to five by the participants, with five being the highest and one being the lowest. [11]

- **Engagement**: It focused on the interaction of the user to the application. The user should be able to find the app to be interesting, interactive (e.g. sends alerts, messages, reminders, feedback, enables sharing) and are well - targeted to audience.
- **Functionality**: It checks if the app is functioning well, simple and and easy to use. Complexity should be the least thing the user will encounter in using the app.
- **Aesthetics**: This checks the overall visual appeal of the application.
- **Information Category**: The information about the app is well - delivered and can be easily understand. The information are from a credible source (FAQs).

4.2. *Results*

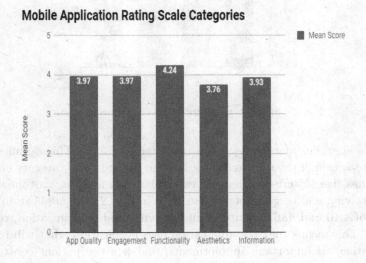

Fig. 1.   Mean Score of the app per categories.

The application was evaluated in four categories, namely engagement, functionality, aesthetics, and information. Based on the results, shown in Fig. 1, the category functionality received the highest score among the four categories. The application got a score of 4.24 for this category. It was followed by engagement category with a score of 3.97, next is information with a score of 3.93, and the category with the least score is aesthetics with score of 3.76. With this, Diabetes Bridge got an app quality score of 3.97. The application quality score of Diabetes Bridge is considerably high considering that five (5) is the highest score a mobile application can attain.

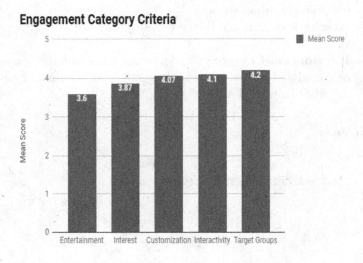

Fig. 2.   Mean Scores of criteria in engagement category.

The engagement category got a mean score of 3.97. This signifies that the interaction of the user to the application is good. The category engagement has five (5) criteria, namely entertainment, interest, customization, interactivity, and target groups. As shown in Fig. 2., the application got a score of 4.10 and 4.07 to criteria interactivity, and customization, respectively. This means that the application uses notifications that will remind the patient of important appointments, and lets the patient control the settings and preferences for the features of the application.

The functionality category got a mean score of 4.24. Functionality got the highest mean score among the 4 categories. Based on the results in Fig. 3., for the five (5) criteria of this category, the application got a mean score of above 4. This implies that the application is functioning well. The application is easy to learn, and navigates consistently to different pages. In fact, all the 30 participants recorded that they don't encounter any crashes during their testing.

Functionality Category Criteria

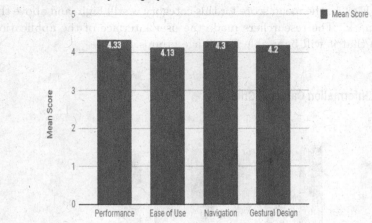

Fig. 3.   Mean Scores of criteria in functionality category.

Aesthetics Category Criteria

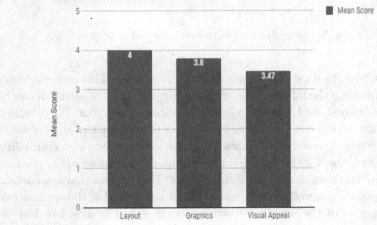

Fig. 4.   Mean Scores of criteria in aesthetics category.

The aesthetics category got a mean score of 3.76. Among the four (4) categories, this category received the lowest mean score. However, as shown in Fig. 4., the mean score for this category is still high, and above the passing mark. The researchers made the user interface of the application simple so that it will be usable for all age groups.

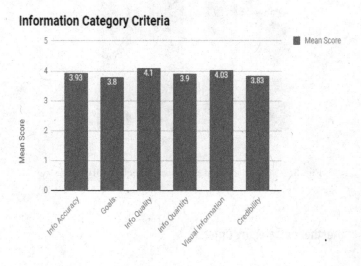

Information Category Criteria

Fig. 5.   Mean Scores of criteria in information category.

The information category got a mean score of 3.93. This category deals on determining if the information on the application is well-delivered, can be easily understood, and if it came from a credible source. For this category, there are six (6) criteria used, namely accuracy of information, goals, quality of information, quantity information, visual information, and credibility. According to Fig. 5., among the 6 criteria, quality of information received the highest mean score with the score of 4.10. This implies that the content of the application is well written, and relevant to the goal of the application.

The results of the usability testing per age group is shown in Fig. 6. The figure showed that people in early adulthood (age 20–39) gave the application higher mean scores for all categories compared to people in middle and late adulthood (age 40 and beyond). For the category engagement, the application got a mean score of 3.98 for people in early adulthood, while it got a mean score of 3.96 for people in middle and late adulthood. For the category functionality, the application got a mean score of 4.34 for people in early adulthood, while it got a mean score of 4.20 for people in middle and late adulthood. While for category aesthetics, the application got a mean score of 3.96 for people in early adulthood, and it got a mean score of 3.68 for people in middle and late adulthood.

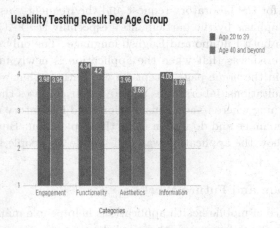

Fig. 6.   Usability testing results per age group.

Lastly, for category information, the application got a mean score of 4.06 for people in early adulthood, while it got a mean score of 3.89 for people in middle and late adulthood. While the application got a higher mean scores from people in early adulthood, there is not much difference on the mean scores from the two age groups. In fact, people in early adulthood gave the application a quality mean score of 4.08, while it received a quality mean of 3.93 from people in middle and late adulthood.

The application got an average 3.7 star rating from the participants of testing. 33% or 10 of the participants answered that they will be using the application for 10 to 50 times for the next 12 months. Overall, from the MARS survey, the application received a quality score of 3.97.

Aside from the scores that the application got from the MARS survey, feedbacks were received from the face-to-face interview. These feedbacks from the interview justifies mostly the scores that the application got from the evaluation in the MARS survey. Most interviewee were older people. The most common feedback of those who participated in the testing is that the application was very simple and easy to use. It did not have complex features that would confuse the user on how to use the application. The input that the application asks from the user is very direct; thus, making it easier for the user to input things such as date and time. The participants said that the application was good on how it was really focused for people with diabetes. Educating the patients more on their illness increases their consciousness and awareness to manage their disease. The what to prepare part for the laboratory request and the frequently asked questions were given emphasis by the participants - especially the FAQs that have a translation in both Filipino and English language. The only difficulty that they encountered was that when the application is newly installed, there was nothing in the home page except for the buttons that would navigate them to consultations, laboratories and FAQs. It confuses them for a little but after learning where to add consultations and laboratory requests, they were able to manage and do well in using the application. But overall, they commended how the application was well - made for people with diabetes.

5. Conclusion and Future Work

The emergence of mobile health applications help people manage their diseases. For the past few years, there is a huge increase in the number of mobile health applications on different application stores, but only few of them have study assessing them. Many mobile health applications have good functionalities, but have poor usability.[9] This leads to people not using these applications as it took a lot of time and effort. Diabetes Bridge was created as a solution for this problem. It has functionalities that satisfy the clinical needs of patients, and a simple user interface.

With the results of the evaluation of the participants to Diabetes Bridge using the MARS survey, the application was well received by the participants. Firstly, as the application was made easy to use, and has a simple user interface, most of the people, especially the elderly, was able to learn the application easily. Based on the comments and suggestions made by the participants of the usability testing, Diabetes Bridge has a potential to be a very efficient healthcare management application for people with diabetes. However, there are still further improvements that can be made to make the application better such as improvement in the user interface in terms of its visual appeal. The interface of the application was made to be simple by the researchers to increase its usability for middle and old age group. By this, the interface can be improved to make it more appealing not only for the older people but for every age group that will use the application.

Many unregulated mobile health applications have no medical professionals involved in the development of the design of medical applications.[4] This is one of the problems that was solved by Diabetes Bridge. In its development process, a healthcare professional was involved. But to further enhance the involvement of the doctors and the caregivers, there should be a way to integrate the records of the patient to the health care system with the consideration of security and privacy. Also, educating the patient is one of the factors that the application considered. With its FAQs and what to prepare for the laboratory requests, information on medication, diet, questions about insulin, and some myths and facts about diabetes can be added to further widen the knowledge of the people about diabetes.

Development in other platforms such as Android would increase the target user of the application as there are a lot of android users now. In addition, it is recommended to conduct further user experience testing with a larger number of participants for a more accurate testing result and for additional comments and suggestions that would improve the features of the application so that it will be a more efficient healthcare management application for people with diabetes.

Overall, Diabetes Bridge is highly recommended for people with diabetes as a tool for them to manage their disease and improve the communication between them and their doctors and caregivers. It is very useful in preparation with the patient's consultation, laboratory requests and results and educating the patient about his/her diseases. In conclusion, Diabetes Bridge is positively received by diabetic people as a mobile health application.

References

1. T. Chomutare, L. Fernandez-Luque, E. Arsand and G. Hartvigsen, Features of mobile diabetes applications: review of the literature and analysis of current applications compared against evidence-based guidelines, *Journal Of Medical Internet Research* **13**, p. e65 (July 2011).
2. I. de la Torre-Diez, M. Lopez-Coronado, B. S. de Abajo, J. Rodrigues and J. A. Basanez (eds.), *Health apps in different mobile platforms: A review in commercial stores* (IEEE, July 2016).
3. K. Terry, Number of health apps soars, but use does not always follow http://www.medscape.com/viewarticle/851226.
4. M. N. K. Boulos, A. C. Brewer, C. Karimkhani, D. B. Buller and R. P. Dellavalle, Mobile medical and health apps: state of the art, concerns,

regulatory control and certification, *Online Journal of Public Health Informatics* **5**, p. 229 (February 2014).

5. O. El-Gayar, P. Timsina, N. Nawar and W. Eid, Mobile applications for diabetes self-management: Status and potentials, *Journal of Diabetes Science and Technology* **7**, 247 (January 2013).

6. B. Holtz and C. Lauckner, Diabetes management via mobile phones: a systematic review, *Telemedicine And E-Health* **18**, 175 (April 2012).

7. M. Arnhold, M. Quade and W. Kirch, Mobile applications for diabetics: A systematic review and expert-based usability evaluation considering the special requirements of diabetes patients age 50 years or older, *Journal of Medical Internet Research* **16**, p. e104 (April 2014).

8. M. Richard, *Software Architecture Patterns* (O'Reilly Media, Inc., California, 2002).

9. M. Jung, S.-M. Park, Y. Ryu, G. Lim and J. Song (eds.), *Understanding Patients' Needs in Diabetes for Mobile Health – A Case Study* (IEEE, August 2016).

10. W. Peng, S. Kanthawala, S. Yuan and S. A. Hussain, A qualitative study of user perceptions of mobile health apps, *Journal of Medical Internet Research* **16**, p. 1158 (November 2016).

11. S. Stoyanov, L. Hides, D. Kavanagh, O. Zelenko, D. Tjondronegoro and M. Mani, Mobile app rating scale: A new tool for assessing the quality of health mobile app, *JMIR mHealth and uHealth* **3**, p. e27 (March 2015).

A Comparison of Filipino and Japanese Facial Expressions and Hand Gestures in Relation to Affective States in Programming Sessions

Thomas James Tiam-Lee* and Kaoru Sumi†

*School of Information Systems Science, Future University Hakodate,
Hakodate City, Hokkaido 041-8655, Japan*
E-mail: g3117002@fun.ac.jp
†*E-mail: kaorus@fun.ac.jp*

This paper presents an analysis of Filipino and Japanese students' facial expressions and hand gestures while solving a series of computer programming exercises. Frequently occurring Facial Action Coding System (FACS) muscle movements such as the widening of the eye (AU-5) and sucking of the lip (AU-28), as well as the occurrence of hand gestures, are identified and discussed in relation to the reported affective states of engagement and confusion. We show that it is possible to build models for predicting engagement and confusion using facial expressions and typing information. We believe that this study can help in the development of affectively aware computer systems for learning programming that can work with different cultures.

Keywords: Affective computing; Facial expression; Gesture; Programming; Education.

1. Introduction and Related Studies

Computer programming is becoming an essential skill in our society. This is evidenced by the fact that several countries have already included programming or computational thinking in their basic education curricula. Computational thinking is already being taught in high schools across the US[1] and EU[2]. Japan plans to make programming mandatory across all public primary schools by 2020[3]. Some high schools in the Philippines have taken the initiative to include programming in their curricula as well[4]. Because of this, it is a timely endeavor to improve the quality of programming education around the world.

One of the ways technology can be used for programming education is by developing computer systems that can support students who are learning how to program. While studies on tutoring systems for programming have been going on since the 1970s[5], the most recent efforts on the field have focused on developing tutoring systems that can respond appropriately to student affect[6-9]. Studies have shown that the emotions students experience while learning programming are correlated with their performance[10-11]. Thus, there is some value for a tutoring system to consider not only the cognitive state of the student, but also the affective state.

A good human tutor can recognize what a student feels during a programming session, and can provide appropriate responses. For example, a student who makes a mistake because he is confused could be given similar examples to clarify his misunderstandings, but a student who makes a mistake because he is frustrated could be given encouraging feedback as well as simpler examples to reinforce his mastery of previous concepts. This kind of affective-based feedback has been implemented in previous intelligent tutoring systems in other domains such as Wayang Outpost[12], but remains to be a challenge in the programming domain.

Previous studies on analyzing student emotions in programming were often conducted on a predominantly Western culture setting. However, we believe it is interesting to explore the occurrence and expression of learner affect on other cultures. While previous studies have argued that facial expressions for basic emotions are universal, triggers for these emotions can vary from one culture to another[13]. Furthermore, cultural display rules could also affect the extent to which these emotions are expressed[14]. In this study we look at Filipino and Japanese students in programming and compare their facial expressions and hand gestures in relation to their affective states in a programming setting. We believe that understanding these similarities and differences is a step towards the development of affectively aware systems that are also culturally sensitive.

2. Data Collection

Two series of data collections sessions were conducted, one for Filipino students and one for Japanese students. The first series was conducted in December 2016 at De La Salle University, Philippines while the second series was conducted in June 2016 at Future University Hakodate, Japan.

2.1. *Participants*

12 Filipino students and 15 Japanese students volunteered to participate in the study. They have already completed or were taking an introductory programming course, which was taught in Java for the Filipino students and in Processing for the Japanese students. The average age was 18.4 (std. dev = 1.31) for the Filipino students and also 18.4 (std. dev = 0.67) for the Japanese

students. For the Filipino group, 7 students were junior students and 5 students were sophomore students. On average, they had around 2 years (junior) and 1 year (sophomore) of programming experience. For the Japanese group, all students were freshmen and had around 2 months of programming experience.

Prior to the experiment, all participants had to sign an informed consent form, which informs them of all the procedures in the experiment and the data that would be collected. All participants have granted us the permission to publish images of their faces on scientific presentations and publications.

2.2. *Programming Phase*

The data collection sessions were held individually for each student. In each session, the student was asked to solve a series of programming exercises, which were of increasing difficulty. For example, in one exercise the student has to write a program that displays the change of a customer, given the price of the item bought and the amount paid. The exercises cover the following concepts: variables, expressions, conditional statements, iterative statements, and arrays.

The same set of exercises were used for all students, but because there are differences with how the introductory programming classes were taught in the Filipino and Japanese universities, the format of the exercises were slightly changed to make the exercises familiar for both groups.

In the Philippine introductory programming class, basic procedural programs were written in Java by getting input from the console, doing some processing, and displaying the result on the console. The Japanese introductory programming class had more focus on graphical user interface (GUI) input and output (they use Processing language which was not designed for console I/O). However, automatic checking of exercises in this approach was unnecessarily difficult. Thus, we changed the format for the Japanese group such that the students simply had to write the body of a function. This removed the part where the students had to get the input and output, since the input is already in the form of the function arguments, and the output is in the form of the return value. To compensate for less typing, the Japanese students had to complete one additional exercise. Figure 1 shows a comparison of the exercise format for the two groups, while Table 1 shows a short description of the exercises.

Write a Java program that gets the price of the item, followed by the amount given by the customer. Display the change.	Complete the Processing function that returns the change of the customer given the **price** of item and the **amount** given.
	
	`int getChange(int price, int amount) {`
	`}`

Fig. 1. Example format of the same exercise for the Filipino (left) and Japanese (right) students.

Table 1. Exercise Problems for the Programming Phase

Description of Exercise	Skills Covered
Display / return the string "Hello World"	Output
Get the change given the price and amount given.	Arithmetic
Convert Fahrenheit to Celsius.*	Arithmetic
Determine if score is at least 60.0 or not.	Conditional Statement
Get the final price of item after applying discounts which based on certain conditions.	Arithmetic, Conditional Statement
Get average of a list of numbers	Arithmetic, Array, Iterative Statement
Given a number, get the sum of all odd digits.	Arithmetic, Conditional Statement, Iterative Statement, Number Theory
Determine if a number is prime or not.	Arithmetic, Conditional Statement, Iterative Statement, Number Theory

*This was an additional exercise for the Japanese students.

The student used a special software to write, test, and submit their code. This software was designed to automatically check the student's solution by running the program and comparing its output to the expected result. The student could only move to the next exercise if he or she has submitted a correct program for the current one. Each session lasted for 45 minutes, or until the student has correctly solved all exercises. During the session, the software also records a video of the participant's face and keeps a log of all the keystrokes and actions done by the student. This allows us to replay each session by reconstructing the history from the actions logged and playing it alongside the video feed.

2.3. *Annotation Phase*

After the programming phase, the student was asked to look at the session replay and report the affective states that they experienced throughout the session. The student identified specific time intervals and annotated them with an affective state label. For this study, we consider the common affective states of engagement, confusion, frustration, and boredom based on the previous study[15]. For the Filipino group, the annotation phase was done manually with the supervision of an assistant. For the Japanese group, because of difficulties with the language barrier, a program was developed for the students to do the annotations on their own, as seen in Fig. 2. For both groups, the role of the assistant is to simply explain the process of annotation, and to answer questions from the students, if any.

Fig. 2. The session can be replayed by playing the video feed alongside the reconstruction of the coding history for the annotation phase. In this image, the slider can be used to play through the session, and annotations can be added by clicking the buttons and dragging the interval.

3. Feature Extraction

Because of some technical problems with the camera setup, data from 4 of the Japanese students had to be discarded. This left us with data from 12 Filipino students (8 male, 4 female) and 11 Japanese students (9 male, 2 female), amounting to approximately 16 hours of video footage and coding logs. Affectiva SDK[16] was used to extract Facial Action Coding Unit (FACS) points from the videos. These are critical points indicating muscle movement, which was used by in previous studies on recognizing emotions from facial expressions[13]. Figure 3 shows snapshots of the video overlaid with FACS points.

Fig. 3. The Facial Action Coding System (FACS) points are extracted using Affectiva SDK.

Fig. 4. Example of AU5 eye widen (left), AU28 Lip suck (middle), and AU27 Mouth open (right)

The video was split into individual frames, or snapshots. In a one second interval there are around 30 frames. Affectiva SDK can analyze each frame and extract the FACS points, as well as the occurrence of Action Units (AU), which are fundamental actions of a set of individual muscles on the face. These actions were described by Ekman and Friesen in their studies on recognizing emotion from facial expressions. Some examples of AUs and their corresponding facial muscle configurations are shown in Fig. 4[13]. Based on its own trained models, Affectiva SDK assigns a score of 0-100 for each type of AU based on its confidence that the AU has occurred on a specific frame. Frames where the Affectiva SDK model is unable to detect the face were discarded.

4. Analysis of Data

This section discusses the occurrence of facial expressions and hand gestures observed from the sessions conducted with the Filipino and Japanese students.

4.1. *Observations on Facial Expressions*

The expressiveness of the face could be measured using Affectiva SDK's "engagement" metric (not to be confused with the academic emotion of engagement), which is based on the amount of facial muscle movements. For each frame, the expressiveness is assigned a score of 0 -100, where 100 is the highest. It was found that all Filipino and Japanese students exhibited expressiveness, which is spread out throughout the entire session. However, the amount of expressiveness could vary among students.

The average expressiveness among students across all frames with an expressiveness score of at least 1.0 is 38.38 (std. dev = 9.4788) for the Filipino students and 28.3 (std. dev = 11.646) for the Japanese students. The average percentage of frames where the students have an expressiveness score of at least 1.0 is 22.62% for the Filipino students and 17.13% for the Japanese students. In this experiment, Japanese students tend to be less expressive than Filipino students, but it is difficult to generalize this due to the small sample size.

The types of AU that were frequently displayed were very similar between the Filipino and Japanese groups. Table 2 shows the most frequent action units across the sessions. To compute for the frequency, we count the number of frames where the AU was detected. We say that the AU was detected in a frame if it has a confidence score of at least 50.0. The percentage values show the ratio between the frames where the AU was detected and the total number of frames (excluding the frames where no face was detected). Although some students tend to display some AUs more than the others, the frequent AUs listed here are generally displayed by a majority of the students and not dominated by just a few.

Table 2. Facial Expressions Commonly Shown by Filipino and Japanese Students

FACS Action Unit	Frequency (Filipino Group)	Frequency (Japanese Group)	Commonly Displayed During
Dimpler (AU14)	21464 (5.1%)	7974 (2.27%)	Brief moments of pondering between typing code
Lip Press (AU24)	16300 (3.87%)	6170 (1.76%)	
Lip Suck (AU28)	18664 (4.44%)	10174 (2.9%)	
Eye Widen (AU5)	20045 (4.76%)	11157 (3.18%)	Thinking, finding a bug, reading problem
Mouth Open (AU27)	12798 (3.09%)	4260 (1.21%)	Reading problem, mouthing code, typing

Dimpler (AU14), Lip Press (AU24) and Lip Suck (AU28), in many occasions, co-occur with one another. Dimpler is an AU characterized by the tightening of the corners of the lips by pulling them inwards, which has been

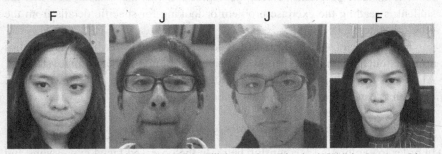

Fig. 5. From left to right: Dimpler (AU14) by Filipino student, Dimpler (AU14) by Japanese, Lip Press (AU24) by Japanese student, Lip Suck (AU28) by Filipino student.

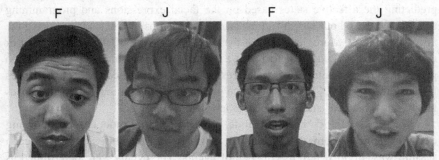

Fig. 6. From left to right: Eye Widen (AU5) by Filipino student, Eye Widen (AU5) by Japanese student, Mouth Open (AU27) by Filipino student, Mouth Open (AU27) by Japanese student

associated with the basic emotion of contempt[13]. Lip Suck is characterized by the pulling of the lips along with the adjacent skin in the mouth, while Lip Press is when the lips are pressed tightly together (see Fig. 5). These AU have been previously associated with the basic emotion of anger[13]. All students have displayed at least one of these AU during the sessions. Both Filipino and Japanese students often display these AU in brief moments of thinking while writing code. It occurs many times during brief pauses while writing a solution, or sometimes while typing a specific of the program with some uncertainty.

Eye Widen (AU5) is an AU described as the raising of upper lids of the eyes so that the eyes appear larger than normal (see Fig. 6). In Ekman's mapping of AUs to basic emotions, AU5 is associated with the emotions of fear and surprise[13]. In the programming sessions, a good number of students displayed AU5, but there were a few who did not. Upon manual observation of the video feeds, AU5 in most cases occurs during 3 types of events. First, AU5 was displayed when the students were finding bugs in the code. This display of AU5 often occurs a few seconds after a wrong compilation or submission. Second, AU5 was displayed when the students were pondering about the next statements to write in their programs. Third, the expression was also displayed when the student is reading the exercise problem or looking for specific details from the problem statement.

Mouth Open (AU27), described as lowering of the lower lip so that the lips are not touching one another, was displayed more by the Filipino students. AU27 was often displayed when the student was reading the problem statement, or when the student was mouthing the code he is typing.

4.2. *Facial Expressions as Predictors of Affective States*

In order to explore the relationship between the observed facial expressions and the affective states experienced by the students, we developed models for predicting the affective states based on the facial expressions and programming activity. We based our classifications on the annotations by the students during the annotation phase. More than 75% of the annotations were labelled engagement or confusion, so this study will focus on these two affective states. For the Filipino group, there were a total of 27 sequences labelled as "confused" and 24 sequences labelled as "engaged." For the Japanese group, there were a total of 20 sequences labelled as "engaged" and 24 sequences labelled as "engaged."

We used a Hidden Markov Model (HMM) to build models for classifying event sequences from the session as engagement or confusion. First, each session was divided into a sequence of events. The events were determined as follows. First, each code compilations and submissions in the timeline were treated as a single event. Next, all intervals where the student was typing were identified and each treated as a single event. A threshold of 3 seconds was used to determine the boundaries of the interval (i.e., if the student was typing, then student did not type anything for the last 3 seconds, it meant that that typing event had ended). Finally, all remaining intervals that were not part of the previous two types of events were each treated as separate events.

Each event was tagged with the type of event, which can be one of the following: (1) "short idle" (short interval with no typing), (2) "long idle" (long interval with no typing), (3) "short typing" (short interval where the student was typing), (4) "long typing" (long interval where the student was typing), (5) "positive compilation" (code was compiled with no errors or submitted correctly), and (6) "negative compilation" (code was compiled with some errors or submitted an incorrect solution).

Each event was associated with an affective state, based on the reported annotations of the students. An event is associated to an affective state if at least 95% of its interval intersects with the student's annotation interval of the said affective state. For example, if the student reported that he was engaged from 200 seconds to 230 seconds, then an event that spans from 210 seconds to 215 seconds will be tagged with engagement. Events that don't get associated this way were tagged with "unknown". An observation sequence for the HMM was obtained by taking the longest possible subsequences of events that fall under the same reported affective state (engaged or confused). Figure 7 shows an example of an observation sequence.

We treated the problem as a binary classification problem, "given a sequence of events, does it likely contain confusion?" (if the answer to this is no, then it is treated as engagement). For each training iteration, HMM models were trained for both classification labels. The best fit model for each classification was chosen based on the number of hidden states that yielded the highest likelihood. Once the best fit models have been determined, a leave-one-out cross fold validation was used to evaluate the classification accuracy of the models. This was chosen due to limited number of instances in the data. To classify a sequence, the log likelihood was evaluated on each model, and the model with the best likelihood was chosen.

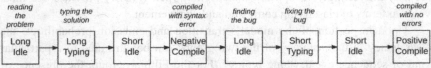

Fig. 7. An example sequence generated from a part of the session. The italic text describe a possible scenario that happened during the session.

The first training round was done without adding any facial expression information, but succeeding rounds were done with additional facial expression information. To do this, each event in the sequences was tagged with additional Boolean information on whether the target facial expression was observed within that event or not. Table 3 shows the accuracy of the different models for the Filipino and Japanese students.

Note that in the table confusion is considered to be the positive class. This means that the true positive (TP) refers to the number of actual confusion sequences that were correctly classified as confusion. The false positive (FP) refers to the number of sequences which were actually engagement, but were incorrectly classified as confusion. The reverse goes for the true negative (TN) and false negative (FN). The accuracy is computed as the total number of correct classifications over all sequences. To measure the likelihood that the performance did not happen by chance, we use the kappa statistic which represents the inter-rater agreement between the model classifications and the ground truth.

Table 3. Performance of Models on Classifying Confusion from Engagement

	Filipino Students						Japanese Students					
	TP	FP	TN	FN	Accuracy	Kappa	TP	FP	TN	FN	Accuracy	Kappa
no AU information	23	6	18	4	80.39%	0.6	14	10	14	6	63.64%	0.28
Dimpler (AU16)	21	3	21	6	82.35%	0.65	13	7	17	7	68.18%	0.35
Lip Press (AU24)	23	7	17	4	78.43%	0.56	12	6	18	8	68.18%	0.35
Lip Suck (AU28)	22	4	20	5	82.35%	0.65	13	9	15	7	63.64%	0.27
Eye Widen (AU5)	22	4	20	5	82.35%	0.65	9	10	11	14	45.46%	-0.08
Mouth Open (AU27)	23	3	21	4	**86.28%**	0.73	15	8	16	5	**70.46%**	0.41

It can be seen from the results that HMM is very promising for modeling affective states in programming sessions. Even without any facial expression information, the model is able to correctly classify confusion from engagement with an accuracy of 80.39% (Filipino group) and 63.64% (Japanese group). Adding facial expression information further increases the accuracy of the models. Interestingly, it appears that Mouth Open (AU27) provides the most value in terms of classifying confusion and engagement.

Upon inspection of the model's transition and emission probabilities, the discrepancy in the accuracy of the two groups can be attributed to a particular kind of sequence event: "long typing". For the Filipino group, the presence of long typing intervals is a good predictor for engagement. However, perhaps because the Japanese students were not as used to typing codes (which are only in English), they did not have too many long typing intervals even in moments of engagement.

4.3. *Hand Gestures*

It is also interesting to observe the hand gestures made by the students during the programming session. A hand gesture in this case refers to visible movements of the hand outside of typing. Because Affectiva SDK does not detect hand gestures automatically, we manually annotated the video feeds with the presence of hand gestures. Figure 8 shows some examples of hand gestures made by Filipino and Japanese students.

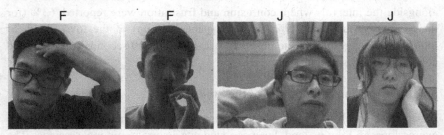

Fig. 8. Examples of hand gestures of Filipino (2 images at the left) and Japanese (2 images at the right) students. From left to right: hand on head, hand on mouth, scratching the head, hand on face.

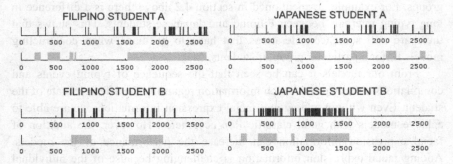

Fig. 9. Frequency of hand gestures, in many cases, coincide with reported confusion and frustration. The top graphs (black) show the hand gestures in one session, the bottom graphs (gray) show the intervals where confusion and frustration were reported.

The most common kinds of gestures were putting the hand on the face, mouth, chin, head or neck. However, the type of gesture that appeared frequently seems to be an individual preference, as it differs from student to student (i.e., some students put the hand on the face a lot, but some put the hand on the chin a lot). Previous studies have associated some of these gestures with negative emotions[17]. Neck touching can take place if there is emotional discomfort, doubt or insecurity. Touching the cheeks or the face, on the other hand, is a way to pacify feelings of nervousness or irritation, while rubbing the forehead area can be an indicator of struggle or discomfort.

While the some students from both groups tend to make significantly more gestures than others, it can be observed that there is a general increase in frequency in hand gestures towards the end of the session for both groups. Furthermore, it can also be observed that the increase of hand gestures, in many cases, coincide with reported states of confusion and frustration. Figure 9 shows the occurrence of hand gestures on the timeline of selected student sessions, alongside the intervals where confusion and frustration were reported. 63% (for the Filipino group) and 78% (for the Japanese group) of the total length of intervals where gestures were observed occurs within 10 seconds from reported confusion and frustration.

5. Discussion and Limitations of the Study

Based on the analysis of the data, there are many commonalities between facial expressions of Filipino and Japanese students in programming sessions. The kinds of facial expressions that were frequently displayed were the same. By analyzing the models it can be seen that there are some differences between the groups. For example, as mentioned in section 4.2 above there is a difference in long typing intervals between Filipino and Japanese students. This shows that there are still some considerations that have to be made when constructing models fit for a particular group of students.

From our models it can be seen that the sequence of typing events and compilations already provide rich information regarding the affective state of the student. Even without adding any facial expression information, we are able to achieve models with good classification accuracies. However, the addition of facial expression information can increase the performance of the models. Adding facial expression information is challenging because of the individual differences among the students. For example, some students tend to display a certain type of expression more than others. More study, preferably with a larger sample size, may be needed to have a better understanding of the relationships between facial expressions and affective states.

One of the limitations of this study is that the facial action units were determined automatically based on the Affectiva SDK model. While this allowed us to process large amounts of data in a short time, it is considered to be less accurate than the judgments of a trained FACS annotator. Another limitation is the granularity and accuracy of the reported affective states by the students. Because the sessions were long, it was sometimes difficult for the students to remember all the emotions that they experienced at different moments. Thus, it is safe to say that the reported annotations only represent the most significant ones that stuck in the students' memories. Future work can explore alternative ways on determining the affective state to make it more accurate and fine-grained.

6. Conclusion and Future Work

In this paper we have analyzed the facial expressions and hand gestures of Filipino and Japanese students in programming sessions. We found that the most common facial expressions are Dimpler, Lip Press, Lip Suck, Eye Widen, and Mouth Open. We showed that HMM models can be used to classify confusion and engagement with high accuracy from programming sessions using programming / typing activity and facial expression information. We also show that while the frequency and types of hand gestures vary from one student to another, there are, in several cases, coincidences between hand gesture frequency and reported states of confusion and frustration.

Some of the future work that can be done on this study are as follows. Alternative ways of determining baseline affective states can be explored to make it more standard and reliable. Using devices for automatic detection of gestures can also be explored, as well as other signals that could be an indicator of affective states. Because typing activity seems to play an important role in recognizing emotion, deeper analyses of typing activity such as keystroke dynamics as a predictor of affective states could also be explored. We believe that the development of an accurate affect recognizer during programming sessions where there are no social interactions can pave the way for the development of better systems that can support students who are practicing or learning programming outside the classroom.

Acknowledgments

Mr. Tiam-Lee would like to thank to Japan's Ministry of Education, Culture, Sports, Science and Technology (MEXT) for providing scholarship for his doctoral program. The authors would also like to thank the research assistants who facilitated the data collection process: Mr. Kim Aguila Oñate for the

Filipino sessions, and Mr. Tomohiro Mori and Mr. Ryo Okuyama for the Japanese sessions.

References

1. J. Wing, Computational Thinking: 10 Years Later, *Microsoft Research Blog*, (2016). https://www.microsoft.com/en-us/research/blog/computational-thinking-10-years-later/
2. A. Balanskat and K. Engelhardt, Integrating Computer Programming / Coding Skills in the Curriculum: Current Situation and Rationale, in *European Schoolnet*, (Brussels, 2014), p. 10.
3. S. Awwal, Japan Plans to Make Programming Mandatory at Schools, *TechMedia*, (2016). https://techmedia.com.ng /2016/05/24/japan-plans-make-programming-mandatory-schools/
4. De La Salle University (2016, February 05). DLSU CCS and Saint Jude Catholic School Collaborate to Implement Computational Thinking Curriculum for K to 12's STEM Strand. Retrieved October 23, 2017, from http://computerstudies.dlsu.edu.ph/post/139091163877/dlsu-ccs-and-saint-jude-catholic-school
5. W. Soloway and L. Johnson-Elliot, Intention-Based Diagnosis of Programming Errors, *Proceedings of the 5th National Conference on Artificial Intelligence*, (1984).
6. J. F. Grafsgaard, K. E. Boyer, and J. C. Lester, Predicting Facial Indicators of Confusion with Hidden Markov Models, in *Affective Computing and Intelligent Interaction Lecture Notes in Computer Science*, (2011), pp. 97 – 106.
7. J. F. Grafsgaard, K. E. Boyer, R. Phillips, and J. C. Lester, Modeling Confusion: Facial Expression, Task, and Discourse in Task-Oriented Tutorial Dialogue, in *Lecture Notes in Computer Science Artificial Intelligence in Education*, (2011), pp. 98 – 105.
8. J. F. Grafsgaard, J. B. Wiggins, K. E. Boyer, E. N. Wiebe, and J. C. Lester, Automatically Recognizing Facial Indicators of Frustration: a Learning-Centric Analysis, in *2013 Humaine Association Conference on Affective Computing and Intelligent Interaction*, (2013).
9. J. F. Grafsgaard, J. B. Wiggins, A. K. Vail, K. E. Boyer, E. N. Wiebe, and J. C. Lester, The Additive Value of Multimodal Features for Predicting Engagement, Frustration, and Learning During Tutoring, in *Proceedings of the 16th International Conference on Multimodal Interaction (ICMI'14)*.

10. M. M. T. Rodrigo, E. S. Tabanao, R. S. Baker, M. C. Jadud, A. C. M. Amarra, T. Dy, et al, Affective and Behavioral Predictors of Novice Programmer Achievement, in *ACM SIGCSE Bulletin*, **41**, 3 (2009), p. 156.

11. D. M. C. Lee, M. M. T. Rodrigo, R. S. Baker, J. O. Sugay, and A. Coronel, Exploring the Relationship between Novice Programmer Confusion and Achievement, in *Affective Computing and Intelligent Interaction Lecture Notes in Computer Science*, (2011), pp. 174 – 184.

12. B. Woolf, W. Burleson, R. Picard et al, Affect-aware Tutors: Recognizing and Responding to Student Affect, *Learning Technologies*, **4**, 3/4, (2009), pp. 129 – 163.

13. P. Ekman and W. V. Friesen, *Unmasking the face: a guide to recognizing emotions from facial clues*, (Cambridge, 2003).

14. D. Matsumoto, S. Takeuchi, S. Andayani et al, The Contribution of Individualism vs. Collectivism to Cross-National Differences in Display Rules, *Asian Joirnal of Social Psychology*, **1**, 2 (1998), pp. 147 – 165.

15. N. Bosch, S. D'Mello and C. Millis, What Emotions Do Novice Experience During Their First Computer Programming Learning Session?, *Lecture Notes in Computer Science Artificial Intelligence in Education*, (2013), pp. 11 – 20.

16. Affectiva Developer Portal. https://developer.affectiva.com/

17. J. Navarro, M. Karlins, P. Constanzo, *What Every BODY is Saying: An ex-FBI Agent's Guide to Speed Reading People*, (2008).

Using Body Posture, Movement and Human Activity to Predict Emotions

E. A. Calapatia and M. C. Suarez

Software Technology, De La Salle University,
Manila, 2401, Philippines
earl.calapatia@delasalle.ph
merlin.suarez@delasalle.ph

Numerous studies on emotion recognition have discovered that facial cues are reliable to distinguish one emotional expression from another. This is useful in highly-controlled environments where the face can easily be tracked. However, this is not true in real-world scenarios, thus, alternative modalities need to be investigated. Bodily expression and human activity can provide additional information to recognize an emotional expression, which will hopefully help create more robust models. Previous works on body movement used acted emotional expressions. To overcome this limitation, this work collected body movement data as human subjects played a game. Subjects are free to move within their assigned space as data was recorded. SVM and Random Forest models predicted valence, arousal and intensity using body posture, movement and activity. Models that reached a validation score of 70% and train-test accuracy of 60% have been analyzed. The best performing model reached a train-test accuracy of 80.2%.

Keywords: Emotion Recognition, Body Movement, Posture, Non-acted Emotions, Activity State.

1. Introduction

Natural emotions can be observed in several cues such as face, voice, and body[1]. The use of body movement for recognizing emotion has generated interest because of its potential role in analyzing depression[2], deception[3], gaming[4] and emotion expression in daily activities[5]. Body movement is a source of additional visual information in scenarios where the face cannot be tracked. The cues which express them may vary in differing conditions. The body can express what the face cannot and vice versa[6,7].

There are several challenges in working with emotional expressions taken in spontaneous and naturalistic situations. Studies conducted with natural emotion produce recognition performances on par with observer scores[8,9].

However, models trained using naturalistic data tend to have "flower" accuracy scores, mainly because differences in emotional expressions tend to be subtle. Performance is based on labels, which are based on observer agreement. Furthermore, the method will likely reflect the perception of emotion more than the actual emotion experienced by subjects.

Unlike acted emotions, natural emotions can also have complex qualities that directly impact their taxonomy and representation. Cam3D is a 3D multimodal corpus using complex mental states to categorize emotion[10]. Various activities were used as stimuli to target specific emotional states. Each activity was able to elicit its own set of target emotions. Activity can also provide cues in recognizing emotions especially for systems in assistive technologies[8,11] and education systems[12]. The proposed approach addresses these issues by focusing on selfreported emotional experience, what the body does to express it and what actions may have led to that emotion.

2. Related Studies

2.1. *Emotions Labels*

In emotion recognition, the emotion label is the target value in classification. Questions of representation and values arise in the design of the labels. Labels may be represented as discrete categories or continuous values. While there is no consensus on which target values will serve best in modelling affect for body movement, dimensional values have gained interest. The effectiveness of using dimensional values, particularly that of arousal, is demonstrated in past studies[13]. Body movement may be best labelled with values that reflect emotion qualities rather than specific emotions. Recognition rates increased when emotion labels of similar qualities were grouped[14].

Complex mental states are a departure from the 6 basic emotions by Paul Ekman. In the Cam3D data set, the cognitive group consist of thinking, concentrating, unsure, confused and triumphant. The second group consists of frustrated and angry. The third consists of bored and neutral and the last consists of the presence and absence of surprise[10].

2.2. *Using Activity in Emotion Recognition*

As demonstrated in the Cam3D methodology, the activity can affect what emotion groups are likely to occur. A learning task for example, will result to the emergence of academic emotions[12] and winning or losing in a game can mental states such as triumph or loss[10]. In their work, the task, goal and state of the tasks have been used as cues for emotion recognition[12]. Activity has been defined as a set of actions taken to fulfill a goal[15]. In gesture recognition systems, activity can provide cues for emotion recognition. There are studies conducted to model emotions in specific activities. Emotions can be recognized through variations in daily tasks such as opening doors[5]. Movement features have also been used to recognize emotion expression in a musical ensemble[14]. The activity constrains which actions can be performed and which are not likely to occur[16].

2.3. *Posture and Movement*

Posture or static features refers to the shape of the body within a single frame. In two dimensional still frames from a video stream, posture can be extracted in the form of blobs, bounding boxes, body shape, body part positions and two dimensional angles. As 3-Dimensional data, posture can be extracted in the form of 3D joint angles, blobs, head to part distance and posture. Movement or dynamic features are extracted from the movement of the body, taking change over time into account. The significance of the temporal quality has been demonstrated in previous studies[4,17]. For For classifiers, continuous data is segmented into frames. Each frame represents the current frame and the previous ones in a sliding window. Determining the sliding window frame is a challenge for extracting movement. In two dimensional and two dimensional data, movement has been extracted in the form of hand trajectories, speed, acceleration, amplitude/oscillation, energy, fluency, shape and curvature. A study that used both posture and movement recognized with a score of 75.41%. They compared this result with classifying with only for posture and only high-level dynamic features, obtaining 68.85% and 57.38% respectively. This finding supports the integration of posture and movement[18].

3. Methodology

Figure 1 illustrates the proposed approach. It begins with data collection, followed by emotion labelling, activity annotations, feature preprocessing and extraction, data set generation, model generation and finally, evaluation. The approach addresses both technical and theoretical challenges for the task of recognizing emotions.

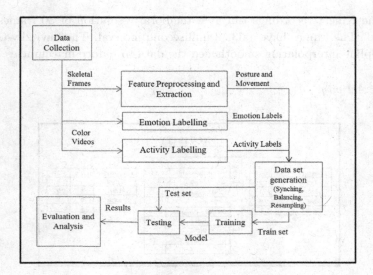

Fig. 1.   Process flow of the proposed approach.

3.1. *Data Collection*

Data is collected from 20 university students, six females and 14 males, ages between 20 to 25 years old. All consented to collect recordings of their data prior to data collection. The activity tasks the subjects to conduct a guessing game in dyads. The host holds the answer. The subject guesses. After the activity, the subject annotates his or her data. The subject is then given an interview which also serves as the debriefing period. Subjects are instructed to annotate Valence, Arousal and Intensity. The post-activity has subjects label their emotions, give feedback, answer an interview and debriefing. Table 1 lists the class labels per dimension.

Table 1.   Class labels per dimension

Dimension	Class Labels	
Valence	Negative	Positive
Arousal	High	Low
Intensity	High	Low

Data is captured by two recording devices, a Kinect v2 sensor and a colour video camera. The subject is free to move within a boundary. The boundary ensures that the subject does not stay out of the view of the video camera and the Kinect camera.

The Kinect recordings run at a temporal resolution of 30 frames per second. The frames have a 33.33 millisecond interval. The Savitzky-Golay and Spline interpolation smoothened the data to reduce inaccuracies.

3.1.1. *Activity*

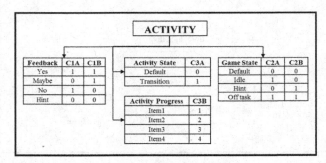

Fig. 2. Values listed for activity. Cn refers to channels while A and B refers to the 1st and 2nd columns of each channel.

Activities are manually labelled after the recording sessions. Activity describes the conditions and events of the activity. These conditions and events consist of the task related categories, activity related categories and feedback. The labels in terms of the game have been identified in pilot experiments. Figure 2 lists the mappings and their corresponding values. Feedback is assigned to Channel 1, Game State is assigned to Channel 2 and Activity State is assigned to Channel 3.

3.2. *Body Features*

The feature extraction step produces four sets of attributes. These are postures, immediate movement, average movement.

3.2.1. *Posture*

Joint positions and segment directions serve as the values computing posture. Both are represented through Euclidean vectors. Figure 3 illustrates the normalized postures.

Equation 1 illustrates a vector v, representing a position of a joint which has the values v_1, v_2 and v_3 corresponding to the horizontal, vertical and depth coordinates of the joint. V is a set containing the direction of all joints.

$$v = [v_1, v_2, v_3] \text{ where } v \epsilon V \tag{1}$$

Fig. 3.   Comparison between initial posture(left) and postures with normalized segment direction(right).

3.2.2. *Movement*

Movement is computed as change in posture over a window period. Studies vary in the window period[4,19]. Five kinds of movement are computed. These are Displacement, Direction, Distance, Speed and Acceleration. Immediate and Average movement have been defined in relation to the window period. Immediate movement measures the movement at the closest observable instant the movement is executed. It is the delta between two posture frames. The recommended time length in measuring temporal data is 0.5 to 4.0 seconds depending on the target emotions[20]. Some emotions in the data set last for no more than 2.0 seconds. Hence, the selected window period for average movement is 1.5 seconds. The framerate of the data stream for joint position and segment direction is 30 frames per second; hence the window period has a frame count of 45 frames.

3.3. *Modelling*

Models are generated with a 7:3 train test ratio. This guarantees that the minimum set of values are met while maximizing the amount of data. Models are trained per subject. Each model uses one feature to recognize one emotion dimension, for example Movement-Valence. Training for classifiers will use two learning algorithms, SVM and Random Forest. SVM is a commonly used algorithm for detecting emotions through body movement[4,5]. It can generalize from high dimensional data. It can generalize from high dimensional data. It can indicate how well the features work together.

Random Forest is less stable and less predictable, but it is capable of emphasizing important features. It is necessary to normalize values for SVM, but not for Random Forests. The discriminant function of Random Forest, the information gain ratio is not sensitive to scale. Hence normalization is unnecessary for Random Forest.

4. Results

4.1. *10 fold cross Validation*

The baseline performance for 10-fold cross validation is set to 70.0%, based on the minimum performance values used for validation in recent studies[9,21]. Table 2 lists the mean performance vectors of all models which performed at or better than 70%. The validation score are further used in the analysis for the subsequent sections of the chapter.

Table 2. Mean performance for 10-fold cross validation.

	Accuracy	Kappa	Rec(1)	Rec(2)	Pre(1)	Pre(2)
Valence	87.05	0.74	86.43	87.67	88.96	87.94
Arousal	84.45	0.69	79.37	89.52	88.69	83.01
Intensity	85.25	0.71	88.28	82.22	85.19	89.12

4.2. *Evaluation*

The evaluation covers models with at least a 10-fold cross validation accuracy of 70.0% and a train-test score of 60.0%. Tables 3, 4 and 5 list the performance vectors of these models. ID refers to the subject ID. Fea refers to the feature group used to train the model. These feature groups are (D)efault, (P)osture, (A)verage Movement, (I)mmediate Movement and A(C)tivity. TT Acc refers to the accuracy of the train-test model. Val Acc refers to the accuracy of the cross validation model. Kappa, Rec(1) and Rec(2) refers to the Kappa coefficient and Class 1 & 2 Recall scores of the train-test models.

Only models produced with the activity and posture groups passed the performance cutoff. Consistent with the established findings such as that of the mean performance and the attribute correlation, activity can be a good indicator for valence. However, models which used activity have a validation score that reaches 84.5% at best while posture at least scores at 91.2%. This means more reliable models can be built using posture.

Table 3. Valence models where validation >= 70 and train-test >= 60

ID	Algo	Fea	TT Acc	Val Acc	Kappa	Rec(1)	Rec(2)
1	SVM	C	70.9	77.3	0.4	88.7	53.0
1	RF	C	76.5	79.1	0.5	100.0	53.0
3	SVM	C	69.9	73.7	0.4	49.2	90.7
3	RF	C	69.9	73.0	0.4	49.2	90.7
4	RF	A	63.1	70.7	0.3	60.6	65.7
5	RF	P	60.0	99.6	0.2	99.0	21.0
6	SVM	C	78.0	84.5	0.6	93.7	62.4
6	RF	C	78.0	83.9	0.6	93.7	62.4
10	SVM	P	61.3	92.8	0.2	83.0	39.5
10	SVM	C	76.0	80.6	0.5	86.2	65.7
10	RF	C	79.1	74.7	0.6	92.5	65.7
11	SVM	P	62.0	98.7	0.2	66.1	57.9
11	RF	P	68.6	91.2	0.4	83.6	53.5
11	SVM	C	75.9	82.2	0.5	100.0	51.6
11	RF	C	64.9	79.9	0.3	78.1	51.6
13	RF	P	70.4	95.4	0.4	78.5	62.2

Table 4. Arousal models where validation >= 70 and train-test >= 60

ID	Algo	Fea	TT Acc	Val Acc	Kappa	Rec(1)	Rec(2)
4	SVM	D	61.1	95.4	0.2	25.1	97.1
4	SVM	P	70.2	98.3	0.4	82.7	57.7
4	RF	P	64.8	87.5	0.3	51.5	78.2
4	SVM	A	64.7	93.8	0.3	31.9	97.4
10	SVM	P	64.6	91.2	0.3	60.8	68.5
10	RF	C	67.8	73.8	0.4	51.0	84.6

Based on the correlations measured and existing studies[8], it is expected that most of the models would use features from the arousal group, however, it is only used once. Due to the lack of useable data for arousal, this is not enough to be generalized.

In contrast to the previous two dimensions, the models use a more diverse group of features for Intensity as seen in Table 5. It is also the only dimension to successfully employ the use features from Immediate Movement. It is likely that the observability of an emotion varies by subject. The emotion expressions in some subjects are easier to read than others. Subject 11, for instance has 4 models within Table 3. Subject 7 has 4 models under Intensity, but none for valence. Finally, Subject 10 has a model for each emotion dimension. However, the experiment is not enough to determine if this is due to the limitations of the features in the scope of the experiment or if this due to the individual tendencies of the subjects.

Table 5. Activity intensity models where validation $>= 70$ and Train-Test $>= 60$

ID	Algo	Fea	TTAcc	Val Acc	Kappa	Rec(1)	Rec(2)
1	RF	A	67.7	81.5	0.4	76.6	58.7
1	SVM	I	61.4	74.6	0.2	84.1	38.7
1	RF	I	62.3	72.8	0.3	76.4	48.3
5	SVM	A	64.4	99.9	0.3	90.2	38.6
6	RF	P	60.4	90.4	0.2	65.5	55.4
7	RF	D	62.4	75.3	0.3	71.1	53.7
7	SVM	P	62.1	82.3	0.2	66.4	57.7
7	RF	A	61.5	75.9	0.2	74.1	48.8
7	SVM	C	80.2	71.2	0.6	66.7	93.7
10	RF	A	71.3	70.4	0.4	74.6	68.0
10	SVM	C	60.4	71.6	0.2	36.4	84.6
10	RF	C	60.4	71.7	0.2	36.4	84.6
13	SVM	P	62.4	96.4	0.3	61.7	63.0

4.3. Analyzing Features

4.3.1. Joints

One of the long running concerns in the filed of study is whether a single body part or a certain set of body parts are used to express emotion and by extension can be used to observe or perceive emotion. The analysis of the joints only cover for models that at least have an accuracy of 70.0% for 10-fold cross validation models and an accuracy of 60.0% for train-test models. Models are referred to by the subject and the first letter of the feature group. These feature groups are (D)efault, (P)osture, (A)verage Movement, (I)mmediate Movement and A(C)tivity. for instance, 4-A refers to the model of subject 4 trained with attributes that only belong to the Average Movement group.

Tables 6 and 7 list the joint used for each subject model and their relative frequencies. The relative frequency is computed from counting how many attributes belong to a certain joint. For example, given that a certain model used 10 attributes and three of them are AC_V_SM_W, AC_P_SM_X, AS_P_SM_Y, the joint SM would have a frequency of 3 and thus, have a relative frequency of 0.3.

Table 6.   Relative frequencies per joint for valence models

	4-A	5-P	11-P	13-P	Mean
SR	0.14	0.07	0.03	0.16	0.10
ER	0.04	0.11	0.10	0.10	0.09
KL	0.07	0.07	0.07	0.10	0.08
EL	0.00	0.19	0.03	0.07	0.07
HR	0.07	0.07	0.03	0.10	0.07
SL	0.04	0.11	0.07	0.03	0.06
SS	0.11	0.04	0.07	0.03	0.06
HE	0.11	0.00	0.07	0.07	0.06
HL	0.07	0.04	0.07	0.07	0.06
WR	0.00	0.07	0.03	0.13	0.06
NE	0.14	0.04	0.03	0.00	0.05
WL	0.04	0.04	0.14	0.00	0.05
SM	0.07	0.04	0.03	0.07	0.05
AR	0.07	0.00	0.10	0.03	0.05
AL	0.04	0.07	0.07	0.00	0.05
KR	0.00	0.04	0.03	0.07	0.03

The last column of tables 6 (Valence) and 7(Intensity) refer to the mean relative frequency of each joint. These tables are ordered from highest to lowest frequency.

The most frequently used joints for observing valence are the elbows, shoulders the left knee and the right hip as seen in table 6. With the exception of the hip and knee, these joints belong to the upper body region.

Table 7.   Relative frequencies per joint for activity intensity models

	1-A	1-I	6-P	7-D	7-A	10-A	Mean
NE	0.12	0.11	0.03	0.12	0.09	0.10	0.10
SM	0.08	0.06	0.14	0.06	0.13	0.03	0.08
HR	0.08	0.09	0.17	0.09	0.03	0.03	0.08
KR	0.13	0.06	0.07	0.03	0.07	0.14	0.08
EL	0.05	0.14	0.07	0.06	0.07	0.03	0.07
HE	0.08	0.17	0.03	0.06	0.00	0.07	0.07
SL	0.10	0.06	0.10	0.12	0.00	0.00	0.06
HL	0.03	0.09	0.00	0.03	0.03	0.21	0.06
SR	0.08	0.03	0.07	0.06	0.10	0.03	0.06
WL	0.05	0.06	0.07	0.12	0.03	0.03	0.06
AR	0.05	0.03	0.03	0.06	0.10	0.07	0.06
WR	0.10	0.00	0.00	0.03	0.03	0.10	0.04
KL	0.03	0.03	0.10	0.00	0.03	0.07	0.04
AL	0.00	0.00	0.00	0.06	0.16	0.03	0.04
SS	0.00	0.06	0.03	0.06	0.07	0.03	0.04
ER	0.05	0.03	0.07	0.03	0.07	0.00	0.04

4.3.2. *Movement*

The analysis of movement covers only for models used to predict the Activity Intesity dimensions as these models are the only models that used movement attributes and have passed the performance cutoff (validation $i =$ 70.0% & train-test $i = 60.0$%). Table 8 lists these movement features and their corresponding relative frequencies, similar in construction to tables 6, and 7 above.

Table 8. Relative frequencies of movement features for intensity

	1-A	1-I	7-D	7-A	10-A	Mean
Displacement	0.00	0.00	0.25	0.00	0.00	0.05
Direction	0.27	0.31	0.07	0.37	0.16	0.24
Distance	0.10	0.14	0.14	0.08	0.11	0.11
Speed	0.31	0.28	0.21	0.08	0.27	0.23
Acceleration	0.31	0.25	0.32	0.45	0.44	0.35

Acceleration is the most frequently used movement feature across the different models while displacement is the least.

5. Conclusion and Recommendations

The results have shown that the current approach is capable of training classifiers that can recognize Valence, Arousal and Activity Intensity from body movement and activity. The approach has three major distinctions; first, the use of non-acted data, second, the investigation as to which and how behavioral movement features can contribute to the prediction of Valence, Arousal and Activity Intensity and third, the integration of activity as part of the stimulus and the feature for prediction. The stimulus was successful in eliciting emotions from the three channels; however these emotions were not balanced. The resulting truncation reduced the number of useable data. The approach employed a Kinect camera, which ensured there will be no need for sensors which may distract the subjects from conducting the activity.

Using Body Posture, Movement and Human Activity to Predict Emotions Activity is an experimental addition to the approach and is suspected to play a key role in the experience, expression and prediction of emotions. The results reveal that it is a strong but inconsistent indicator for Valence and Activity Intensity. While it can give accurate predictions in many cases, it fails for the rest. Furthermore the effectiveness of activity as a feature is highly dependent on which classifier is being used.

In the attempt to model with user-specific and natural data, the research made contributions in three areas. Firstly, it integrates activity in terms of the design of the emotion stimulus and as a feature for classification. A conceptual model and representation is developed to give structure to the data that is used as activity. Second, the research used a dimensional representation of affect from non-acted data. The models are trained to use bodily expression and activity in classifying Valence, Arousal and Activity Intensity values. Finally, it explores the relationships between the features and the emotion labels of each dimension.

The relationships describe the bulk of what can be observed with the data and the results. Given the right configuration, models can reach accuracies between 60% and 80%. However, these models were produced through a wide variety of configurations, which is contingent. User-specific feature selection is a possible extension. User modeling and user stereotyping can be used to determine the tendencies of the subject and help in narrowing down which features to use. The approach did not use functional movement (semantic gestures, intended body language) and instead employed the use of kinematic features. The existing approach can be modified so that it also uses functional and kinematic movement. This can be further enhanced when the approach can narrow down the behavioral tendencies of the user. Finally, a system should be developed for recognizing the activity. Currently, the activity data is made by manual annotation. The system should employ voice to text conversion and activity recognition to recognize all the relevant information. This can be extended to include other kinds of information, especially when the learning task is applied in a different domain.

References

1. L. Constantine and H. Hajj, A survey of ground-truth in emotion data annotation, in *Pervasive Computing and Communications Workshops (PERCOM Workshops), 2012 IEEE International Conference on*, 2012.
2. J. Joshi, A. Dhall, R. Goecke and J. F. Cohn, Relative body parts movement for automatic depression analysis, in *Affective Computing and Intelligent Interaction (ACII), 2013 Humaine Association Conference on*, 2013.
3. P. Ekman and W. V. Friesen, Detecting deception from the body or face., *Journal of Personality and Social Psychology* **29**, p. 288 (1974).

4. N. Savva and N. Bianchi-Berthouze, Automatic recognition of affective body movement in a video game scenario, in *Intelligent Technologies for Interactive Entertainment*, (Springer, 2012) pp. 149–159.

5. D. Bernhardt and P. Robinson, Detecting affect from non-stylised body motions, in *Affective Computing and Intelligent Interaction*, (Springer, 2007) pp. 59–70.

6. B. de Gelder, Why bodies? twelve reasons for including bodily expressions in affective neuroscience, *Philosophical Transactions of the Royal Society B: Biological Sciences* **364**, 3475 (2009).

7. A. Kleinsmith and N. Bianchi-Berthouze, Affective body expression perception and recognition: A survey, *Affective Computing, IEEE Transactions on* **4**, 15 (2013).

8. M. Karg, A.-A. Samadani, R. Gorbet, K. Kuhnlenz, J. Hoey and D. Kulic, Body movements for affective expression: a survey of automatic recognition and generation, *Affective Computing, IEEE Transactions on* **4**, 341 (2013).

9. A. Kleinsmith, N. Bianchi-Berthouze and A. Steed, Automatic recognition of non-acted affective postures, *Systems, Man, and Cybernetics, Part B: Cybernetics, IEEE Transactions on* **41**, 1027 (2011).

10. M. Mahmoud, T. Baltrušaitis, P. Robinson and L. D. Riek, 3d corpus of spontaneous complex mental states, in *Affective computing and intelligent interaction*, (Springer, 2011) pp. 205–214.

11. Z. Zeng, M. Pantic, G. I. Roisman and T. S. Huang, A survey of affect recognition methods: Audio, visual, and spontaneous expressions, *Pattern Analysis and Machine Intelligence, IEEE Transactions on* **31**, 39 (2009).

12. C. Conati, Probabilistic assessment of user's emotions in educational games, *Applied Artificial Intelligence* **16**, 555 (2002).

13. A. Kleinsmith and N. Bianchi-Berthouze, Recognizing affective dimensions from body posture, in *Affective computing and intelligent interaction*, (Springer, 2007) pp. 48–58.

14. A. Camurri, G. Varni and G. Volpe, Towards analysis of expressive gesture in groups of users: computational models of expressive social interaction, in *Gesture in Embodied Communication and Human-Computer Interaction*, (Springer, 2010) pp. 122–133.

15. Y. Li and J. A. Landay, Exploring activity-based ubiquitous computing: interaction styles, models and tool support, *computing* **11**, p. 13 (2006).

16. D. Bernhardt, Posture, gesture and motion quality: A multilateral

approach to affect recognition from human body motion.

17. L. Omlor and M. A. Giese, Unsupervised learning of spatio-temporal primitives of emotional gait, in *Perception and Interactive Technologies*, (Springer, 2006) pp. 188–192.

18. J. Lange and M. Lappe, The role of spatial and temporal information in biological motion perception, *Advances in Cognitive Psychology* **3**, p. 419 (2007).

19. W. Wang, V. Enescu and H. Sahli, Towards real-time continuous emotion recognition from body movements, in *Human Behavior Understanding*, (Springer, 2013) pp. 235–245.

20. R. W. Levenson, Emotion and the autonomic nervous system: A prospectus for research on autonomic specificity. (1988).

21. J. L. Hagad, R. Legaspi, M. Numao and M. Suarez, Predicting levels of rapport in dyadic interactions through automatic detection of posture and posture congruence, in *Privacy, Security, Risk and Trust (PASSAT) and 2011 IEEE Third Inernational Conference on Social Computing (SocialCom), 2011 IEEE Third International Conference on*, 2011.

Online Legal Case Management for a Multi-Tiered Organization

Trishia Denisce Tubojan,

Jonathan John Yacapin, and Jaime D.L. Caro

Department of Computer Science,
University of the Philippines Diliman
Quezon city, Philippines
Email: jdlcaro@up.edu.ph

The researchers attempt to create a Case Management System that could better represent and better assist workflow environments currently in use by most multi-tiered Organizations. The Office of the Vice President for Legal Affairs in the University of the Philippines, one such office, will be used as the pilot office. The Case Management System will be based on the needs of the said office and the comments, ideas and suggestions of their employees, as well as incorporating modern studies on functional Information Systems into the design.

Keywords: Legal Management, Case Management, University Information System

1. Introduction

Information Systems (IS) pertains to any organized flow of processes, storage, and distribution of data. A more modern definition of an Information System, however, is more specific in defining it as a computer based set of applications that, in organizing the flow of data, aids end-users by way of simplifying tasks, keeping easily accessible and understandable records, as well as allow said data to be modified easily as needed, to name a few. Most institutions and enterprises nowadays, no matter how big or small, often have one or more Information Systems in place to facilitate a lot of processes, as well as store most of the data relevant to the aforementioned institution. Thus it can be inferred that implementing Information Systems, although sometimes costly, are often worth the investment.

A Case Management System is one example of an Information System. Case Management Systems specifically assist legal offices by keeping track of cases, managing paperworks and documents, and manages schedules, among other things.

However, while Information System implementations are now very common among big organizations, it is very important to have an Information System that accurately fits an organization's workflow. That is, an Information System should be able to accurately mimic how paperwork was being done before the Information System is implemented. This is because mimicking the workflow of the organization means converting as much human work as possible into a computer-assisted process.

1.1. *the UP-OVPLA as a Pilot Office*

The University of the Philippines - Office of the Vice President for Legal Affairs (UP-OVPLA) was an office created so as to facilitate all legal processes of the UP System. Thus, the OVPLA has long been UP's representation in legal court affairs. Aside from legal representation, the OVPLA still has a long list of other duties, including the giving of legal counsel and guidance to University Officials, serving as the point of contact between the University and other government agencies as circumstances warrant, as well as the management of all contracts wherein the UP System, or one of its constituents, is an entity of said contract.

However, OVPLA is a massive office encompassing multiple campuses in the University System. The office is subdivided into offices for each of the 8 University Campuses across the Philippines, with one head office situated in the Diliman Campus of the University system. Essentially, cases are handled at campus level, with more severe or critical cases being escalated to the head office to be resolved. Being an office that encompasses multiple campuses, the amount of material that the OVPLA have to work with is staggering, which means that employees, as well as the people who are part of the legal team, often deal with far too lengthy work hours, as well as a large amount of stress. Data filing, organizing, and tracking of files, while debatably inconsequential, definitely contribute to the aforementioned problems. Another problem often encountered in the legal office is that most cases often span a long amount of time, and thus are often handled by multiple lawyers and multiple legal teams. With multiple cases being passed on from one legal team to the other, tracking cases, their statuses, supporting documents and other files related to the case are often very tedious.

Thus, the researchers chose the OVPLA as a pilot office as it not only represents a multi-tiered organization, despite having only two tiers of office, the massive workload of the office definitely underscores an immediate need for an Information System that will help mitigate some of the workload of the OVPLA. Currently, UP OVPLA still has archaic methods of maintaining and organizing files, as well as outdated means of tracking legal cases, their statuses, and their supporting documents. Without utilizing the modern trends of Information Systems, the office suffers from a significant loss of productivity due to the work hours allotted to maintaining obsolete workflows. Maintaining the current work methods of the office is also a priority as offices like the OVPLA do not have the luxury of time enough to change their flow of work based on the Information System. Specific to this is in ensuring that disruption of office workflow due to introducing new technology is kept to a minimum. This can only be achieved by making the Information System feel as intrinsic to the office as possible, as well as making sure that the interface of the system is as user friendly as possible. Lastly, the researchers also have to ensure that the Information System will not buckle under stress from the standard workload of the office. This means ensuring that the users of the Information System will not experience a drastic reduction in speed, accessibility and reliability when there is an increased number of clients simultaneously using the system.

Thus, the goal of this project is to create an Multi-Tiered Case Management System to track and manage cases and their statuses, supporting documents, as well as all other related information that might prove useful to the case. This includes understanding the current workflow processes of the OVPLA, so as to translate it into an application as accurately as possible, designing a database for the use of the Information System, designing the flow of data within the Information System, and designing the interfaces with which both administrators as well as the end-users, interact with the Information System. The design of the components of the Information System should also be as efficient as possible, with data and studies to back up such a claim. Lastly, the interfaces of the application should be made to be as intuitive as possible, with none to minimal training needed for the satisfactory usage of all the functionalities of the application.

Through this study, the researchers plan on developing a functional multi-tiered Case Management System that is capable of achieving some sort of data integration across multiple branches of the same offices spread apart geographically. This also means establishing a framework to assist the flow of data across the multiple offices, and will allow for more connected functions in the future. By doing so, the researchers will also have made a Legal Information System that more accurately represents and mimics how the office itself is organized, thus allowing for a workflow that more closely resembles the system that is meant to be replaced. Designing the new Information System with this mentality should effectively create a more efficient workflow in handling the tracking of cases, which will save on both time and material resources. Not only that, this study also plans on facilitating for how data across multiple OVPLA offices across the different campuses interact with each other, thus effectively becoming one big Legal Information System that encompasses multiple office, paving the way for increased data integration across the regions.

The researchers plan on finishing the thesis by creating and implementing a highly efficient Information System that will assist and trivialize the processes involved in tracking cases and storing its data securely. The Information System should also be have frameworks in place for future Data Integration across the multiple tiers of the system. A secondary goal is for the planned Information System to be easily understandable and very user-friendly, with an intuitive interface for end users so as to minimize disruption to the workflow of the office.

The study was motivated by the fact that the UP OVPLA, despite being one of the busiest offices in the system, are often not considered from ease-of-life system upgrades simply because it is quite hard to find market ready software that directly benefits the office without changing the current workflow culture set by the office. Legal offices are very resistant to changes in the workflow because, as often said before, the material that the office works with are almost always sensitive. Simply put, all the work is still being done manually because the impact of wrong decisions in such a line of work is oftentimes disastrous. Thus, the systems in use by the OVPLA has stayed archaic even as systems among other offices have evolved through time.

The scope of this study encompasses the specific set of processes concerning case management systems that are specifically designed for multi-tiered organizations that is unique to the UP OVPLA. As such, the application created from this study will only be useful for the aforementioned office, and may be somewhat beneficial to offices of similar nature. However other entities can glean from this study how a multi-tiered legal information system can function, and how data between multiple tiers of the system may interact. Also, the primary focus and concern of the researchers in this study is to migrate the unique processes into a computer assisted workflow, and by extension to create a far more efficient system than the current manual system put in place. Thus, while, say, basic security will be implemented, there will be no further analyses on things such as security threats and vulnerabilities of the application.

2. Review of Related Literature

2.1. *Information Systems and The Paperless Office*

An Information System, at its most basic form, is any organized system that facilitates for the movement of data or information. This generally includes processes that serve to move or modify data in terms of collection, storage, organization, modification, and communication. Information Systems are the most basic and most commonly used method in order to become a paperless office.

The Paperless Office is a modern concept which is defined as either the elimination or a large reduction in the use and dependency on paper in an office or other similar setting. This is mostly done by converting or adapting documents and other such papers into digital form, which is then stored in servers.

There are many advantages to the so called paperless office. Benefits include the practical elimination of storage costs, improved employee productivity, improved customer satisfaction, as well as the elimination of the risk of lost or misfiled files and the ability for data to be backed up. To put in perspective, In the United States, companies, on average, spend 20$ in labor to file a document, 120$ to find a misfiled document and 220$ in labor to reproduce a lost document. Also, on average, 7.5 percent of all documents get lost, while another 3 percent of the remainder get misfiled, for a total of roughly 10 percent of documents[1]. On the case of the planned Case Management System, given the importance of legal documents and their impact on an institution for possibly many years, it is especially important for files to always be available, un-tampered, and easily accessible, albeit to the right people[2].

Fiorenza adds that going paperless allows for automation of tasks, which can allow multiple workers to work on different parts of the project simultaneously, share project status easily, and track project needs far better. Fiorenza also interjects that these leads to better morale in the workplace, as employees are spared from time intensive yet droning tasks which are essential in most offices. Paperless systems also empower potential field workers, who can access vital information at ease. On the other hand, paperless systems allow for self-service opportunities for both clients and constituents, saving time and effort not only for clientele but also for the people manning the office, as they would have needed to allocate precious employee time to satisfy the needs of the client. Lastly, migrating to a Paperless system serves as a framework for possible methods and requirements of data integration in the near future[3].

However, it should be noted that not only is it more likely that data can be manipulated should it be transferred online, the impact, say the amount of data unlawfully retrieved, manipulated, or deleted, is far greater. To say that legal records can make or break an institution is not too far from the truth. Thus, it has not been uncommon in recent years for certain people to hack Legal Information Systems to retrieve highly confidential information, be it for monetary purposes, personal reasons or otherwise. Recent cases include the hacking of the top law firms in New York who specialize in merger advise where hackers made more than 4 million dollars from information obtained from the hack[4]. While this specific situation will likely not be any cause for concern due to the fact that what the researchers are handling are of a far smaller scale and far less public, it is still important to note that hacks on Legal Information Systems are not unheard of.

2.2. *Legal Information System*

Legal Information Systems pertain to Information Systems created and adapted for the use of offices and firms that handle legal cases; The office of the Vice President for Legal Affairs is one such office. There is no proper definition as to what a Legal Information System should be, or what fundamental processes it should contain. Rather, the term 'Legal Information System' is used rather loosely to summarize all Information Systems that either help a legal office, provide legal information, or serve as a point of contact between a legal office and its clients, among others.

There have been many implementations of Legal Information Systems abroad, and now there are a few such Legal Information Systems being implemented in the Philippines. One example is the Department of Agrarian Reform's Legal Information System, known as the DAR-LIS project. The Department of Agrarian Reform – Legal Information System was developed as part of the former president Aquino's initiatives so as to maintain an "open-door and disclosure" policy in government. However, while the DAR-LIS can still be categorically considered as a Legal Information System, it was created with the primary purpose of being an access point for the Filipino people, rather than an Information System that helps its employees in their daily routine. Specifically, DAR-LIS functions as a source of Legal Information by making laws and Presidential Issuances concerning Agrarian Reform available for reading and downloading. The DAR-LIS also contains download links to their publications and lectures, as well as forms and templates that can be used by regular citizens in filing for minor legal cases such as applications for livestock exemptions, applying for retention rights, among others[5].

2.3. *Free or Open Source Legal Information Systems*

Typical legal offices are, more often than not, highly lucrative ventures. As such, there is a significant lack of Open Source Information Systems for legal offices available in the market. Nevertheless, there are a few open source legal software tools , and maybe some other partially-free tools that can be used to help a legal office. Of these, the researchers collated the most highly rated of the set and scrutinized both available functions as well as the user experience and usability of said softwares. The softwares selected for scrutiny are as follows: "Jarvis Legal, Open Source Law, CiviCRM, LegalSuite, ClinicCases, and CaseBox."

Jarvis Legal is a legal tool primarily made to assist lawyers in terms of time-keeping, billing as well as document management. Time-keeping is mostly tracking working billable time spent by lawyers on cases. Billing, on the other hand, allows you to set your rates based on work, and thus allow you to create a bill instantly when needed, as the software tracks your billable hours, as well as documents created for the case. Lastly, and what is relevant to our Case Management System, is it provides for an intuitive way to collaborate with colleagues concerning legal documents. This includes functions for selective sharing of documents with teammates, which include a way for teammates to only review a paper. Leaving of bulletins as well as task assignments are also provided for by this software. The software is not open-source, but it has a free version which is limited to 5 cases and 5gb of storage.

Open Source Law is slightly different, in that while it can still be classified as a Legal Information System, it works rather differently.Open Source Law is more a wiki where both lawyers and law students can share each other's documents within a central repository. Offering Version control, this allows bonafide lawyers to assist law students with their cases by editing the source material, and commenting on the changes. With version control capabilities, the document can simply be reverted to a previous version should their be unwanted and/or unwarranted changes to the document.

CiviCRM is a closer approximation to the Case Management System being developed by the researchers. While technically a 'Constituent Relationship Management' software, it has a solid Legal Information Subsystem for managing cases, with rather important functionalities. Primarily, their Legal Information Subsystem allows for the tracking of events that occurred with a specific case, as well as events scheduled to occur. Aside from this, CiviCRM also provides for a robust contacts management that allows the users of the software to maintain contact with, say, legal clients.

The LegalSuite is a full blown Legal Office Tool, and is probably the most comprehensive free (although not open-source) Legal Information System available in the market today. The software is marketed as a swiss-knife software for legal offices, and manages to do as such. It maintains records of full client information and their pictures, notes and TO-DOs, documents per case. Not only that, but it also maintains records and information concerning opponents in the case and even map entries, issues, evidences, witnesses and so on, not to mention the fact that it also has billing functionalities as implemented on Jarvis Legal. Lastly, LegalSuite also maintains records of the office staff. However, the LegalSuite software is regarded rather poorly by users, due to a noticeable lack in useability. The user interface design is very outdated, and information is packed and cluttered too tightly across the screen. The software is being updated, however only bug fixes and enhancements being introduced, with no clear hope of the interface ever being updated. Another problem with the LegalSuite is that it is not network compatible, in that only one PC will have access to the database, which consequently means only one PC can add, edit, view and generally use the information on database entries. Essentially, LegalSuite is only suitable for solo lawyers or small offices, who don't mind the clutter of data and the outdated interface of the program.

ClinicCases, while still considered a web-based case management system, is a system designed specifically for law school clinics. Though while it was intended as a teaching and guidance tool, the software still boasts robust functionalities, which include file management capabilities, along with a great calendar and event tracking module. With the target audience being students, the software prioprietor also took pains to make the program look as sleek and modern as possible. While ClinicCases might only sport a few parallels with the intended Information System being developed, it is important to note that ClinicCases is open-source, and can thus be a source of information regarding database and application design for the researchers.

Lastly, CaseBox is one of the more promising Legal Information tools available. It is free and open-source, is network ready, and has a large following of users with it's sleek, modern and simplistic design. It's user interface resembles typical file management systems currently in use today. While it has a limited amount of functions, users believe that the functions encompassed by CaseBox are the only functions critically needed by a legal office. It can be said, therefore, that Casebox made the decision to only include the most important of functions, thus highly maintaining the usability of the system. CaseBox allows an administrator to create a case, a task or a link. Creating a case is basically creating a folder, inputting the data related to the case, as well as allowing the administrator to specify tags, what type of case it is, and the status of the case, which simplifies sorting and searching later on. The administrator could then set permissions on the case, specifying which users can access the case, and how much access is given; whether the user can only read the files, or whether they edit or even delete files. Within the case, permitted users can upload files, create contacts and fill in appropriate information, or create an organization entry whenever appropriate. Outside of the case, users can also create tasks which they can assign to others, and casebox groups up tasks assigned to you as well as tasks you created. Tasks also give out notifications based on the date and reminders set by the task creator. Lastly, while inconsequential, users can create a clickable link that could serve as a bridge to a file available online, or an online resource.

2.4. *Legal Information Retrieval*

Legal Information Retrieval pertains to the science of how legal information is located or accessed. In a legal setting, it is crucial to retrieve all information pertaining to a search query. However, a key problem with current commonly used search algorithms is that currently used search algorithms have retrieval rates of as low as 20 percent when dealing with legal texts, which means that during a search of legal documents, only 1 in 5 of relevant documents sought for are actually retrieved. An even bigger problem is that during these searches, it has been found out that the population of the research believed they have retrieved 75% of the relevant documents being retrieved, which means that most of the people who were retrieving said documents would then be satisfied of their results, and thus stop further attempts to retrieve more[6]. The implication of the research is that common search algorithms may result in failing to retrieve cases and documents of relatively relevant import.

As such, studies in Legal Information Retrieval aims to increase the effectiveness of legal search queries by increasing the retrieval rate of relevant documents as well as reducing the retrieval rate of irrelevant documents, often by using artificial intelligence to optimize search results. However, optimizing search queries in a legal application is hard due to the fact that law rarely has an inherent taxonomy. Another problem is the legal field's heavy usage of jargons and polysemes, as well as the fact that each legal office tends to have their own specific jargons known only to them[7]. Yet despite the difficulties of devising a workaround to increase retrieval rate, there are some techniques commonly in use in search queries pertaining to legal information, with varying degrees of difficulty, complexity and efficacy.

The most basic Legal Information Retrieval implementation is to make the search algorithm Boolean in nature, where the user, essentially, is allowed to include Boolean Logic phrases as search parameters. This typically includes the use of 'AND' and 'OR' to keywords, as well as negating certain keywords with the 'NOT' operator. While there are countless types of Boolean Search Algorithms being implemented for Legal Information Retrieval, the general concept of Boolean Search Algorithms stays the same, and thus can be classified as such. Now the problem with Boolean Searches concerning Legal Information Retrieval is that studies have shown while it did indeed improve recall rate and precision when used by non-legal professionals, it had either no effect, or even having inverse effects when run by legal professionals. This could be attributed to the fact legal professionals know their complex terms, and thus have no need for a Boolean Search Algorithm and that, furthermore, the addition of the Boolean Search Algorithm may have only served to increase the technological barrier to use the Information System[8].

Another implementation of Legal Information Retrieval is through manually classifying data. This is done by having legal professionals manually classify and categorize cases, and/or manually connecting multiple keywords, creating something of a legal encyclopedia that, although it can be used in other legal offices, is still highly unique to the office that initiated such a project, or from where the legal professionals hailed from[9]. While this implementation does have very significant improvement when it comes to recall rates and recall precision, the obvious drawback to such an implementation is that highly skilled legal professionals have to devote a large amount of time to classify text, and have to continue to do so as the amount of legal entries in the database increases. Researchers believe that as the amount of text continues to increase, manual classification becomes unsustainable[10].

Researchers are currently working on a third implementation that involves classifying legal data through the use of Artificial Intelligence. While this will probably not achieve the levels of success that Manual Classification manages, it does relieve the need for skilled legal professionals to do the classifying, and thus also make it feasible for a persistent Legal Information database. Current experimental implementations generally employ Natural Language Processing (NLP) techniques. The most advanced implementations of such a method have so far only yielded 30 percent recall rate and precision, which is probably much lower than what might be considered an acceptable rate for general usage[11].

2.5. *Data Integration*

Data integration is the process of standardizing definitions and structures of said data by using common conceptual schema across big collections of data sources. Integrated data will naturally be consistent and logically compatible with different systems and/or databases. This means that data can be used across multiple users.

However, in order to integrate data properly, there are multiple factors to address first. Key factors would be the level of noise and distortion of data due to the integration process, computational efficiency of the integrated data in terms of achieving user end-goals, spatial capacity of storage systems and natural accuracy of the data[12].

We can, however, remove these factors such as noise and distortion of data by instead, creating just one massive Information System, separated into tiers. The major benefit of a single comprehensive information system comes from the ability to share or aggregate information across tiers or divisions of an organization. This will lead to two different impacts that data integration might have on an organization. The first is an improved managerial information for the organization. The second is the operational coordination between interdependent parts of the organization[13].

Benefits of the Data Integration Process also include the alleviation of the burden of duplicated data gathering efforts, as well as create more avenues for the extraction of information[12].

Data integration would also allow for a bigger data set for data mining purposes. That is, having a bigger data set would mean that patterns and knowledge in the data set would become more apparent, and may prove useful in the future.

2.6. *Data Mining and Analytics*

Data Mining is the process of analyzing data from a massive dataset of different perspectives and inferring from it or summarizing it into useful and useable information. This information can then be used to increase revenue, cut costs, or in a legal office setting, gain valuable info on key personnel within the legal community, such as judiciary tendencies. Technically, data mining is the process of finding useful relations and correlations and or patterns within related or unrelated fields in a big data set [14]. The product of analysis and presentation of meaningful patterns in the aforementioned data can henceforth be referred to as analytics.

However, Legal Information Analytics have only very recently gained traction within the Legal Circle. Legal Offices have long relied on human decision making since the creation of the office, and for good reason; the material handled by Legal Offices are often very sensitive in nature, and automation has long been shunned by a paradigm built on tradition that are centuries-old. LexisNexis, one of the biggest Legal Information Systems provider in the world, has only recently integrated legal analytics functionalities from their research arm wholly dedicated to Legal Analytics; Lex Machina.

2.7. *Legal Analytics: A Closer Look at Lex Machina*

Until recently, traditional legal research tools only proceeded to extract data, leaving processing to human hands. This roughly translates to collating hundreds and upto thousands of cases, and yet leaving the sifting through of Valuable Information to Legal Assistants. This poses problems because not only are Legal Assistants a potential source of errors, it also means that using such a massive amount of data and drawing patterns from it through statistical analysis is simply not possible.

Lex Machina, on the other hand, is a module that sifts through such data using Artificial Intelligence. Essentially, their engine crawls through millions of pages of cluttered litigation dockets. Then, using Natural Language Processing, along with Machine Learning, the engine cleans, tags, and structures data. The engine basically automates what used to be done by hand for centuries, eliminating error resulting from human input. This process is essentially an automated Legal Information Retrieval function, and is only made possible due to the amount of data that is made available to Lex Machina.

With such amount of data, the engine can even infer data patterns from seemingly insignificant information. To emphasize, Lex Machina has a company database that paint a somewhat accurate picture of Judges' personal behavioral patterns. For example, you could determine the percentages a specific judge deviates from the average rate for granting or denying specific motions, or the likelihood for said judge to find infringement in patent or trademark cases. Lex Machina keeps such tabs on judges, lawyers, parties, and even case subjects themselves. Not only that, but the Lex Machina database even track crucial insights on the opposing legal counsel, such as their track record or experience on specific judges or cases. Such analytics would provide a very subtle, yet not insignificant advantage to the Legal Office that decides to use such a powerful tool[15].

However, as mentioned before, this was only made possible due to the amount of court data that is made available to Lex Machina's Engine, which means that the engine is powered by the number of clients that it directly services. Such an arrangement shows how data integration and data mining does not necessarily mean allowing others to access information on your private cases. This plays perfectly into a multi-tiered Information System. Access to cases does not necessarily have to be shared between the multiple tiers, and yet their data could be mined regardless, and correlations could still be drawn between cases without exposing sensitive case data. Still, it cannot be stressed enough that the effectivity of such analytics only become significant when there is a big enough inflow of data to support it.

2.8. *Statistical Analytics*

Statistical Analytics is another form of analytics that could be implemented within the multi-tiered Case Management System. While Statistical Analytics does not help improve the success rate of handled cases, it does immensely help in the management of the multi-tiered office.

Statistical Analytics, rather than Legal Analytics, would be the higher priority in implementation within the Case Management System. This is because Legal Analytics would require a large amount of data to be inputted in the system, across multiple organizations, to be of some use and have significant impact. Meanwhile, statistical analysis can be implemented within just one organization, and would provide significant impact on management and administration of the organization, with little to no impact on application workflow.

3. Requirements Analysis

The researchers interviewed Atty. Hannibal Bobis, who serves as the University Legal Counsel and is associated with the Office of the Vice President for Legal Affairs, to have him discuss the process of case handling within the OVPLA and to ask for specific features that their office will need in a case management system.

According to the Attorney, a case that has just been filed by the OVPLA is handed to a lawyer for initial review. That lawyer will be keeping notes and important documents and information related to the case while trying to resolve the case. The lawyers keep these loads of documents in folders. According to the Attorney, the lawyers who receive a case file need to update on the status of the case as early as possible. If they cannot resolved the case, the case will undergo edit reviewing. The lawyer will pass the folder to another lawyer, usually to a senior, and that lawyer will review the case and try to resolve it. If the case is not yet resolved during the edit review, the folder will be passed to another lawyer for final review. If the case is not yet resolved during the final review, it will be given back to the lawyer who received the case for initial review. The Attorney also stated that the number of days that a lawyer spends in reviewing a case is important. Lawyers who are reviewing a case are usually asked to give an update 3 days after they received the case. The OVPLA can also escalate cases to the Office of the President or receive cases from the Legal Offices of the UP constituents.

Two common functionalities of case management systems namely, records management and document handling, will be able to aid the lawyers in their work. A centralized storage of cases and case documents will provide the lawyers a way to share the "folder" with everyone who is handling the case.

For the specific system requirements, the Attorney stated that there should be four types of system users namely, the administrator, the senior lawyer, the lawyer, and the staff. Each user type has their own level of access within the system. The Attorney wants to have the usernames of the users to be email addresses. That way it is easy to contact and send notifications to a user. The administrator will provide their passwords for them upon creation but the user will be prompted to change their password on their first login.

Due to the nature of the data stored in the system, user access must be controlled. The attorney believes this can be achieved by only having the administrator be allowed to open or delete case records, while the other users can freely view the cases in the system. The non-administrator users will only be able to edit a case if they were assigned for initial, edit, final, or loop review. In line with this, the Attorney also wants a generated audit trail of all user actions committed in the system. This will be made available for the administrators to view and scrutinize. This way every user can be held accountable for changes they commit to the system.

Process ID	Modules	Role	Functionality	Functionality Type	Comments/Remarks
010000	USER				
010101	User Authentication	Users	Enter User Credentials	Login	For system security.
010201	Profile	Admin, Senior Lawyer, Lawyer, Staff	Prompt for Change Password	View	User must also be prompted to change their password at their first login.
010202		Admin, Senior Lawyer, Lawyer, Staff	View Profile	View	User must be able to view the recorded information about them: Email, Name, Phone
010203		Admin, Senior Lawyer, Lawyer, Staff	Edit Profile	Edit	User must be able to modify their email, first name, last name, phone, and password. User must enter their current password to change their password.
020000	ADMIN				
020101	User Management	Admin	View System Users	View	View all system users.
020102		Admin	Search System Users	Search	Search user by name or email.
020103		Admin	Add System Users	Add	Enter email, password, first name, last name, phone, type. For type, admin can choose between Staff, Lawyer, Senior Lawyer, Administrator.
020104		Admin	Edit System Users	Edit	User must be able to modify name, address, phone, type of a system user.
020105		Admin	Enable/Disable System User	Activate/Deactivate	If a user is deactivated, credentials remain in the system but must not be able to access the system.
020106		Admin	Delete System User	Delete	User record will be erased from the database.
020201	System Settings Management	Admin	View Case Categories	View	
020202		Admin	Add/Edit/Delete Case Categories	Add/Edit/Delete	Enter case category name.
020203		Admin	View Case Subcategory	View	
020204		Admin	Add/Edit/Delete Case Subcategory	Add/Edit/Delete	Enter case subcategory name.
020205		Admin	View Case Tags	View	
020206		Admin	Add/Edit/Delete Case Tags	Add/Edit/Delete	Enter case tag name.
020301	Audit Log	Admin	View Audit Log	View	
020302		Admin	Search Audit Log	Search	Search through action description and name of user.
020303		System	Add Audit Log from User Actions	Add	Record user actions within the system.
030000	CASES				
030101	Case Management	Admin, Senior Lawyer, Lawyer, Staff	View List of Cases	View	For Admin, Lawyers, and Staff, view all cases that their office handles. For Senior Lawyer, view all cases that his office handles and cases his office escalated and/or de-escalated.
030102		Admin, Senior Lawyer, Lawyer, Staff	Search Case	Search	Word-based search. Search through Name, Decision, Judge, Type, Tags, Names of parties involved, Role of parties involved, Title of case notes, Contents of case note, Title of tasks/events, Details of tasks/events of a case.
030103		Admin	Open Case	Add	Enter name of the case. Select category and subcategory of case. Select tags. Assign to a user for initial review.
030104		Admin	Edit Case	Edit	Edit name, category, subcategory, status, decision, judge. User can also close the case here.
030105		Admin	Delete Case	Delete	Deletes case record. Delete all notes, parties, contacts, tasks, events, and documents related to the case.
030106		Senior Lawyer	Escalate Case	Escalate	All user access in current office will be removed. However, senior lawyers can still view the case details after escalation.
030107		Senior Lawyer	De-escalate Case	De-escalate	All user access in current office will be removed. However, senior lawyers can still view the details, notes, etc of the case after de-escalation.
030201	Case Details	Admin, Senior Lawyer, Lawyer, Staff	View Case Details	View	View status of case, open date, close date. View last update date and last user who updated the case. View number of days past the last status update. For cases that are escalated, only this will be viewable by the senior lawyer.
030301	Assigned Users	Admin, Senior Lawyer, Lawyer, Staff	View Assigned Users	View	View list of all users assigned in a case.
030302		Admin, Senior Lawyer, Lawyer, Staff	Assign User for Edit/Final/Loop Review	Add	Only admin and assigned users have access to this functionality. Select one from list of Senior Lawyers, Lawyers, and Staff. List of users must only contain users that are from the same office as the Admin. Assigned users can add, edit, and delete parties, notes, contacts, tasks, events, and documents of the case.
030401	Case Parties Involved	Admin, Senior Lawyer, Lawyer, Staff	View Parties Involved	View	View list of parties involved in a case created by the assigned users
030402		Admin, Senior Lawyer, Lawyer, Staff	Search Parties Involved	Search	
030403		Admin, Senior Lawyer, Lawyer, Staff	Add Party	Add	Enter name and role of party.

Fig. 1.   Requirements Traceability Matrix

Next, there must be a search function that searches through all the information of all the cases, and should not be limited to only searching for keywords in, say, just the title. The Attorney said that lawyers usually only remember the names of the parties or certain keywords that may appear in the case notes. An effective search function is important for retrieval of information.

Lastly, the Attorney wants the users to start receiving email notifications when a case they are handling has reached 3 days in review. The users must also receive email notifications to when an event is about to begin or a task is about to reach its deadline.

Process ID	Modules	Role	Functionality	Functionality Type	Comments/Remarks
030404		Admin, Senior Lawyer, Lawyer, Staff	Edit Party	Edit	Edit name and role of party.
030405		Admin, Senior Lawyer, Lawyer, Staff	Delete Party	Delete	
030501	Case Notes	Admin, Senior Lawyer, Lawyer, Staff	View Case Notes	View	View list of all case notes of a case created by the assigned users
030502		Admin, Senior Lawyer, Lawyer, Staff	Search Case Notes	Search	
030503		Admin, Senior Lawyer, Lawyer, Staff	View Case Note Details	View	More detailed view of the case note. Can download attachement, if any.
030504		Admin, Senior Lawyer, Lawyer, Staff	Add Case Note	Add	Enter title, note, and attachment.
030505		Admin, Senior Lawyer, Lawyer, Staff	Edit Case Note	Edit	
030506		Admin, Senior Lawyer, Lawyer, Staff	Delete Case Note	Delete	
030601	Case Contacts	Admin, Senior Lawyer, Lawyer, Staff	View Contacts	View	View list of contacts of a case created by the assigned users
030602		Admin, Senior Lawyer, Lawyer, Staff	Search Contacts	Search	
030603		Admin, Senior Lawyer, Lawyer, Staff	View Contact Details	View	More detailed view of a contact. View name, phone, email, description, role
030604		Admin, Senior Lawyer, Lawyer, Staff	Add Contacts	Add	Enter name, phone, email, description, role of contact
030605		Admin, Senior Lawyer, Lawyer, Staff	Edit Contacts	Edit	
030606		Admin, Senior Lawyer, Lawyer, Staff	Delete Contacts	Delete	
030701	Case Tasks and Events	Admin, Senior Lawyer, Lawyer, Staff	View Case Tasks/Events	View	View list of tasks and events in a case created by the assigned users.
030702		Admin, Senior Lawyer, Lawyer, Staff	Search Case Task/Event	Search	
030703		Admin, Senior Lawyer, Lawyer, Staff	View Case Tasks/Events Details	View	More detailed view of a task/event. View activity name, description, type, date, time, and attachment.
030704		Admin, Senior Lawyer, Lawyer, Staff	Add Case Task/Event	Add	Enter name, description, date, time of task/event. Select whether it is a task or an event. Can attach document.
030705		Admin, Senior Lawyer, Lawyer, Staff	Edit Case Task/Event	Edit	
030706		Admin, Senior Lawyer, Lawyer, Staff	Delete Case Task/Event	Delete	
030801	Case Documents	Admin, Senior Lawyer, Lawyer, Staff	View Folders and Documents	View	View list of all folders created and documents uploaded by the assigned users. View size and upload date of documents.
030802		Admin, Senior Lawyer, Lawyer, Staff	Create Folder	Add	
030803		Admin, Senior Lawyer, Lawyer, Staff	Delete Folder	Delete	
030804		Admin, Senior Lawyer, Lawyer, Staff	Upload Document	Upload	Can upload multiple files at the same time. Can only upload Word documents, text files, pdfs, spreadsheets.
030805		Admin, Senior Lawyer, Lawyer, Staff	Download Document	Download	
030806		Admin, Senior Lawyer, Lawyer, Staff	Delete Document	Delete	
030807	Notification	Senior Lawyer, Lawyer, Staff	Receive Email Alerts	Notification	Send email alerts to user when a case that they are assigned to has reached 3, 5, 7, 10 days in its current status.
040000	CALENDAR				
040101	Calendar	Admin, Senior Lawyer, Lawyer, Staff	View Month	View	View calendar of user for the current month. Highlight days with tasks/events and show number of tasks/events for that day. The calendar for lawyers and staff must show only the tasks/events from the cases they were assigned to. The calendar for admin and senior lawyer must show all tasks and events for all cases in his office.
040102		Admin, Senior Lawyer, Lawyer, Staff	View Day	View	View list of tasks/events for a specific day. View details of tasks/events too.
040103		Admin, Senior Lawyer, Lawyer, Staff	View Previous/Following Year	View	View the same month of the previous/following year.
040104		Admin, Senior Lawyer, Lawyer, Staff	View Previous/Following Month	View	
040301	Notification	System	Receive Email Alerts	Notification	Send email alerts to user when a task's deadline or an event's date is near. The users will receive an email 2 weeks, 1 week, 5 days, 3 days, 2 days, 1 day before the date. The user will also receive an email on the day.

Fig. 2.   Requirements Traceability Matrix contd.

The attorney stressed however that what the office wanted was an "open architecture that they can easily enhance and configure to better suit the office's needs." The researchers added functionalities to complement the requirements of the Attorney. A system settings management was included to add flexibility to the system. For more information about the requirements, see the requirements traceability matrix (Figs. 1 and 2). The document also captures the purpose of a use case diagram.

The design of the application will be largely guided by the principles of sprint. That is to say, we develop an initial application, and then consult the concerned end users on further design decisions weekly. This largely means that we constantly alternate between specification and development phases all throughout the project. This will ensure an application heavily grounded on the direct and practical uses of the pilot office.

4. Database Design

Open source case management systems like CaseBox, ClinicCases, and Civi-CRM all use RDBMS – MySQL to store their data. This is why the researchers were inclined to use RDBMS for the Case Management System.

The tables in the schema are as follows: the 'offices' table is where the different offices that are going to use the system within an organization

188

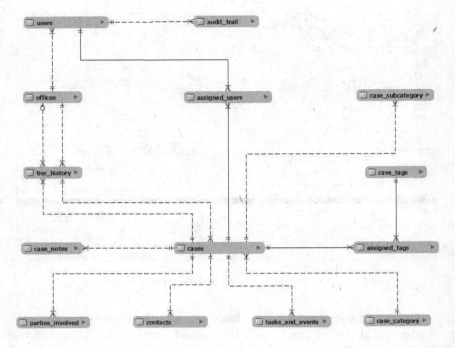

Fig. 3. Database Schema Diagram.

are defined. The 'head_office_id' column references an entry in 'offices'
which represents the immediate head office of an office. This table can
only be accessed by the system admin. A record in the 'cases' table stores
the details of a case in the system. The 'curr_tier' column references a
record in 'tier_history' table which will be explained next. A record in
the 'tier_history' table represents a certain step that the case has gone
through in the escalation system. 'prev_office_id' refers to the id of the
office where the case came from and 'curr_office_id' is the id of the office
where the case went to after escalation. These records are useful to track
where the case came from if it is needed to be brought back to the lower
offices for review. The 'users' table keeps the records of all the system
users. It has a field called 'office_id' to know which office the user belongs
to, thus limiting what cases a user can view. The 'assigned_users' table
is needed since there is a many-to-many relationship between 'cases' and
'users'. A record contains the id of the case and the id of the user assigned
to the case. 'case_category', 'case_subcategory', and 'case_tags' are where

Table Name	Column Name	Data Type	References: table_name.column_name	Constraints	Default / ENUM Values	Comments
offices	id	INT		PK, NN, UN, AI		
	name	VARCHAR(50)		NN		
	head_office_id	INT	offices.id	NN, UN		Immediate head office
audit_trail	id	BIGINT(10)		PK, NN, UN, AI		
	object_id	BIGINT(20)	users.id, cases.id, case_tags.id, case_category.id, case_subcategory.id, case_notes.id, tasks_and_events.id, parties_involved.id, contacts.id	NN, UN		
	action_by	BIGINT(20)	users.id	NN		
	action_time	DATETIME		NN		
	action_details	MEDIUMTEXT		NN		Include name of object in case the object was deleted.
users	id	BIGINT(20)		PK, NN, UN, AI		
	office_id	INT	offices.id	NN, UN		
	email	VARCHAR(100)		NN		Serves as username
	password	VARCHAR(100)		NN		
	type	ENUM		NN	Admin, Senior Lawyer, Lawyer, Staff	
	status	TINYINT(1)		NN	1	0 - disabled, 1 - enabled
	changed_password	TINYINT(1)		NN	0	0 - false, 1 - true
	firstname	VARCHAR(50)		NN		
	lastname	VARCHAR(50)		NN		
	phone	VARCHAR(11)				
cases	id	BIGINT(20)		PK, NN, UN, AI		
	name	VARCHAR(100)		NN		
	case_category_id	BIGINT(20)	case_category.id	NN, UN		
	case_subcategory_id	BIGINT(20)	case_subcategory_id	NN, UN		
	status	ENUM		NN	For initial review, For edit review, For final review, For loop review, Closed	
	last_status_change	DATETIME		NN		
	decision	VARCHAR(50)			NULL	
	judge	VARCHAR(50)			NULL	
	curr_tier	BIGINT(20)	tier_history.id	NN, UN		
	esc_status	TINYINT(1)		NN	0	0 - not escalated/de-escalated, 1 - escalated, 2 - de-escalated; needed for senior lawyer view
	open_date	DATETIME		NN		
	opened_by	BIGINT(20)	users.id	NN, UN		
	close_date	DATETIME			NULL	
	updated_by	BIGINT(20)	users.id		NULL	
	updated_date	DATETIME			NULL	
tier_history	id	BIGINT(20)		PK, NN, UN, AI		
	case_id	BIGINT(20)	cases.id	NN, UN		
	prev_office_id	INT	offices.id	NN, UN		
	curr_office_id	INT	offices.id	NN, UN		When case is newly created, this value is null
assigned_users	case_id	BIGINT(20)	cases.id	PK, NN, UN		
	user_id	BIGINT(20)	users.id	PK, NN, UN		
	date_assigned	DATETIME		NN		
case_tags	id	BIGINT(20)		PK, NN, UN, AI		
	name	VARCHAR(50)		NN		

Constraints Reference:	
PK	Primary Key
FK	Foreign Key
UQ	Unique
NN	Not Null
ZF	Zero-Fill
AI	Auto-increment
UN	Unsigned

Fig. 4. Data Dictionary.

the categories, subcategories, and tags of a case are stored, respectively. Only the admin can change the records in these tables. And because a case can have multiple tags, a separate table called 'assigned_tags' is needed. The tables 'parties_involved', 'case_notes', 'contacts', and 'tasks_and_events' contains all the records of the parties, notes, contacts, tasks, and events of all the cases in the system. Each record in these tables has a column that references a record in 'cases' to indicate the case it belongs to. The 'audit_trail' table records all the activities of all the users within the system. It stores the id of the object that was accessed, the id of the user who did the action, the time when the action was done, the type of the action, and remarks about the action. Only the admin can view the records of this table in the system. For more information on the columns and relationship of the tables, refer to the attached schema diagram and data dictionary (Fig. 3 and Fig. 4,5).

Table Name	Column Name	Data Type	References: table_name.column_name	Constraints	Default / ENUM Values	Comments
assigned_tags	case_id	BIGINT(20)	cases.id	PK, NN, UN		
	case_tags_id	BIGINT(20)	case_tags.id	PK, NN, UN		
case_category	id	BIGINT(20)		PK, NN, UN, AI		
	name	VARCHAR(50)		NN		
case_subcategory	id	BIGINT(20)		PK, NN, UN, AI		
	name	VARCHAR(50)		NN		
case_notes	id	BIGINT(20)		PK, NN, UN, AI		
	case_id	BIGINT(20)	cases.id	NN, UN		
	title	VARCHAR(50)		NN		
	notes	VARCHAR(1000)		NN		
	file	VARCHAR(50)				Path to attachment
parties_involved	id	BIGINT(20)		PK, NN, UN, AI		
	case_id	BIGINT(20)	cases.id	NN, UN		
	name	VARCHAR(50)		NN		
	role	VARCHAR(50)				
contacts	id	BIGINT(20)		PK, NN, UN, AI		
	case_id	BIGINT(20)	cases.id	NN, UN		
	name	VARCHAR(100)		NN		
	description	VARCHAR(100)		NN		
	role	VARCHAR(50)		NN		
	phone	VARCHAR(50)		NN		
	email	VARCHAR(50)		NN		
tasks_and_events	id	BIGINT(20)		PK, NN, UN, AI		
	case_id	BIGINT(20)	cases.id	NN, UN		
	name	VARCHAR(50)		NN		
	details	VARCHAR(1000)		NN		
	date	DATE		NN		
	time	TIME		NN		
	type	TINYINT(1)		NN	0	0 - event, 1 - task
	file	VARCHAR(50)				Path to attachment

Fig. 5.   Data Dictionary contd.

5. Design, Functions and Features of a Case Management System: A Closer Look at CaseBox

CaseBox has appealed to a somewhat large number of users, primarily due to the fact that it has one of the simplest, and sleekest designs among free or open-source Legal Information Systems. Quite minimalistic in design, CaseBox is designed to provide a clutter free, yet thorough environment to store comprehensive legal information as it stands.

The interface of casebox looks like a file system. It has breadcrumbs at the top of the page, beside a search bar, a notifications tab, and a profile tab. The breadcrumbs allow the user to always know where he is relative to the file system, the search bar allows searching through the cases, and the profile tab allows customizing ones' personal information, as well as contain language settings, and personal preferences such as themes. Below that, there are three buttons namely: New, upload and clipboard. New creates either a Case, a contact, an organization, a task, a link, or a new internal folder, within the directory. The upload button uploads a file from the user's computer to the directory, and the clipboard just keeps track of the last text the user copied or cut. To the rightmost of these buttons are buttons that control the displayed table, commands such as refreshing the table, changing the view to a grid, setting the number of displayed rows, expanding folders, exporting the table, and opening a preview tab. To the left of the three buttons, on the other hand, is the full directory you can use to navigate around your Information System, much like windows explorer.

Each case has a unique identifying case number, the value of the case for prioritization, the case name, its status, the tags associated with the case, the type of case, the date of the case, a short description, the country of the case, a list of contacts associated with the case, files you can upload directly to the case description, and lastly, comments concerning the case. A case acts much like a folder, but has details inherent to the case. As such, users can still create cases, contacts, organizations, etc. within the case, although the uses of creating a case within a case is questionable at best.

Creating a contact entry will record the name, title, organization, email, phone, and country of a contact. Likewise, creating an organization will record the name, email, phone number, country, website, facebook link, and twitter link of the organization. You can also create a link that will record the type, URL, description, and tags of the link. links, contacts and organizations will also keep files uploaded to their specific entry, as well as user comments meant for working in a team environment. Lastly, you can create a task and set its title, the due date and due time, to whom it is assigned, the importance, and the description of the task. Approaching the due date would notify the user assigned.

Administrators are the only users who can naturally create cases or files by the onset. However, once a user is assigned a case file, they can create cases within that file or folder by themselves. The administrators will also be the only users who can create other users, and assign them authorization levels.

6. Application Design

The design of the program is a meld between the needs of the office, ascertained from the interview with Attorney Bobis, with functionalities and design choices that the researchers believe are imperative to have on the Legal Information System, drawing significant inspiration from CaseBox's design.

Firstly, while the researchers did implement a file system within each case, the researchers did not implement the Case Management System as a file system clone. That is, a user cannot create cases within a case. Essentially, we have done away with the organizational functionality of a file system as the researchers believe it is of relatively low import to the intended client of the system. Consequently, this change did away with the relevance of breadcrumbs or the ability to create folders. Creating contacts and organizations, while modified in its implementation, have been adapted into the new system. Creating links have also been removed, although a user can add a link by simply creating a note, the note system being one of the many enhancements the researchers introduced to the system. The case details however, and even contacts and organization details, do differ from CaseBox, as the researchers prioritized the findings from the systems requirement interview with Atty. Bobis. Permission system was expounded with the Case Management System, due to the nature of the escalation and de-escalation system, adding a significant tier difference among users. However, having the administrator be able to give users access to cases, as well as creating new user accounts were both observed in CaseBox, as well as requested by Atty. Bobis. The calendar system is a more advanced version of the notifications system implemented by CaseBox, and lastly, the audit trail available to administrators is a significant improvement as well.

The interface design is aimed to be simple and intuitive, which means features had to be reduced to bare essentials, based on the requirements interview with Atty. Bobis, so as to not clutter the interface, and thus make it a lot more user-friendly.

The application starts out in a login page. After successfully logging in, the user is redirected to the case list page. For regular users, there will be three items in the toolbar, just below the titular Case Management System header, which consists of: the profile page, the calendar page, and the cases page, with the logout button on the opposite side. The Profile Page is where a user can edit their user information, such as their first name, last name, and phone number. The profile page is also where a user can change their password. The calendar page is where a user can view the events related to the cases that the user handles. Lastly, the cases page will show the list of all the cases handled by the office. The user will readily see the number of days that has passed since the case was handed to a user for review. While the user can see every case, they will only be able to edit the information when they are assigned to review the case. The user can then add or edit an involved party's name and role in the case, add or edit case notes (attaching a document when needed), add or edit case contacts, consisting of a contact's name, phone number, email address, description, and role in the case, adding or editing events related to the case, specifying activity name, the description, whether it is a task or an event, the date and the time of the event/task, and a related document if needed, and lastly, add, organize, and retrieve documents within the case's own file system.

Administrators will have two extra panels in the toolbar, as well as extra actions. Firstly, administrators will have access to the users page, where they can view the list of all users. This is also where administrators can add new users to the system. Administrators will also have access to the audit log, essentially recording every action done within the system. As for extra actions, only administrators are allowed to create or delete cases. Lastly, administrators can add new categories, subcategories, and tags of cases, all of which are used when creating new cases.

Senior Lawyers, on the other hand, will have access to all cases within the specific tier of the organization. Additionally, Senior Lawyers will also be the only users authorized with escalating or de-escalating a case. Once escalated, edit access to the case will be removed from users hailing from the specific tier of the organization, and the case is moved up to the next tier, should the case prove too critical or sensitive for the current tier. Conversely, the Senior Lawyers of upper tiers can also de-escalate a case, sending it down for review. Lastly, Senior Lawyers will also be able to see all the events of all the cases within their tier.

In essence, the regular user has access to two main module clusters: the case handling module and the calendar. All of the cases that the user's office is handling will be listed however, the user can only edit the cases that he is assigned to handle. Files relevant to the case could be attached, and the Case Management System also keeps track of the notes the lawyers have of the case, as well as the events related to the case, and a list of contacts that are relevant to the case.

The calendar module, on the other hand, basically functions as a schedule tracker, tracking all events that a user needs to attend. The Calendar is automatically updated whenever an event is added to a case of which a user is handling. The user is reminded of the event via email at pre-set intervals before the event occurs.

Administrators will then have access to most management modules as well as generally important functions such as case creations. Lastly, Senior lawyers would be the only role able to escalate or de-escalate a case.

7. Analytics Implementations

While the pilot office, the UP-OVPLA, did not request for analytics, the researchers still developed a framework for possible future analytics implementations. While these are rather simple statistical analytical implementation frameworks, nevertheless the researchers know the value that such a framework can provide in the future.

The researchers have added a framework that collates the number of cases filed by the University and cases filed against the University, subdivided into the type of case. Another framework was added that collates data to help visualize the number of cases for filing, pending cases, and closed cases. Yet another framework was designed to display workload over a year, to help ascertain heavy work months, and lastly, one was designed to collate data concerning the average time a case is spending in court, measured by the number of days from the moment a case is opened until a case is closed.

These frameworks could be used in the future by outputting their results into graphs and charts, for easier visualization. It would then be made available only to the senior lawyer, unless otherwise required.

8. Case Workflow

A typical case starts with an administrator creating the case file. The administrator inputs the name, category, and subcategory of the case. They may choose to select tags to help the users identify and categorize the case. The administrator will also select either a senior lawyer, a lawyer, or a staff that will be assigned for the initial review of the case. Upon creation of the case, the system will automatically record the administrator who created the case and when it was created. The system will also automatically set the status of the case into 'for initial review'. The assigned user will have the ability to edit the list of involved parties, notes, contact list, events, tasks, and documents of the case. If the case is not yet resolved and has to go to edit reviewing, the user may assign another user for edit review. Doing this will change the status of the case to 'for edit review' and the newly assigned user will now have access to edit the case information. If the case is still not resolved and needs to go to final review then the previous users can assign a new user for final review. If the case is still not resolved during the final review, then a user will be assigned again for the loop review. Once the case is finally resolved, the administrator will close the case and the edit access of the handling users will be removed.

Alternatively, a case could be too critical to be handled by the campus office and thus, could instead be escalated to the head office by a senior lawyer. Once a case is escalated, editing access is removed from the lower

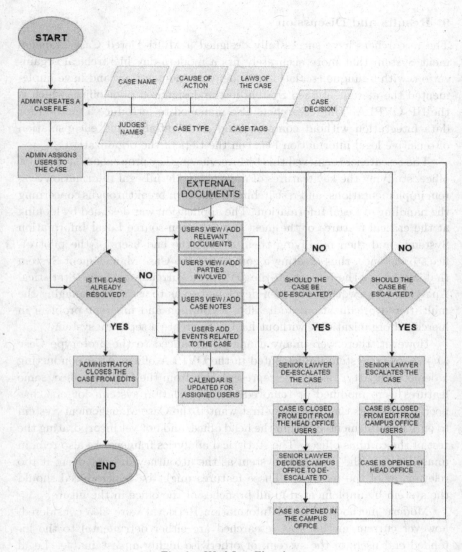

Fig. 6. Workflow Flowchart.

office, and the case is moved towards the list of escalated cases found only on the interface of the head office. Alternatively, the head office could also send a case back to a campus office for review, much like de-escalation. This can also only be done by designated senior lawyers within the head office (Fig. 6).

9. Results and Discussion

The researchers have successfully designed a Multi-Tiered Case Management System that more accurately fits a modern-day hierarchical organization, with a unique escalation and de-escalation system, and have implemented the aforementioned System in the designated pilot office, which is the UP-OVPLA. The researchers also managed to introduce a method for data integration without compromising confidentiality and encapsulation of sensitive legal information between the tiers of the organization.

The researchers achieved this by interviewing key proponents of the pilot office, studying the key features of multiple modern Legal Information System implementations, and researching on modern breakthroughs concerning the handling of Legal Information. The application was designed by looking at the critical features of the most favored open-source Legal Information Systems, and then modifying them to suit the end users of the pilot office's preference, thus creating a comprehensive Case Management System that minimizes the impact on the OVPLA's current workflow. Statistical Analytics frameworks were then developed so as to assist in managing the multi-tiered organization, addressing a common and inherent problem in hierchical organizations, without having to create a separate system.

However, there were many changes introduced to the prototype Case Management System implemented in the OVPLA office. After conducting a demo with Atty. Bobis, the representative from the OVPLA office, some features were modified or removed. The escalation system, for one, has been removed as the Attourney first wanted the Case Management System to only be implemented within the head office, and not yet incorporating the rest of the campus offices. The statistical analytics frameworks also remain unused within the prototype system as the attourney did not deem it too relevant as of the moment. These features might be reintroduced should the system be implemented in all branches of the office in the future.

Modern methods of Legal Information Retrieval were also considered, however current methods as researched are either detrimental to the intended end users of the system, or otherwise highly unsustainable. Legal Information Retrieval could be revisited should more research be done on the field itself, specifically advancements in the field of Natural Language Processing.

Legal Analytics were also considered, however the idea was quickly scrapped due to the fact that, even if the technical know-how was there, the amount of data that the system is projected to handle will unlikely be enough for Legal Analytics to be of significant help to the office.

References

1. J. F. Mancini, "10 fast facts about document management," 2008. [Online]. Available: http://info.aiim.org/digital-landfill/newaiimo/\\ 2008/10/27/10-fast-facts-at

2. D. Kempner, "Ten benefits of going paperless," 2014. [Online]. Available: http://community.aiim.org/blogs/dennis-kempner/\\2014/ 07/29/ten-benefits-of-going-paperless

3. P. Fiorenza, "10 benefits of going paperless," 2014. [Online]. Available: https://www.govloop.com/resources/10-\\benefits-going-paperless/

4. S. Randazzo and D. Michaels, "U.s. charges three chinese traders with hacking law firms," 2016. [Online]. Available: https://www.wsj.com/articles/u-s-charges-three-\ \chinese-traders-with-hacking-law-firms-1482862000

5. Department of Agrarian Reform, "Department of agrarian reform – legal information system." [Online]. Available: http://lis.dar.gov.ph

6. D. C. Blair and M. E. Maron, "An evaluation of retrieval effectiveness for a full-text document-retrieval system," *Communications of the ACM*, vol. 28, no. 3, pp. 289–299, 1985.

7. W. Peters, M.-T. Sagri, and D. Tiscornia, "The structuring of legal knowledge in LOIS," *Artificial Intelligence and Law*, vol. 15, pp. 117–135, 2007.

8. M. Saravanan, B. Ravindran, and S. Raman, "Improving legal information retrieval using an ontological framework," *Artificial Intelligence and Law*, vol. 17, pp. 101–124, 2009.

9. K. T. Maxwell and B. Schafer, "Concept and context in legal information retrieval," in *Proceedings of the 2008 conference on Legal Knowledge and Information Systems: JURIX 2008: The Twenty-First Annual Conference*. IOS Press Amsterdam, 2008, pp. 63–72.

10. E. Schweighofer and D. Liebwald, "Advanced lexical ontologies and hybrid knowledge based systems: first steps to a dynamic legal electronic commentary," *Artificial Intelligence and Law*, vol. 15, pp. 103–115, 2007.

11. K. D. Ashley and S. Brninghaus, "Automatically classifying case texts and predicting outcomes," *Artificial Intelligence and Law*, vol. 17, pp. 125–165, 2009.

12. J. Zeng, "Research and practical experiences in the use of multiple data sources for enterprise level planning and decision making: A literature review," 1999. [Online]. Avail-

able: https://www.ctg.albany.edu/publications/reports/multiple\ _data_sources?\\chapter=5\&PrintVersion=2

13. D. L. Goodhue, M. D. Wybo, and L. J. Kirsch, "The impact of data integration on the costs and benefits of information systems," *MIS Quarterly*, vol. 16, pp. 293–311, 1992.

14. J. Frand, "Data mining: What is data mining?" 2011. [Online]. Available: http://www.anderson.ucla.edu/faculty/jason. frand/teacher/technologies\\/palace/datamining.htm

15. Lex Machina, "Lex machina: What's unique?" [Online]. Available: https://lexmachina.com/what-we-do/whats-unique/

Bisociative Serendipity Music Recommendation

Sirawit Sopchoke*

*Graduate School of Information Science and Technology, Osaka University,
Suita, Osaka, 565-0871, Japan*
* E-mail: sirawit@ai.sanken.osaka-u.ac.jp

Ken-ichi Fukui and Masayuki Numao

*The Institute of Scientific and Industrial Research, Osaka University,
Ibaraki, Osaka, 567-0047, Japan*
E-mail: {surname}@ai.sanken.osaka-u.ac.jp

With the traditional similarity-based approaches to recommender systems, it is unlikely to discover truly novel things. Users no longer find the outputs interesting or surprising since the outputs are locked into clusters of similarities on single domain. To make recommendations more attractive to the users, the system must provide a serendipitous recommendation list which is new, exciting and unexpectable. Serendipitous recommendation increases the chance of discovering music that is truly novel and unexpectedly useful leading to better performance and higher efficiency. In this paper, we propose a bisociative based approach to automatically generate a serendipitous recommendation list for particular users. The unexpected interesting links crossing different context domains are found by applying bisociative knowledge discovery concept and inducting the rules for generating the serendipitous list using probabilistic logic framework. For the music recommendation on subset of Amazon product dataset including users' music and movie preferences, we are able to achieve a recommendation list with 60% accuracy. The list includes recommendations which are not found in the single-domain based systems.

Keywords: Recommender System; Serendipity; Bisociations.

1. Introduction

People are increasingly overwhelmed by information available on online channels which seem to provide ample choices. It has become more challenging for people to find the choice that will perfectly satisfy their needs. In addition, some may have insufficient experience to make right decisions.

Hence, it becomes necessary to have a tool which can scope or screen choices for the users or suggest other alternatives that users do not even know that they exist. With this tool, users will have more chances to make a better decision or select a better choice. Such tool is known as "Recommender System".

In developing a recommender system, the traditional techniques including content-based and collaborative filtering commonly perform on a single domain. Both techniques assume that users want to see the content which is similar to what they already rate highly (content-based) or similar to the content their friends rate highly (collaborative filtering). With these techniques, users are locked into the clusters of similarity with no or low chances of discovering things that are truly novel to them. The recommendations might be boring since they are too predictable, especially for the music recommender system. The recommended music is basically similar to the previous set of music in users' activities either based on music contents (i.e., rhythm pattern, melodiousness) or music context (i.e. artist, tags).

To broaden the choices, increase the chances for users to discover music that is unexpected and truly novel and to open up a whole new musical universe to users, the notion of "serendipity" has recently been proposed. However, to generate an unexpected recommendation list in most existing algorithms requires user interaction.

In this paper, we, therefore, propose an alternative automatic serendipitous music recommendation algorithm inspired by bisociative knowledge discovery concept and implemented using probabilistic logic framework.

2. Related Work

In this section, some of the recent work on serendipitous music recommender systems and bisociative knowledge discovery are discussed.

2.1. *Serendipity*

Serendipity is currently a hot topic in recommendation systems. A number of different approaches to serendipitous recommender systems have been proposed including [1,2]. However, there are two problems commonly found when introducing serendipity into recommender systems. One problem is that the quality of predictions becomes progressively worse, so there is a need to find the right balance between similarity and novelty, and between the immediate surrounding and the periphery [3]. The other problem is that the proposed algorithms mostly require users' interaction to generate unexpected recommendation lists, e.g., Stober, et al. [4] proposed a music recommendation using MusicGalaxy, an adaptive user interface application for exploring music collections.

2.2. *Serendipity in Music*

The methodologies currently used to develop music recommender systems can be classified into three different categories [5]: music content-based, music context-based, and collaborative filtering-based. All of them share the common concept which is to create the recommendation lists based on the musical similarity.

In content-based, the similarity may be computed on some sort of acoustic features extracted from the audio signal via signal processing techniques. Alternatively, context-based approach or collaborative filtering-based approach derives the musical similarity from listening co-occurrences among users.

However, each approach has its own disadvantages. For example, the recommendation list by music content-based approach is too perfect or homogeneous and boring since the recommendations, while they should be similar, they should not be too similar. In music context-based, most data is at artist level, thus too similar and no novelty. Likewise, collaborative filtering-based typically analyzes only one aspect of all users' model globally, for example, listening or buying. Both music context-based and collaborative filtering-based are also faced with the lack of data problem or cold-start problem, like the other researchers in the field. Cold-start problem has a big impact on the quality of recommendation.

Improving recommendation performance no longer depends only on the efficiency of the similarity algorithms. The serendipitous music recommendation becomes an option for users to increase the chances to discover music that is truly novel and unexpectedly useful.

Zhang, et al. [6] introduced the Auralist recommendation framework which attempted to inject serendipity into recommendations whilst limiting the impact on accuracy. The two novel serendipity-enhancing techniques, Community-Aware Auralist and Bubble-Aware Auralist were presented. Both could be combined with the existing ranking methods through hybrid recommendation approach.

Community-Aware Auralist interpolates a new item-based collaborative filtering algorithm called Artist-based LDA. Artist-based LDA is based on Latent Dirichlet Allocation and is combined with Listener Diversity. Bubble-Aware Auralist is the combination of Artist-based LDA and Declustering algorithm. Community-Aware Auralist and Bubble-Aware Auralist effectively boost novelty, diversity and serendipity scores, with the latter offering a better trade-off with regards to accuracy. However, these

202

serendipity-enhancing methods still neither include the explicit user feed-back to shape the algorithm interpolation for individual users nor allow the system to adapt to the adventurousness and mood of different personalities.

In this paper, we present an alternative solution to the serendipitous mu-sic recommendation problem using probabilistic logic framework to model and to generate the recommendations. This framework also provides a mechanism to extend the system by incorporating and reasoning over cur-rently unspecified types and similarity measures of additional information collected from several sources. We also define the relations or links crossing different context domains. Thus, it leads to the use of bisociative knowl-edge discovery concept to find yet unexpected interesting links to generate the serendipitous recommendation lists. The details of our methodology will be discussed in the third section.

2.3. *Bisociations - Unexpected Interesting Links*

Bisociations focus on the discovery of surprising relations in the reposito-ries coming from diverse origins or heterogeneous data sources, forming a different domain [7].

The idea of bisociations was first introduced by Arthur Koestler in 1964. It is defined as an association that can directly connect objects from differ-ent domains or connect those of the same domain via an object of another domain (or other domains) (Fig. 1). The promising approach for bisocia-

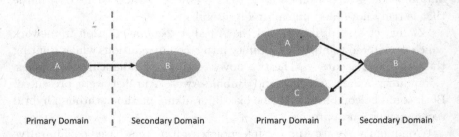

Fig. 1. Bisociative Knowledge Discovery concept.

tions data exploration is the graph structure [8].

As mentioned above, Stober, et al. [4] proposed a serendipitous music recommendation using MusicGalaxy application. They turned their mu-sic discovery application into an environment that supported bisociative music discovery. The idea is to combine two distinct domain views into one visualization using the secondary focus to highlight connections to the nearest neighbors in a different domain than the one used for projection. The "primary domain" is directly visualized by the projection and contains the displayed tracks connected by neighborhood relations that are implicitly induced between each track and its neighbors in the projection. The "secondary domain", however, is used to identify nearest neighbors for the secondary focus distortion and not directly visible to the user. A bisociation occurs in this setting if two tracks are not neighbors in the projection domain but are connected in the secondary domain.

Nonetheless, Stober, et al. [4] focused only on the field of bisociative music collection exploration using a user interface which integrated the music graph information for each user's interaction and led to the highlighted secondary domain focusing for serendipitous music discovery.

In this paper, after thoroughly exploring the dataset, we found that properties of the items or those of the users can lead to some relationships which subsequently provide us with the unexpected recommendation results.

Figure 2 shows examples of association via item property. In this example, Emitt Rhodes and Paul McCartney are linked by their physical characteristics while Yoko Ono and John Lennon are linked by their relationship. Figure 3 shows examples of association via user property. On the left, user and "The cup of life" are linked since user was a soccer fan and the song was a theme song for France 98 World Cup. On the right, user is linked to "Candle in the wind" because user was an admirer of Princess Diana and the song was performed at Princess Diana's funeral.

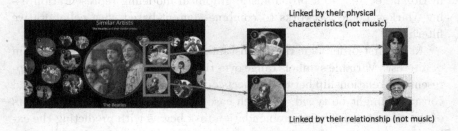

Fig. 2. The examples of association via item property.

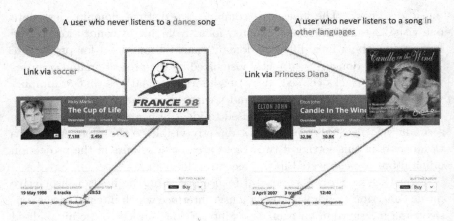

Fig. 3.   The examples of association via user property.

3. Method

To reach our goal in designing and building an automatic serendipitous music recommender system based on bisociative knowledge discovery concept, the designed algorithm using probabilistic logic framework was implemented.

The success of Inductive Logic Programing and Statistical Relational Learning has been shown in a number of researches. For example, the recent work of Hoxha and Rettinger in 2013 [9] and Kouki et al. in 2015 [10] which applied Inductive Logic Programing and Statistical Relational Learning to the hybrid recommendations proved that incorporating additional information for users and items was beneficial to the cold-start settings in particular [11]. The recent progress in relational learning was presented in Hoxha, et al. [9], a probabilistic graphical modeling representation using Markov Logic Networks to combine content-based with collaborative filtering.

In the first-order logic rules, constants represent the objects in a domain of interest. Variable symbols range over the objects. Predicate symbols represent the relationship between objects or features of objects. Variables and constants might be typed, in which case variables only range over objects of the given type. The recommendation task begins with predicting the existence probability of a relation between a particular user and a particular item. Then, returning the recommendation for the query predicate, (e.g., rates(userA, book1, rating), by choosing the items with the high probability according to the specified threshold.

In 2015, the study by Kouki, et al. [10] showed that Statistical Relational Learning framework could be used to develop a general and extensible hybrid recommendation system framework called Hybrid Probabilistic Extensible Recommender. This framework also provided a mechanism to extend the system by incorporating and reasoning over currently unspecified types and similarity measures of additional information collected from several sources. A learning method used to appropriately balance the different input signals from many information sources was also discussed.

The evidences from the researches by Hoxha, et al. [9] and Kouki, et al. [10] discussed above indicate that relational learning provides a better recommendation performance by incorporating additional information compared to a traditional method with a single dyadic relationship between the objects i.e. users and items. Hence, the relational learning captured our interest to model and provide a potential solution for serendipitous music recommendations.

We use probabilistic logic framework, a kind of relational learning in which some of the facts are annotated with probabilities, since it is suitable for representing and solving bisociative knowledge discovery problem for music recommendations. ProbLog [12], a probabilistic logic tool, is chosen for our implementation. ProbLog is a tool that allows us to intuitively build programs that encode complex interactions between large sets of heterogeneous component and inherent uncertainties that are presented in real-life situations. With ProbLog, it is also easier to describe the relations between the items in dataset than other representation methods such as matrix.

In our initial implementation, we first demonstrated how a musical taste related to other facets of users' life and preferences. In other words, we used a user's taste of another type-level item, movies for example, to predict the user's music taste.

Our proposed approach to music recommendations on cross domains using items is designed based on a traditional recommendation approach using Pearson correlation to find similarities between users, then deduce the certain recommendation rules. For the user-based recommendation, the similar taste on movies will lead to a similar taste on music. For the item-based recommendation, the high confidence of the defined rule results in a music recommendation. The ProbLog syntax is used to describe the model. The approach can be performed in three steps, define rule, query and select outputs. Only the output that is greater than or equal to the desired threshold will be selected.

An example of the dataset containing the preferences on music and movies of the users is the following.

```
A likes song1
A likes movie1
A likes song2
A likes movie2
B likes song1
B likes movie1
B likes song3
B likes movie3
...
```

Examples of user-based recommendation and item-based recommendation are shown respectively below.

Example: User-based recommendation
Define rule: `likedMusic(U2, Music) :- influencesUser(U1, U2),`
`likedMusic(U1, Music).`
Query: `query(likedMusic(U2, Music)`
Outputs $\geq$ Threshold will be selected.

Example: Item-based recommendation
Define rule: `likedMusic(U2, Music) :- influencesItem(Movie, Music),`
`likedMovie(U2, Movie), likedMovie(U1, Movie),`
`likedMusic(U1, Music).`
Query: `query(likedMusic(U2, Music)`
Outputs $\geq$ Threshold will be selected.

The initial experiment for proof of concept will be discussed in the next section.

4. Experiment for Concept Proof

Our approach was designed to build a more flexible model for serendipitous music recommendations by combining the incorporated data from different aspects or different levels. The unexpected interesting links were found using bisociative knowledge discovery. We used ProbLog, the probabilistic logic framework, to implement and test serendipitous music recommendation results. The datasets, evaluation metrics and data partitioning, and experiment results are described in this section.

4.1. *Datasets*

Our initial experiments were mainly conducted over two datasets: user's preferences and item attributes. User's preferences dataset contained music preferences and movie preferences with ratings obtained from Amazon product dataset provided by UCSD [13]. Only the top 1,000 reviewers were extracted to be used in our initial experiment.

The original dataset contained product reviews and metadata from Amazon, including 142.8 million reviews spanning May 1996 - July 2014. This dataset included reviews (ratings, text, helpfulness votes), product metadata (descriptions, category information, price, brand, and image features), and links (also viewed/also bought graphs).

The item attributes dataset contained attributes of music and movies listed in the first dataset. This dataset was developed using Amazon Product API.

4.2. *Evaluation of Serendipity*

For evaluation metrics and data partitioning, the evaluation was performed by precision evaluation metric and rank-based evaluation metric as per the traditional evaluation method for recommender systems. Partitioning technique was hold-out setting. In this setting, test reviews were sampled and hidden from our dataset without partitioning the users (Fig. 4).

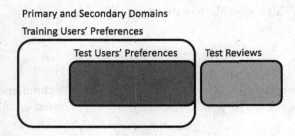

Fig. 4.   Hold-out data partitioning technique.

Adomavicius, et al. [14] suggested that recommender systems should be evaluated not only by their accuracy, but also by other important metrics such as serendipity, unexpectedness, and usefulness. In order to accurately and precisely measure the unexpectedness of candidate items and generate recommendation lists, the metric introduced by Ge, et al. [15] was used to evaluate our method. The unexpected set of recommendations can be calculated as follows:

$$UNEXP = RS \setminus PM \tag{1}$$

where PM is a set of recommendations generated by a primitive prediction model and RS is the recommendations generated by our serendipitous recommendation. Any RS element which does not appear in PM is considered as unexpected.

As Ge, et al. [15] argued, unexpected recommendations might not always be useful and, hence, they also proposed a serendipity measure as:

$$SRDP = \frac{|UNEXP \cap USEFUL|}{|N|} \tag{2}$$

where USEFUL is the set of useful items and N is the length of the recommendation list. For instance, the usefulness of an item can be approximated by the users' feedback.

4.3. *Initial Experiment Result*

Our initial experiment result on subset of Amazon product dataset which included users' music preferences and movie preferences is 60% accurate. The SRDP result which is the measure to evaluate our model which recommends the music that user does not expect but may find it interesting is 21%. These recommendation results contain recommendations which are not found in single-domain based system (Fig. 5).

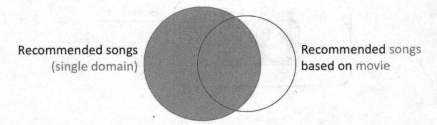

Fig. 5.   The recommendation results contain recommendations which are not found in single-domain based system.

Therefore, it is promising and encouraging to generate the novel recommendation music based on a user's movie preference. To generate an even better recommendation, our music recommendation result is merged with the result from a traditional method on users' music preference only (single domain).

5. Conclusion

To satisfy the user with the new and exciting recommendation, the serendipity list is our proposed solution. To generate truly serendipitous recommendation, the bisociative knowledge discovery concept is used to properly link the items, and the ProbLog, the probabilistic logic framework, to generate the accurate recommendation rules. To generate the recommendation list with more coverage for the particular user which will better satisfy the user, we plan to generate probabilistic recommendation rules using the relationships between users and items plus the item attributes.

Acknowledgement

This work was supported by JSPS Core-to-Core Program, A. Advanced Research Networks. In particular, we would like to express our deepest thanks and appreciation to Professor Dr. Luc De Raedt for his invaluable guidance and advice and to Dr. Anton Dries for his support throughout the program.

References

1. G. Shani and A. Gunawardana, *Evaluating Recommendation Systems*, in *Recommender Systems Handbook*, (Springer, 2011), ch. 8.
2. L. Iaquinta, M. d. Gemmis, P. Lops, G. Semeraro, M. Filannino and P. Molino, Introducing serendipity in a content-based recommender system, in *HIS '08 Eighth International Conference on Hybrid Intelligent Systems*, Sept 2008.
3. P. Adamopoulos and A. Tuzhilin, On unexpectedness in recommender systems: Or how to better expect the unexpected, *ACM Trans. Intell. Syst. Technol.* **5**, 54:1 (December 2014).
4. S. Stober, S. Haun and A. Nürnberger, *Bisociative Knowledge Discovery: An Introduction to Concept, Algorithms, Tools, and Applications* (Springer Berlin Heidelberg, 2012), ch. Bisociative Music Discovery and Recommendation, pp. 472–483.
5. M. Schedl, D. Hauger and D. Schnitzer, A model for serendipitous music retrieval, in *Proceedings of the 2Nd Workshop on Context-awareness in Retrieval and Recommendation*, CaRR '12 (ACM, 2012).

6. Y. C. Zhang, D. Ó. Séaghdha, D. Quercia and T. Jambor, Auralist: Introducing serendipity into music recommendation, in *Proceedings of the Fifth ACM International Conference on Web Search and Data Mining*, WSDM '12 (ACM, 2012).

7. U. Nagel, K. Thiel, T. Kötter, D. Piatek and M. R. Berthold, *Proceedings of the Advances in Intelligent Data Analysis X: 10th International Symposium (IDA)* (Springer Berlin Heidelberg, 2011), ch. Bisociative Discovery of Interesting Relations between Domains, pp. 306–317.

8. M. R. Berthold (ed.), *Bisociative Knowledge Discovery: An Introduction to Concept, Algorithms, Tools, and Applications* (Springer-Verlag, 2012).

9. J. Hoxha and A. Rettinger, First-order probabilistic model for hybrid recommendations, in *12th International Conference on Machine Learning and Applications (ICMLA)*, Dec 2013.

10. P. Kouki, S. Fakhraei, J. Foulds, M. Eirinaki and L. Getoor, Hyper: A flexible and extensible probabilistic framework for hybrid recommender systems, in *Proceedings of the 9th ACM Conference on Recommender Systems*, RecSys '15 (ACM, 2015).

11. Z. Gantner, L. Drumond, C. Freudenthaler, S. Rendle and L. Schmidt-Thieme, Learning attribute-to-feature mappings for cold-start recommendations, in *IEEE 10th International Conference on Data Mining (ICDM)*, Dec 2010.

12. L. De Raedt, A. Kimmig and H. Toivonen, Problog: A probabilistic prolog and its application in link discovery, in *Proceedings of the 20th International Joint Conference on Artifical Intelligence*, IJCAI'07 (Morgan Kaufmann Publishers Inc., 2007).

13. J. McAuley, C. Targett, Q. Shi and A. van den Hengel, Image-based recommendations on styles and substitutes, in *Proceedings of the 38th International ACM SIGIR Conference on Research and Development in Information Retrieval*, SIGIR '15 (ACM, 2015).

14. G. Adomavicius and A. Tuzhilin, Toward the next generation of recommender systems: A survey of the state-of-the-art and possible extensions, *IEEE Trans. on Knowl. and Data Eng.* **17**, 734 (June 2005).

15. M. Ge, C. Delgado-Battenfeld and D. Jannach, Beyond accuracy: Evaluating recommender systems by coverage and serendipity, in *Proceedings of the Fourth ACM Conference on Recommender Systems*, RecSys '10 (ACM, 2010).

Redesign of WappenLite: A Localhost Web Application Framework for Web-based Programming Environments

Koji KAGAWA

Faculty of Engineering, Kagawa University,
2217-20 Hayashi-cho, Takamatsu, Kagawa 761-0396, JAPAN
E-mail: kagawa@eng.kagawa-u.ac.jp

WappenLite is a platform to provide Web-based programming environments mainly for JVM-based programming languages. Since the deprecation of Java applets, we must redesign some aspects of WappenLite. This paper reports the structure and the features of renewed WappenLite and explains its usage along with its future plans.

Keywords: Computer Science Education, Web-based, Java, Programming Paradigm.

1. Introduction

It is more or less a headache for teachers to explain relatively minor programming languages and related tools. For popular languages such as C, Java and Python, it is possible to spend plenty of time and therefore possible to explain the usage of compilation tools and the syntax of the language in details. For minor programming languages, in general, it is not possible to spend such a long period of time. In many cases, we can devote only a hour or two to explain each programming language. Still, sometimes we want to explain, for example, functional languages and logic languages which are somewhat off from the main stream, for some computational algorithms are best expressed in such languages and only poorly expressed in major programming languages.

To remedy such a situation, we have proposed using Web-based programming environments and WappenLite[3] to provide a uniform interface to various programming language implementations for Web-based programming environments. WappenLite is mainly designed for Java Virtual Machine (JVM)-based language implementations.

Before WappenLite, we first constructed an EclipseRCP-based framework called Wappen[5]. However, the JavaScript platform has matured and has become powerful enough. We have switched to WappenLite, which can use AJAX-based user interface. WappenLite has been used in the author's classes for compiler and programming paradigms for several years.

During this period, the situation has changed in several aspects. We have proposed WappenLite applications to be used as a Java applet. However, Java applets have lost momentum for security reasons recently and are currently not available on most of major Web browsers. Therefore, it is a time to redesign the structure of WappenLite by simplifying some aspects and providing new features.

In this paper, we will explain new features of WappenLite introduced recently and their design rationals. The rest of this paper is structured as follows. First, we will introduce WappenLite in its original design and in its renewed design in more details in Section 2. Then, in Section 3, we will explain how to use WappenLite from teachers' perspective. Section 4 explains related work. Finally, we concludes and discuss future directions in Section 5.

2. The Structure of Redesigned WappenLite

In this section, we will explain briefly the structure of original WappenLite which uses Java applets as its platform, and then that of redesigned WappenLite.

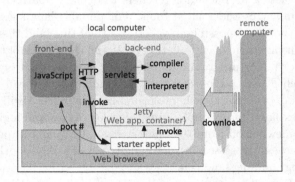

Fig. 1.   Old Structure of WappenLite.

A WappenLite application behaves as an HTTP server which runs in the local computer (i.e. the same computer as the Web browser is running) as is show in Fig. 1. Since it runs in the client-side computer, its TCP port cannot be determined in advance. The applet version had a mechanism to let

Web pages know its TCP port using so-called "LiveConnect." More specifically, the applets uses the `netscape.javascript.JSObject#eval` method to communicate with JavaScript programs running in Web pages. They use LiveConnect for informing the TCP port to JavaScript in the beginning only and communicate via HTTP only in the rest of their lifetime. Though it reduces learners' labor, it somewhat complicates the structure of JavaScript programs since they must communicate with both applets and servlets.

Since Java applets are now deprecated, we will simplify this part altogether. The TCP port is not informed to the JavaScript component automatically. The WappenLite application displays its port number in its window or in the console window where it is invoked and then the user must copy and paste it manually into the Web page as is show in Fig. 2.

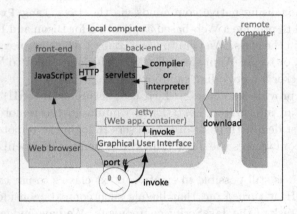

Fig. 2. New Structure of WappenLite.

When the WappenLite application accessed by a Web page via Ajax (i.e. `XMLHttpRequest`), it first receives some configuration parameters. It also creates a working temporary directory and download required JAR files and source files. In a case of interpreter-based implementation, it also starts an interpreter at this moment and records its process id in a session attribute. Then, it is attached to the console component in the Web page via the WebSocket protocol.

2.1. *Discontinued Features*

With the applet component, we decided to discontinue some of the features of WappenLite to keep the JavaScript component simple. We will explain such features in the following in turn.

In order to communicate with the compiler or the interpreter, we have to write a class which we call "context" for each language implementation to provide a uniform interface to the servlet classes. We have provided several context classes mainly for JVM-based language implementations. Some programming languages, however, do not have popular JVM-based implementations. In such a case, we provided a context which uses `java.lang.Process` to invoke external processes. This approach has some obvious deficiencies. First, it is platform-dependent. The context can run, for example, on Windows, but not on Linux. Second, it cannot provide sandboxes to safely run programs. And finally, it is sensitive to the change of environments such as the version up of the compiler toolkit. Though such a context using native commands via the `java.lang.Process` class was adopted to provide a Web-based application for Bison and Flex, it is no longer used in the class. We plan to use a context which employs server-side compilation, or to use WappenLiteDocker[4] which is similar to WappenLite but uses Docker for providing sandboxes.

We also provided a context which uses secure shell (SSH) to communicate with an interpreter (i.e. REPL) running in the remote computer. Then, it must deal with passwords for users to login the remote computer, which also complicates the JavaScript component of WappenLite applications.

Though it is still possible to create context classes to use external processes or SSH, it turned out that having such contexts considerably complicates the task of the JavaScript components. We have judged that such contexts are not a good idea and we will concentrate on contexts which use JVM-based language implementations and use server-side programs for compilation only.

2.2. *New Features*

In this subsection, we will explain some new features which are introduced with the discontinuation of the applet.

First, we explain how WappenLite applications are distributed to learners in place of Java applets. Since WappenLite is an Eclipse project, we can use the runnable JAR format for this purpose. Therefore, we create a runnable JAR file which contains several servlet classes and at least one context class as well as all the necessary libraries such as Jetty and make it downloadable from Web pages. Though Java Web Start applications may seem to be another appropriate option, they must be signed with a code signature obtained from a trusted certificate authority since Java 7 update 51. This is a very tedious task for teachers and there is no merit for WappenLite to use the Web Start technology.

We introduced a generic context class for JVM-based interpreters. There are many JVM-based languages implementations which act as interpreters (e.g. Clojure, core.logic, Frege (a variant of Haskell), Kawa Scheme, miniKanren, SISC Scheme, tuProlog). They all have similar behaviors and can be uniformly operated by simply changing parameters. Other standard context classes we provide with WappenLite are those for Java, Oolong (an assembler for JVM) and NestedVM. NestedVM is a compiler for the C language targeted at JVM[1]. Since the NestedVM compiler itself is not implemented in JVM but is a native Linux application, the compiler is offered as a Web service and the NestedVM context communicates with the Web service for compilation. Those standard contexts run interpreters or compiled (assembled) JVM code as a separate process using `java.lang.Process` and invoking the `java` command while specifying a policy file with the `-policy` option. This option lets Java programs run in a sandbox with some permission. We need to grant some permissions to run JVM-based interpreters introduced above.

It is worth noting here that WappenLite applications run programs in sandboxes so that learners can convince that source codes modified by them do not do harm by mistake. Since WappenLite allows considerable amount of customization by teachers, it does not consider the case where teachers try to do something evil to learners' computer. A WappenLite application checks the URLs of `referer` of Ajax calls and those of the source and library files so that it is not abused by (possibly malicious) users other than the teacher who has created it.

We have added new buttons "Information" and "Open Directory" to the graphical user interface of WappenLite. The "Information" button shows some information about the running context and "Open Directory" button opens the working directory of the context by using the native file explorer via `java.awt.Desktop` class. These buttons play important roles when some troubles happen in learners' programs or in JavaScript programs of Web pages. It is impossible to completely avoid the troubles caused not only by bugs introduced by learners but also by bugs in JavaScript programs of Web pages introduced by teachers. In order to avoid depressing learners in such cases, WappenLite enables learners to run programs also in the console (Command Prompt or PowerShell for Windows and bash or other shells in Linux). (In Windows, we can type "cmd" or "powershell" in thr address bar of the explorer window to start Command Prompt or PowerShell respectively, using the folder displayed in the explorer as the current directory.)

Though WappenLite applications are supposed to run in the local computer (i.e. the same computer as the Web browser is running), it seems to have some benefits to run WappenLite applications in the remote computer (i.e. the server). Especially, if we consider using smart devices (with iOS or Android) as learners' machines, naturally, we cannot run WappenLite applications in the client machine. In servers, though we may use other sandbox mechanisms such as Docker, JVM-based approach may have some advantages such as amount of load on the server. To accommodate such "server-side mode," we would like to augment WappenLite with some features to avoid troubles caused by runaway programs. Currently it has a mechanism to kill the process of the interpreter or the compiled program when the session is invalidated due to timeout (i.e. when the user does not perform any action during some interval).

3. Usage after Redesign

With the redesign of WappenLite, the JavaScript component of the front end is substantially simplified. We can dispense with the part that communicates with the applet. Besides, we also reviewed other inflated parts at the same time.

A Web page using WappenLite includes some JavaScript files which offer WappenLite utility methods, then usually shows a link to a runnable JAR file of WappenLite and suggests learners to download and to execute the file. It should also have the console component to show the result of program execution and the editor component to edit the source codes. When the WappenLite application is executed and its URL is given in a text field, it first connects to WappenLite with configuration parameters such as `class` (the name of the context class), `sources` (the URLs of the source files), `jars` (the URLs of the required JAR files), `encoding` (the character encoding of the source files) and other context-specific parameters. We can use a JavaScript method `WappenLite.configure` for this purpose. Then, we use `WappenLite.assignCallbacks` to connect the WebSocket downstream channel to the console component. That is, we can register several callback functions such as `consoleAppend` which are called when data packets arrive from the WappenLite application via WebSocket. On the other hand, we use `WappenLite.write` to send data to the WappenLite application via the WebSocket upstream channel. When the source codes in the editor component are modified, we call `WappenLite.save` to send the modified source codes to the WappenLite application. In case of compiler-based context, they are compiled automatically, while in case of interpreter-based context they are reloaded to the interpreter. Finally, in case of compiler-based context, we use `WappenLite.run` to send command-line arguments and to run compiled programs. There are also some other miscellaneous methods such as `WappenLite.abort`, the details of which are omitted here.

4. Related Work

In this section, we will explain some systems which resemble WappenLite in some aspects.

4.1. *Web-based Programming Environments*

There are a lot of Web-based programming environments such as `paiza.io`, `repl.it`, codepad (`codepad.org`) and `ideone.com`. They all execute users' programs on the remote computer (the server computer). They are not intended as a platform where teachers can freely prepare programming language environments and customize such environments as they like.

4.2. *Python Tutor*

Python Tutor[2] is a Web-based program visualization tool. At first, it is designed for Python, then, later is extended to other programming languages such as Java, JavaScript, TypeScript, Ruby and C/C++. Its back ends for various programming languages are developed independently and are intended to run on the remote computer.

4.3. *Jupyter Notebook*

Jupyter Notebook is a Web-based environment for creating "notebook" interfaces. Jupyter Notebook has evolved from IPython Notebook[6]. A notebook document typically includes live code, visualizations and explanatory text, It supports more than forty programming languages. It runs its back ends on the local computer and therefore it has something in common with our system. Jupyter Notebook requires Python runtime to run back ends.

It would be interesting to add APIs to support a notebook interface to WappenLite and to provide a generic back end for JVM-based languages

5. Conclusion and Future Work

In this paper, we have explained the redesign of WappenLite. It can provide back ends for Web-based programming environments. It uses the Java runtime and especially supports JVM-based programming language implementations. Its usage has been simplified as a result of redesign.

Currently, we run WappenLite applications on the local computer (the same computer as the Web browser is running.). It has an advantage that teachers do not need to prepare dedicated server hardware. We plan to use WappenLite in the classes of "compiler" and "programming paradigms" and continue to improve user interface, which is made feasible thanks to the simplified JavaScript library.

Since smart devices employing iOS or Android are now getting popular, we would like to add features to support "server-side mode" of WappenLite applications and design user interfaces that fit such devices.

Acknowledgment

This work is supported by Kakenhi JSPS KAKENHI Grant Number 15K01075.

References

1. B. Alliet and A. Megacz. Complete translation of unsafe native code to safe bytecode. In *Proceedings of the ACM 2004 Workshop on Interpreters, Virtual Machines and Emulators*, pages 32–41, 2004.
2. P. J. Guo. Online Python Tutor: Embeddable web-based program visualization for CS education. In *Proceedings of the 44th ACM Technical Symposium on Computer Science Education*, SIGCSE '13, pages 579–584, New York, NY, USA, 2013. ACM.
3. K. Kagawa. WappenLite: a Web application framework for lightweight programming environments. In *9th International Conference on Information Technology Based Higher Education and Training (ITHET 2010)*, pages 21–26, Apr. 2010.
4. K. Kagawa, H. Nishina, and Y. Imai. WappenLiteDocker — a interface program between a web-browser and a Docker engine. In *The*

Third International Conference on Electronics and Software Science (ICESS2017), pages 152–155, July 2017.

5. Y. Mimoto and K. Kagawa. A framework for Web-based applications for learning programming using Eclipse RCP. In *World Conference on Educational Multimedia, Hypermedia & Telecommunications (ED-Media 2008)*, pages 2253–2264, June 2008.

6. F. Pérez and B. E. Granger. IPython: a system for interactive scientific computing. *Computing in Science & Engineering*, 9(3), 2007.

Evaluating RoboKuma: A Serious Game to Measure Cognitive Abilities

Angelo Christian Matias, Angelo John Amadora, Kurt Neil Aquino, Matthew Seaver Choy, and Rafael Cabredo

De La Salle University,
2401 Taft Avenue, Manila, Philippines
{angelo_matias, angelo_amadora, kurt_aquino, matthew_choy,
rafael.cabredo}@dlsu.edu.ph

Cognitive abilities are brain-based skills needed to carry out any task. These are measured using cognitive tests generally designed to be administered by an expert, which consequently makes experience less engaging. Gamification, or the application of game elements in a non-game context improves the experience and the engagement of the user while doing mundane tasks. RoboKuma is a serious game platform that incorporates gamified cognitive tests to measure a person's cognitive abilities to improve the engagement and overall experience when taking the tests. This study evaluates the effectiveness of the system for use in measuring a person's cognitive ability. Upon the deployment of the system, the collected data from select participants were observed and analyzed to assess the system's replay value and effectiveness as a clinical tool. Based on the analysis performed, it can be concluded that the system is an effective tool in measuring a person's cognitive abilities.

Keywords: Gamification; Cognitive Ability Testing; Serious Games.

1. Introduction

A game, as defined in [1], is an activity where individuals seek to achieve certain objectives in some context as a form of entertainment. Serious games however have more explicit and carefully thought out educational purpose and are not intended to be played primarily for amusement. Considering its differing intention from the root definition of a game, serious games are designed and developed for use in fields such as education, training, health, research, military, and the likes.

Considering that games by nature, engage the player by providing difficult challenges to overcome along with the use of a good narrative structure, complex graphics, as well as interesting rules and objectives, this further immerses the players with whatever they might be playing within game, even beyond the purpose of entertainment. In addition, considering that games help increase several skills like working memory, attentional capacity, and problem solving, it can also be used as a medium to provide a range of benefits [2].

The overall engagement of the participants is especially important in the field of psychology as the accuracy of the data gathered is integral to the accurate assessment of a person's cognitive functions. In [3], they were able to show that motivational incentives are associated with better performance and greater cognitive control which emphasizes the importance of keeping the participants motivated and engaged while performing tests that would measure their cognitive abilities. The presence of a clear task or goal, progressive balance or hierarchy of skills and challenge, and immediate feedback were identified as some of the factors which contribute to the level of engagement a player may invest towards a game [4] [5] [6].

In this study, the researchers developed a game platform for gathering and collecting data about a person's cognitive abilities. Game elements were added into existing cognitive ability tests that were commonly used by professionals in the field of psychology. These gamified tests were then incorporated into a game platform that featured additional game mechanics that would increase the game's overall replay value.

Incorporating gamification concepts and proper game design elements into cognitive ability tests improves the overall experience and engagement of the participant, which would therefore enhance the quality of the data being measured. Ensuring the replayability of the game would allow the collection of data from the users at various times of the day which would provide researchers in the field of psychology a new interactive medium for the collection of data related to a person's cognitive abilities. Furthermore, a tool which extracts the data collected within the game is also made available to researchers so that experts within the field of cognitive science would be able to perform further in depth analysis with the measured data.

2. Related Literature

Cognitive Ability is the person's ability to perform mental operations, to pay attention, to remember and to communicate about something that a person learned [7].

Cognitive abilities are brain-based skills needed to carry out any task from the simplest to the most complex. They have more to do with the mechanisms of how we learn, remember, problem-solve, and pay attention, rather than with any actual knowledge [8].

2.1. *Cognitive Ability Testing*

Cognitive Tests also known as Cognitive Ability Tests are tests designed to measure an individual's cerebral activities, which encompass reasoning, memory, attention, and language, in a specific area such as verbal reasoning and awareness. There are many tests that measure a person's cognitive ability and each with its own purpose.

In this study, we are interested in measuring four of the player's core cognitive skills:

(1) Working memory
(2) Response selection
(3) Speed
(4) Accuracy

These cognitive skills are measured by using mini-games based on existing cognitive ability tests. The researchers chose cognitive tests that were widely used in the field of Cognitive Science, namely, Go/No-Go Visual Reaction for the measurement of response selection, N-Back Task for the measurement of working memory, and speed and accuracy, Corsi Block-Tapping Task for the measurement of working memory and Eriksen Flanker Task for the measurement of response selection, and speed and accuracy.

2.2. *Playability Heuristic*

Considering that user engagement and replay value, or better known as "replayability", are key considerations towards the progression of the development of the system, the evaluation process as well as the criteria on what makes a game or a system playable should be first defined. Once defined, these criteria will then be verified by both the target participants as well as the consultants of the research in order to assess and determine how the development process of the system should proceed.

Playability is a term used to measure the three main components of a game, namely, Game usability, Mobility, and Gameplay [9]. If a game has good playability, the gameplay of the game is considered enjoyable [10]. Game usability relates to how the player interacts with the game. The interaction depends upon the visual design of the game and how the game presents relevant information to the player. Game usability also evaluates how the player is able to navigate through the game screens. Finally, game usability also evaluates the feedback of the game as well as how the game keeps the player's attention.

Mobility is defined by how easily the game helps immerses the players into the game world and how the game creates a diverse and interesting environment for the player. The game should be able to allow freedom in the game experience.

Testing the gameplay requires the evaluators or the players to at least have some degree of game design expertise. The gameplay of the game is not dependent on the platform of the game, but it is dependent on whether the target players can actually follow and have fun with the game.

3. RoboKuma System

RoboKuma is a game that allows players to perform various cognitive ability tests in the form of mini games, as well as to provide researchers and experts within the field of Cognitive Science the raw, quantified data gathered from the players.

The game provides the player a virtual pet, as shown in Fig. 1, to serve as a representation of the player's likeness by reflecting their cognitive skill level and capabilities which are defined by a combination of the different attributes. For the pet to properly reflect the player's current aptitude, various mini-games based on the cognitive ability tests will be available for the player to access.

3.1. *Virtual Pet*

One of the objectives of the player is to monitor and maintain their virtual pet. This game feature mostly embodies game elements such as pet interaction, customization, achievements and objectives, as well as some few narratives which will motivate user engagement.

For the pet interaction, the virtual pet will act accordingly depending on the player's performance on the mini-games, which are represented as cognitive assessments. Other interactions include swiping, tapping, or holding the virtual pet, who will then respond with varying reactions depending on the pet's current cognitive state.

Fig. 1. RoboKuma allows players to take care of a virtual pet.

3.2. *Mini-games*

RoboKuma includes gamified cognitive ability tests, as shown in Fig. 2, in order for players to level up their virtual pet as well as determine the player's cognitive performance. The cognitive ability tests present within the system were implemented such that it would incorporate various elements from game design and engaged learning theories, to ensure player motivation and engagement. The cognitive ability tests were implemented as follows:

3.2.1. *Go/No-Go Visual Reaction*

The player taps the positive stimuli whenever it appears while ignoring the negative stimuli. The difficulty of this minigame increases through the introduction of positive stimuli and negative stimuli in the game. The player should not respond to the negative stimuli and continually respond to the positive stimuli as the mini game progresses in difficulty.

3.2.2. *N-Back Task*

A series of stimuli will be presented at the screen one at a time, and the player taps the corresponding stimuli if it has appeared a specified n number of times before. As the player progresses, the difficulty of the N-Back tasks increases by increasing the value of n, requiring the player to remember more stimuli as well as take into account which ones have appeared before.

3.2.3. *Corsi Block-Tapping Task*

The player taps the correct boxes in correct sequence which was shown to the player before the game starts. The difficulty of the Corsi Block-Tapping task increases as the player progress through the mini-game. The difficulty is increased by lengthening the sequence that the player has to remember and to tap in the correct sequence.

3.2.4. *Eriksen Flanker Task*

The player has to swipe in the direction that the arrow at the center of the screen is pointing to. As the player progresses through the mini-game, its difficulty increases by introducing additional incongruent arrows, arrows that does not point to the same direction with the arrow in the center, making the arrow at the center of the screen less noticeable.

3.3. *Cognitive Assessments and Data Gathering*

The system collects data about the various cognitive functions of the player for research analysis. Considering that the mini-games implemented into the system are the gamified versions of their respective cognitive ability tests, each corresponding mini-game yields different cognitive attributes depending on the test being represented. The player's performance or result from playing the mini-games are reflected into the listed attributes as follows:

- Response Selection - The consistency of the speed in which the player responds to the stimuli, regardless of correctness, within the player's average Speed.
- Memory - Rate of successfully recalling past stimuli.
- Speed - Average response time to given stimuli regardless of correctness.
- Accuracy - Rate of correct responses towards incoming stimuli.

Once the corresponding data has been collected, the cognitive skill level of the player will then be reflected onto their virtual pet in the form of status ailments such as: when the player has weak short-term memory, the pet will be forgetful; when the player has slow reaction time, the pet will move slowly; when the player is impulsive, either with negative or positive stimuli, the pet will be fidgety; when the player has low accuracy, the pet will be clumsy; when the player has low average response times, the pet will act listless. The status ailments would be caused by the imbalance of its attributes, which could be the result of playing a specific mini-game too much.

Stabilizing the condition of the virtual pet would require the player to play other mini-games in order to balance out its set of attributes, which would therefore encourage the players to play the minigames in equal or sequenced intervals.

Other forms of replayability mechanics implemented into the system is the customization feature which involves the modification of the virtual pet's equipped accessories. The accessories are unlocked as the virtual pet levels up and can be bought with points earned from playing the mini-games or accomplishing achievements.

Fig. 2. From left to right: Go/No-Go, N-Back Task, Corsi Block-Tapping Task, and Eriksen Flanker Task.

In order to ensure consistent gameplay from the players, daily objectives were set as well which would incentivise players to regularly visit the system and play the mini-games on a day to day basis. In addition to that, an attribute deduction mechanic was introduced such that if the player fails to play any of the mini-games for a certain amount of time, a random value will be decreased to all of the cognitive attributes which would then in turn affect the cognitive state of the virtual pet, thus potentially inflicting a status ailment.

None of the implemented replayability mechanics however affect the integrity of the data being gathered in term of the player's performance in the mini-games, as well as other player data such as their most active hours, play time duration and frequency, and most and least played mini-games.

3.4. *Measured Data*

As mentioned before, the system collects relevant data from the player in each of the mini-games which could be used for further in depth analysis. Listed as follows are the relevant data that the system collects which could be used in the analysis of the player's cognitive abilities as specified by [11] as well as by the psychology consultant, Dr. Adrianne Galang:

3.4.1. *Go/No-Go Visual Reaction*

The performance of the player in this mini-game affects the pet's response selection, speed and accuracy attributes. For this mini-game, the system collects:
- Number of correct Go responses
- Number of correct No-Go responses
- Average response time on reacted stimuli
- Total number of trials

3.4.2. *N-Back Task*

The performance of the player in this mini-game affects the pet's memory, speed and accuracy attributes. For this mini-game, the system collects:
- Average response time on reacted stimuli
- Number of correct responses
- Size of n
- Number of unique elements presented
- Total number of trials

3.4.3. *Corsi Block-Tapping Task*

The performance of the player in this mini-game affects the pet's memory attribute. For this mini-game, the system collects:
- Number of completed trials

- Longest completed sequence length
- Total sequence length
- Total number of trials

3.4.4. *Eriksen Flanker Task*

The performance of the player in this mini-game affects the pet's response selection, speed and accuracy attributes. For this mini-game, the system collects:
- Number of correct congruent responses
- Average response time on correct congruent responses
- Number of correct incongruent responses
- Average response time on correct incongruent responses
- Total number of congruent trials
- Total number of trials

3.4.5. *General Player Data*

Other relevant miscellaneous player data to be recorded which will be necessary for the analysis and assessment of the player's cognitive ability as well as overall engagement and interactivity.
- Best scores per mini-game
- Most played mini-game
- Least played mini-game
- Mini-game Logs (date and time started and ended)

3.5. *Data Extraction Module*

The system provides a tool for extracting game statistics for research analysis. With the game statistics being the collected cognitive ability measurements from the players, this system feature will only be available for authorized specialists within the field of psychology. Although technically still part of the overall system, this tool was implemented as a separate app from the game itself. It is an application that allows authorized users to view, extract, and export raw data collected from the players which have not been analyzed nor preprocessed. Player data will of course be recorded as anonymous and will not contain any personal information about the players themselves. Although playing the game system itself does not require online functionality, it will however attempt to upload data to the online database periodically once enough data has been collected or a certain time frame has passed.

4. Results and Analysis

Over the course of the research, the game had several iterative cycles of testing and development. The researchers took note of the feedback from the participants and performed the necessary revisions.

Prior to proceeding with any of the usability testing methodologies for the system, the integrity of the gamified cognitive ability tests were first verified with the help of an expert. The effects of the incorporated game elements, the modified aesthetics and visuals of the tests, and most importantly, the data being gathered by each individual mini-game were all evaluated and considered with respect to the original methodology and implementation of the tests themselves. In summary, considering that the researchers have consistently taken into account the mechanics of the original tests when developing their gamified counterparts, the consultant has confirmed the validity and effectiveness of the gamified tests, even with the incorporated game design elements, such as the point/scoring system, altered visuals, as well as the overall game platform in which the tests has been implemented in.

For testing the user interface and the user experience, ten (10) select participants, aged 19-21, with a background in Computer Science, were given a set of tasks to perform while operating the system without aid or supervision. They were then asked to provide feedback as well as suggestions with regards to their overall experience of using both the system and playing the mini-games. Considering that basic feedback regarding the system's general user interface, art style, and user experience.

Most of the problems encountered by the participants were related to understanding the mechanics of the minigames. For Go No-Go some of the participants had a hard time distinguishing between the positive and negative stimuli, as seen on Fig. 3, based on the description given to them in the mini-game's instructions. The researchers realized that the problem could be attributed to the fact that a visual indicator would be better to show than simply describing the task to the player. Thus, the researchers decided to show them the visual indicator that would indicate the difference between the positive and negative stimuli instead of simply describing it to them.

Fig. 3. The respondents had a hard time distinguishing the difference between the positive (left) and negative (right) stimulus based on the instruction given due to a lack of visual content.

Most of the participants also had a hard time understanding the mechanics of N-back task given the instruction to tap the object that had appeared 2 objects before. This prompted the researchers to give the players a demonstration for them to get a better grasp of the mechanics of the mini-game. As for the data gathering itself, the researchers selected twenty (20) participants, aged 18 and above, were selected to use the system for a period of 3 weeks. 10 of these participants were students from De La Salle University, 5 of them were working adults while the rest were students from outside the university.

The participants were asked to play the game at their own leisure during the designated period, using their own mobile devices. The researchers were then able to collect data from the participants from the system which could be used for an in-depth analysis.

Using the collected player logs, the researchers were able to identify the replay value of the game with respect to the developed and evaluated components of playability heuristics. Figure 4 shows that the game was well received by the participants during their first week of playing. The participants played as much as 74 mini-games on day 1 and 114 mini-games on day 4 with a total of 356 played mini-games combined during the first week of the long term testing. In comparison, the second and third week of testing only had a total of 290 and 301 mini-games played combined respectively.

From Figs. 4 and 5, it could be observed that the player activity of the participants greatly vary. This could be attributed to a number of outside factors that might affect their motivation to play the game such as being busy with work or studies.

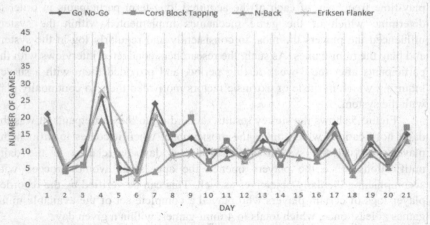

Fig. 4. The number of games played by the participants during the three weeks of deployment.

Based from the data gathered, the N-back task was the least engaging game while Go No-Go is the most engaging game because N-Back was the least played while Go No-Go was the most played by the participants. These observations reflects the results gathered from the UI/UX testing where the participants and the consultants had commented on the difficulty in understanding the mechanics, and performing the N-back task itself.

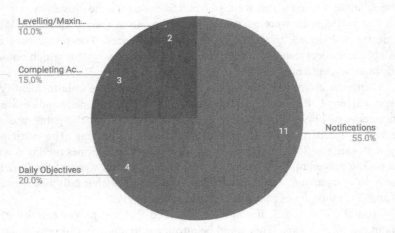

Fig. 5. Participant feedback regarding replayability.

Referencing the collected player logs, the researchers also verified the play-time frequency of each of the acquired long-term participants in order to determine which of the game mechanics implemented within the system influenced the players the most to consistently and regularly log-in the system and play the mini-games. As such, the researchers conducted interviews with the participants after the 3-week testing period, and provided them with a survey inquiring which intrinsic or extrinsic factors motivated them to continually play with the system.

Figure 5 shows the survey results. According to the participants, it was the daily notifications which made the most impact when it comes to influencing players to visit the system at least once a day. In relation to the daily notifications, once the players opened the app, some would proceed with accomplishing the daily objectives as well. This can be verified by the recorded player logs of certain players who played a complete set of the available mini-games at least once, which totals to 4 mini-games, within a given day.

It should be noted however, that notifications only pop-up after 24 hours have passed after the player's last logged mini-game. As such, player activity and consistency was not determined by whether or not a player has visited the system continually every single day throughout the 3-week testing period, but rather, it was determined by the consistency of the number of mini-games the player has performed with respect to their average session activity; with the session activity being the average active hours and average play time of the player.

Other factors which influenced the players to consistently play the mini-games, as they have mentioned during their respective interviews, was their desire to complete all of the available achievements as well as maxing out the level and attributes of the virtual pet. This can be observed by the spike of the number of games played as shown in Figure 4 as quickly leveling the virtual pet and its attributes would require the players to play the mini-games as much, and as frequent, as possible.

5. Conclusion

Based on the analysis performed on the collected data, both in terms of frequency and consistency of the participant activity, it can be concluded that the system is an effective tool in gathering data related to a person's cognitive abilities. Thus demonstrating the feasibility of the use of serious games in measuring a person's cognitive abilities.

By evaluating and analyzing the list of existing cognitive ability tests, the researchers were able to select cognitive tests which were most commonly used by experts within the field of cognitive science to incorporate into the system. This was done in order to determine the quality as well as the usefulness of the macro data being collected per basic or standard cognitive ability test. Upon determining that all of the recorded data per base test was of use, with the guidance the psychology consultant, it has been verified that it would also apply and scale as well to the other variations of the selected tests as they would generally be measuring the same data.

Upon selecting the base cognitive tests to include in the system, the researchers were able to incorporate game elements into the mechanics of each test, and in turn, integrate the gamified tests, in the form of mini-games, into a virtual pet platform. Various game mechanics such as daily objectives, achievements, rewards and leveling, as well as personalization of the virtual pet were all implemented within system in order to improve the replay value of the system, and ultimately, encourage player interaction and engagement, which is the overall goal of this research.

After the gamified system had been developed, with the help of the psychology consultant, Dr. Adrianne Galang, the overall accuracy and validity of the data which is being measured by each of the gamified cognitive tests were verified. This includes the verification of the usefulness of the miscellaneous player data being collected such as their active play hours, their average play time, and their most and least played mini-games. The consultant also confirmed that the data could be used for in-depth analysis by the experts within the field of cognitive science. Furthermore, the researchers were also able to develop a tool for previewing and extracting the collected data for the use of the aforementioned experts.

6. Future Work

Additional features to RoboKuma can still be developed to further encourage players to continually use the app. For example, some games use a daily, weekly, or monthly reward system. Additional items and customization features that are more expensive than current items can also be introduced as gold sinks and encourage players to earn more Bearya (in-game currency) to buy these items. Finally, it is also interesting to explore features that encourage social interactions between other RoboKuma users. This would allow players to share their virtual pet's progress to other players which could lead to competitions and other game mechanics.

The possible effects of the addition of game elements into the mechanics of the selected cognitive ability tests and the effects of taking the test without the supervision of an expert could also be looked into. The results of taking the original cognitive tests and their gamified versions as well as the results of tests taken with and without supervision of an expert could be compared and analyzed to determine the effects of the said changes.

Acknowledgments

We would like to thank our consultants, Dr. Adrianne John Galang from the Department of Psychology, College of Liberal Arts, as well as Mr. Briane Paul Samson from the Department of Software Technology, College of Computer Studies, De La Salle University, for their expertise and insights in developing this project.

References

1. Abt, C. (1970). Serious Games. University Press of America 1987.
2. Lumsden, J., Edwards, A. E., Lawrence, S. N., Coyle, D., & Munaf'o, R. M. (2016). Gamification of cognitive assessment and cognitive training:

A systematic review of applications and efficacy. JMIR Serious Games, 4 (2), e11.

3. Locke, H., & Braver, T. (2008). Motivational influences on cognitive control:Behavior, brain activation, and individual differences. Cognitive, Affective, and Behavioral Neuroscience, 8 (1), 99112.

4. Bowman. (1982). A pac-man theory of motivation: Tactical implications for classroom instruction. Educational Technology, 22 (9), 14-17.

5. Malone, T. (1981). Toward a theory of intrinsically motivating instruction. Cognitive Science, 33, 333-369.

6. Provenzo, E. (1991). Video kids: Making sense of nintendo. Cambridge, MA: Harvard University Press.

7. Oswald, A. (2010). Intelligence: The measurement of cognitive capabilities. Retrieved from https://www.mentalhelp.net/articles/intelligence-the-measurement-of-cognitive-capabilities/

8. Michelon, Pascal. (2006). What are cognitive abilities and skills, and how to boost them? Retrieved 08-07-2016, from http://sharpbrains.com/blog/2006/12/18/what-are-cognitive-abilities/

9. Korhonen, H., & Koivisto, E. M. (2006). Playability heuristics for mobile games. In Proceedings of the 8th conference on Human-computer interaction with mobile devices and services (pp. 9-16). ACM.

10. Jrvinen, A., Heli, S., and Myr, F. (2002). Communication and Community in Digital Entertainment Services Prestudy Research Report. University of Tampere, 2002.

11. Cognitive Group (2006). Test summary. http://www.cogtest.com/tests/cognitive int/cpt fv.html. (Accessed: 2016-11-17)

Hacking Contest Rule and an Official Practice of Information Security Event with Attack and Defense Style on a Game Website

Makoto Nakaya and Hiroyuki Tominaga

Kagawa University
2217-20 Takamatsu, Kagawa 761-0396, JAPAN
†E-mail: s15g479@stu.kagawa-u.ac.jp

Practical education about information security is needed for system developers and administrators in Web service suppliers. We propose a hacking contest CTF as attack and defense style with a website for a multiple online game. The contest organizer prepares a game server site as a contest environment which contains several vulnerability. The contest participants are divided into an attacker team as game players and a defender team as game Website operators. While the attackers access the game site with normal actions, they find vulnerabilities and try cheating actions. While the defenders monitor server logs, they detect illegal events and prevent them for maintenance. An action of each side is calculated as a point and makes each score for victory or defeat by the contest rule. The contest organizer reviews the progress situation with all participants. In this paper, we introduce several functions of the system and discuss the result of an official practice in Security Camp 2016 in Japan.

Keywords: Security Learning, Hacking Contest, Capture the Flag, Attack and Defense.

1. Introduction

Incidents about cracking systems of computer and network have been increased. Vicious crackers use many kinds of malware. Web services by public institutions and large business enterprises are often targeted and damaged by cyber attack. Moreover, web sites of small companies and personal web pages may also be invaded. These accidents are sometimes reported as big and bad social news. For examples, "Targeted threat mail" with computer virus has a significant social impact to ICT engineers and general users. Especially, in May 2017, the notorious ransomware "WannaCry" raged all over the world. It demands a ransom money of locked information of victims.

With such background, information security has become one of necessary infrastructure in the modern society. Governments of many countries have urgent tasks to foster. In Japan, it is very important before the Olympic games in 2020.

System administrators and website developers must learn information security very well. The learning contents contain knowledge of network and server management. Of course, information ethics is required. Moreover, they must have an educational opportunity of practical skills. An effective exercise is to have an experience that a learner acts both roles of an attacker and a defender. It cultivates good hackers as "white hat".

2. CTF styles and the features

Recently, a hacking contest CTF has been paid attention. CTF means "Capture The Flag". The flag is a hiding message in a website. It is a simulation game between network attackers and security defenders on a system or a web server. Most of CTF is for group counter and online participation. "DEFCON CTF" is the most famous and large CTF in USA. It has been held every year since 1996. In Japan, "SECCON CTF" has been held every year since 2012. The other contests are widely held all over the world in (Table 1). Most of them are introduced in the summary website CTFtime.org. There are mainly 3 styles of CTF, shown in (Fig. 1), such as, "Jeopardy" (JPD), "King-of-the-Hill" (KoH) and "Attack-and-Defense" (A&D).

2.1. JPD style (Jeopardy)

JPD style (a) is a simple CTF like a difficult open quiz. A contest organizer prepares several problems to participants in a website. A problem has a hiding message with some unkind hints in a web page. Participants access the web page and find the flag from sentence, keywords, image and binary data. The problem genres contain cryptogram, calculation about information mathematics, phishing by fake URL, forced browsing, directory traversal, binary reading, forensics, packet capturing, and so on. Elucidation tasks needs trial-and-errors and information retrieval from outside websites. So, sharing and cooperation of members in a team is very important.

JPD style is the most popular contest. Beforehand, contest contributors must register many problems in database. They are separated by genre, difficulty, required time and point. An organizer can construct a contest in various levels for the target participants form novices to hackers for the purpose. While a contest has about 10 to 20 problems, the contest period is also widely from 2 hours to 72 hours. A team has about 3 to 6 members. The progress situation is exhibits by ranking table in the contest page. After the contest, they have review time. This style is often used in a preliminary round of a large contest because of the scalability. However, almost problems only need partial knowledge of a given genre. Skills of a defender are difficult to treat. So, it lacks a little reality.

2.2. KoH style (King-of-the-Hill)

KoH style (b) is more practical than JPD style. A contest organizer prepares some web servers with several vulnerabilities like honeypots. Each server has a flag with given point. Participants attack any server and find the flag. A team captures the flag by his sign and gets the point in the occupied server. The sign means falsification of a web page. Moreover, other team can access opponent server to plunder the flag with another point. This style treats real simulation by attackers to find the vulnerability. The required skills are quite high. They are concerned with SQL injection, OS command injection, buffer overflow, back door, directory traversal and XSS (cross site scripting). The target participants must be in the next grade of JPD style. However, it treats only skills of the attacker side. Before the event, an organizer must show the guideline about information ethics. Participants must pledge not to abuse. the organizer may need to control network traffic and truly illegal access without rules. The KoH style is used in "SECCON finals" and "PhDays CTF 2012". However, it is not so used in the other events.

2.3. A&D style (Attack-and-Defense)

A&D style (c) is near to a simple cyber range. A cyber range is a virtual environment that is used for cyberwarfare training and cyber technology development. It treats both skills of an attacker and a defender. A contest organizer prepares several web servers of each team. A server manages web services by client-side scripts and CGI with a database manger. It has the same condition in vulnerability. Team members share roles as an attacker and a defender. The attacker members get success points by cheating actions and penetration to the opponent server. For examples, they may crash web services and destroy database. They may also tamper a web page and steal information. On the other hand, the defender members get maintenance points by preventing some troubles and keeping the own server normal. They may detect cheating actions and banish illegal users. They may revise vulnerabilities quickly and recover database and web pages. They may need stop their services temporarily.

A&D style is a very exciting and useful contest. All skills of information security are needed. Especially, the practical experience in real-time and both side is important for participants. Moreover, the game score can be regarded as a virtual money in a cyber-space. However, the style is quite difficult by the organizer to prepare and hold the event. It must also require information ethics not to abuse. It is necessary of the organizer not to leave unexpected vulnerability. It may mangle the event itself. The event may hold in distributed network environment not to affect the business. It is important of the organizer to adjust the game point rule for the balance. This style is usually held by two teams of both sides. A simple version is held by two teams of defender side and attacker side. The usual A&D style is often used in "DEFCON CTF finals" and "SECCON CTF finals".

Table 1. CTF events in the world

CTF	Country	Year	Style	URL
DEFCON	USA	1993-	A&D	https://www.defcon.org/
UCSB iCTF	USA	2002-	A&D	https://ictf.cs.ucsb.edu/
US Cyber Challenge	USA	2005-	JPD	https://uscc.cyberquests.org/
picoCTF	USA	2014-	JPD	https://picoctf.com/
PhDays CTF	Russia	2011-	JPD, A&D KoH	https://www.phdays.com/program/ctf/ http://2012.phdays.com/ctf/king/
RuCTF	Russia	2010-	JPD, A&D	https://ructf.org/
panda challenge	Spain	2009, 2010	JPD	http://www.pandasecurity.com/
Nuit du Hack	France	2010-	JPD, A&D	https://www.nuitduhack.com/
CCCAC (29C3 - 33C3)	Germany	2012-	JPD	https://32c3ctf.ccc.ac/
InCTF	India	2010-	JPD	https://junior.inctf.in/
NetAgent Security Contest	Japan	2008-2010	JPD	http://www.netagent-log.jp/archives/ 51498926.html
SECCON CTF	Japan	2012-	JPD, A&D KoH	http://2016.seccon.jp/
CTF ChallengeJapan	Japan	2012	JPD	http://2013.seccon.jp/meti-ctf/
BeeCon in OSC Tokushima 2015	Japan	2015	JPD	http://chausson4.eng.kagawa-u.ac.jp/ App/SecExrc/BeeCon/
Security Camp 2016	Japan	2016	A&D	https://www.ipa.go.jp/jinzai/ camp/index.html
CODEGATE	Korea	2004-	JPD	https://www.codegate.org/
ISEC CTF	Korea	2009-	JPD	https://wowhacker.com/
HITCON CTF	Taiwan	2014-	JPD, A&D	https://hitcon.org/

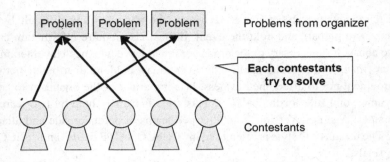

(a) Jeopardy style (JPD)

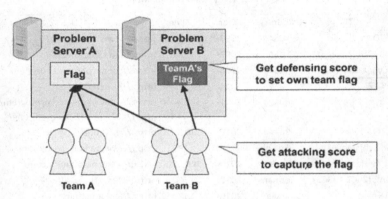

(b) King-of-the-Hill style (KoH)

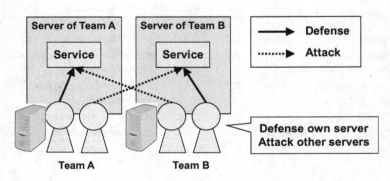

(c) Attack-and-Defense style (A&D)

Fig. 1. CTF styles.

3. CTF events for the purpose of security education

3.1. *Related events*

CTF event is regarded as a useful approach to security education for end-users and ICT engineers. Some international conferences about CTF events and security education are often held in recent years. Especially, 3GSE (Gaming, Games and Gamification in Security Education) held in 2014 and 2015 by USENIX of USA is very important. From 2016, it will be held by renamed ASE (Advances in Security Education) [1][2]. Some educational organization in USA held CTF as educational events for high school and college students. "picoCTF" (Zhang 2013) is the most famous event. Cisco Cyber Range provide a real world cyber threat training of internet security. "CTF365" in Poland manages security training platform. Hematite LLC in Japan offers "CTF kit". Both sites provide services for a price.

In our study, we have also proposed an easy CTF event of Jeopardy style for beginners (Nakaya 2015). It is for an introductory educational experience about information literacy and security. The main target users are novice students in a college and a high school. We developed a contest management server "BeeCon" (Nakaya 2016). BeeCon offers several functions about user and team management, problem database, contest construction and result log. It exhibits contest progress and a ranking table as an open event. We classified genres and grades of CTF problems of Jeopardy style for novices. We held several contests as trial practices for entrance students in our college (Nakaya 2017a).

In BeeCon, we introduce a supporter role besides a contestant in a main CTF. The supporter decides a cheering team and participates an accessory event as a player of an assistive game. The assistive game has a point rule like a card game or a board game. A supporter tries to answer security quizzes and takes a game action. These points are added to each team score in the main CTF. We plan to extend BeeCon as virtual environment system. We will offer it as a rental service on Web cloud for business use in some enterprises.

The purpose of BeeCon is to promote concern and awareness about information security to general end-users. However, it seems trivial and lack of interesting for ICT experts, who are strongly interested in information security for necessity of business. In this study, we propose a CTF event of A&D style about web services. The purpose is to offer challenging opportunity of practical training with game feeling. The target users are system administrators, web service developer and website operators. Ethical hackers so called "white hat" are also included. They are heavy users or free programmers, who find some vulnerabilities in open web site and report them to a website manager not to attack. They may be personal website managers for own original online game. Malicious crackers of an online game access to the game website by illegal tricks and get some lucre by cheating actions. They are common enemies for good game players and earnest website manager.

3.2. Related researches

Many of related studies could be classified to the method of education, operation and effectiveness for security. Recently, studies about the method of education are more active. We think the reason that taking measure by companies is not enough to prevent the security incidents and general people is needed to know and study about security literacy. About studies of operation the contest, there are many devises to rise up their motivation and stable or effective operation.

Cowan joined to DEFCON CTF and was well scored using the Immunix (Cowan 2003). The Immunix is a host based linux application security system. In this result, reliability of the Immunix was raised up and they got some feedback about improvement. They also discuss the various defense technique and strategy used by Immunix. The DEFCON CTF's level is very high and many experts joined this CTF. Immunix was successfully demonstrated.

Eagle describes that CTF can be good opportunity to get the ability of finding vulnerability (Eagle 2004). There are two points of view, constructor and defender. This paper introduces the third point of view, named destructor. Destructor is needed to know unknown vulnerability. It is focused to find vulnerability on the computer system. Destructor collaborates with constructor and defender to construct more secure system.

We need to be known the CTF to many people for the future participants to spread CTF. However, the CTF is hard to know how is it on the outer sight. In addition, although CTF often takes a team-based competition, there are many individual work and it is difficult to understand the activities of team members. Therefore, Harada discusses visualization of the CTF (Harada 2014). They use cameras to understand participants' situation and share the status of the answer throughout the whole team. It seems that it is under consideration how much effect this is.

Recently, many CTFs incorporating gamification have been studied. Zhang implemented picoCTF for high school students and received a positive questionnaire evaluation (Zhang 2013). Chapman disclosed picoCTF as open source. It reports that it is used by many educational institutions (Chapman 2014). Boopathi discusses cases of learning security through gamification, using InCTF as a case (Boopathi 2015). In both cases, subjects are divided for each level while incorporating game like UI, and ingenuity to concentrate on themes is tackled. The game story is interwoven. The participants' feeling of immersion is also enhanced. PicoCTF has a large-scale exhibition of more than 10,000 people.

Facebook published a CTF system compatible with JPD and KoH format on open source. Development is actively, UI and others are refined. Procedures for environment construction are easy to understand. Management screens are well maintained. It is easy to organize. Although it supports multilingualization, it does not correspond to Japanese as June 9, 2017.

UC Santa Barbara Seclab which organizes iCTF has opened the CTF system of A&D format in open source (Vigna 2014). Generate servers dedicated to all teams as VMs. It also generates a VM for the score server. Based on this source, the versions running on Docker rather than VM are being developed as InCTF by Amrita University and Amrita Center for Cybersecurity Systems and Networks (Raj 2016).

4. Our proposed CTF event "CtFrog" of simple A&D style

We have proposed a CTF event "CtFrog" of simple A&D style (Nakaya 2017b). CtFrog is a battle event between a defender team and an attacker team. Our CtFrog treats an original web game "Capture the Frog" of multiple users as a subject of CTF. We show the progress flow on (Fig. 2). The contest organizer prepares a game website as contest environment which has some remained vulnerabilities in client side and server side with database management system. The contest participant has either role. One is a game website operator in a defender team. Another is a game website user in an attacker team. The defender team must have more technical skills than the attacker team. The organizer assign members of each team by hearing their choice and skills. Each team must have at least 3 persons.

After team assignment, the organizer gives operating permission of the game site "Capture the Frog" to the defender as a site operator. The attackers access the game site as site users. If they find security holes, they try cheating actions and obstruct the site operation like crackers. While the defenders monitor system logs, they revise vulnerabilities and prevent cheating actions. The organizers calculate each side score and exhibit them the contest progress. After the event, the organizer comments and discusses for contest review. In the case of many participants, both teams have each own website. Members in a team are divided into attackers and defenders as the role. The battle is carried out each other.

In educational seminars of information security like "Security Camp" in Japan, the theme about web games has gained a very popular for young students. They are interested in the lecture of methods of attacking and defending for web game site. Many of them usually play web games and sometimes meet the experience as victims by cheating actions. They may have discontent and regard the counterplan as familiar issues. The subject is not so difficult than other web services for target users widely. It can be carried out as a compact size in scripts and codes. So, we adapt the subject for a CTF event of A&D style.

The system configuration of CTF event CtFrog is shown in (Fig. 3). The game website "Capture the Frog" is a virtual subsystem in CtFrog. The client side in the game website is written in HTML and JavaScript. The server side is implemented by Node.js with Express and Socket.IO. It uses SQLite as DBMS. This game has some vulnerabilities shown in (Table 2). These vulnerabilities should be treated with considering cost effectiveness by the fixing difficulty and effect. The amount of scripts is approximately 300 lines in each server and game client JavaScript file.

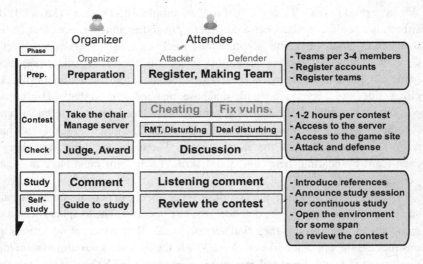

Fig. 2. The progress flow of the contest event CtFrog.

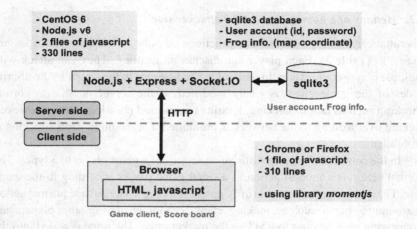

- CentOS 6
- Node.js v6
- 2 files of javascript
- 330 lines

- sqlite3 database
- User account (id, password)
- Frog info. (map coordinate)

Node.js + Express + Socket.IO ↔ sqlite3

Server side

HTTP

User account, Frog info.

Client side

- Chrome or Firefox
- 1 file of javascript
- 310 lines

Browser

HTML, javascript

- using library *momentjs*

Game client, Score board

Fig. 3. The system configuration of CtFrog.

5. The outline of the web game "Capture the Frog" in the CTF event

We describe the web game "Capture the Frog". The GUI is shown in (Fig. 4). It includes a game client window with a game field and a score board. A game user in an attacker team has a game player account. A player has a game character as an avatar in the game field. When the player acquires many points, the corresponding character changes as level-up according to the score grade.

The game field is 2D grid plain, the player moves a from the current cell to an adjacent cell horizontally and vertically. The player can capture a from in the same cell and remove it. New frogs sometimes appear in random cells. The player must capture necessary frogs to level-up. Players in the game field are individuals as rivals. The player gains score to sell own character on virtual RMT (Real Money Trading). The market price of the character is depended on the level. The money in virtual RMT is the score of the game. They are summed up in an attacker team. After selling the account, the game user gets a new account as another player.

5.1. *Management of the contest organizer*

On the organizer side, this game is rather difficult to make game balance stabilized because of cheating. Normal players feel not good and stop playing. High level character with cheating assist is traded by actual money and it causes heavy damage to the website operator. It also often leads to other criminal actions. Examples of cheating are auto playing BOT (macro script), speed hacking, memory hacking, packet hacking and modification of client program.

5.2. *Actions of a game player in the attacker side*

The attacker may do some cheating actions or policy violation. The rules are shown in (Table 3). Each player can discuss on chatting. They can attack with multiple player cooperation. In particular, sending data to the server by JavaScript codes of the game client is easily modified. If the server doesn't do correct checking such as range checking, it omits unexpected cheating action. However, making over loading to the network is prohibited. For example. DoS attacking is prohibited.

In the contest CtFrog, we distinguish actions of a game player to 3 types. The normal action is a modest action as a usual game player according to the game rule. The inside normal action is of "Capture the Frog". The outside normal action is around the game, such as, making a new account, chattering other players and exchanging own account to RMT as the market price. The price is added into the game score of the attacker side. The loophole action is just a cheating action as an attacker against the game rule. The tricky getting price is also added into the game score. The overlooked loophole action is no problem. The illegal action is a really unacceptable action in the contest, such as, cracking the game score server, increasing the network traffic and disturbing the contest organizer. The player is banished and the game score has large distraction points. The behaviors of the game players as the attacker side are shown in (Fig. 5).

5.3. *Actions of a website operator in the defender side*

The defender team can read these source code before the CTF event. They should found vulnerabilities and start fixing on this time. After starting the contest, they should monitor the game website and system logs. They must find malicious movement of game users and prevent them as soon as possible. They not only fix vulnerable bugs, but also disable illegal result. They also suspend invalid activity and banish accounts with policy violation. They may reset database and logs, or stop the service temporary if they needed. The behaviors of the website operators as the defender side are shown in (Fig. 6).

A modest game player with only normal actions must be protected. while normal game players play without some troubles, the defender side as website operators gains ordinary points constantly. If the website operator stop the game server or the online game doesn't work, modest players don't enjoy the game. During the disturbed time, the defender side must have some distraction points. The detected loophole action by the attacker side is getting points of the defender side and canceling points by the attacker side. Moreover, when the defender side detects cheating actions and banishes the attacking players, the side gets some large points.

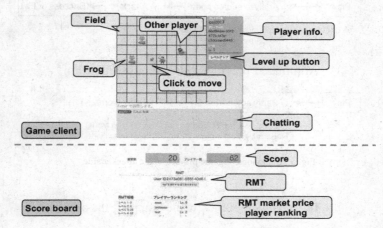

Fig. 4. The GUI of the web game "Capture the Frog".

Table 2. The prepared vulnerabilities by the contest organizer

Vulnerability (No check)	Side	Difficulty	Effect
Distance of player and frog	S	Normal	Large
Moving speed of player	S/C	Hard	Middle
Continuous posting to chat	S/C	Normal	Small
Level-up condition of character	S	Normal	Large
Collision with other players	S	Normal	Small
Returning all information of overall map	S	Normal	Middle
Logging about player actions	S	Easy	Large
Obfuscation of source code	S/C	Easy	Middle

Table 3. The action type of the attacker side

Normal actions	Loophole actions	Illegal actions
- Modest actions of the game - Making a new account - Chattering other players - Exchanging own account to RMT	- Falsification of sending data - Modifying other player's data - Trolling chat - Disturbing other players - Getting multiple accounts - Running the game client multiple	- Cracking the game score server - Distubing the organizer - Increasing the network traffic

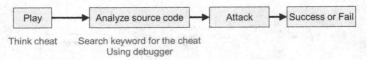

To analyze source code and send malicious traffic

Play → Analyze source code → Attack → Success or Fail

Think cheat   Search keyword for the cheat
              Using debugger

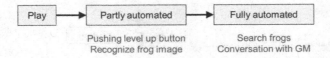

Automated playing with a simple algorithm

Play → Partly automated → Fully automated

Pushing level up button   Search frogs
Recognize frog image   Conversation with GM

Fig. 5. Behavious of game players as the attacker side

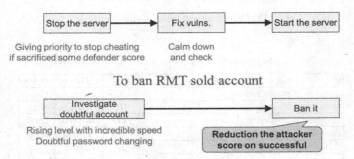

To fix vulnerabilities while stopping the server

Stop the server → Fix vulns. → Start the server

Giving priority to stop cheating   Calm down
if sacrificed some defender score   and check

To ban RMT sold account

Investigate
doubtful account → Ban it

Rising level with incredible speed
Doubtful password changing   Reduction the attacker
                                  score on successful

Fig. 6. Behavious of website operators as the defender side.

6. The point rule and game score in the CTF event

We regard scores of both attack and defense side as virtual money on the game. The defender gains defense points to keep game server normal. They prevent the attacker's cheating action by banishing violated player account. The attacker gains attack points by selling own account with the character level on virtual RMT.

We make a rule of changing the market price of virtual RMT on real-time. It is depended on 2 factors, character level k and elapsed time t. When a character level is higher, the relative value of the account must be higher. However, the average of character level may be higher by elapsed time and the relative value of the account must be may be discounted. Now we define the market price $P(k,t)$ in virtual RMT by the expression. E_i means required amount of experience point for level-up from $i-1$ to i. It is decided in advance. *R(t)* is reduction ratio of elapsed time to the total contest time *T*. *R(t)* is set to 0 at the end of the contest.

$$P(k,t) = R(t) \sum_{i \leq k} E_i \quad ; \quad R(t) = 1 - \frac{t}{T}$$

The score server manages the score of the defender team and the attacker team. It accesses to the game server every fixed interval to check creation of account and signing in correctly. The defender team gains 10 points if passed these checks as normal running. If it failed 4 times continuously, they lose points as the same of failure number on every check. This makes penalty of long time service down larger.

In this version, if the defender team banishes a sold account on virtual RMT, the attacker team loses the half of its score. This purpose is to give the defender team a chance to win if the attacker team gets a big lead by virtual RMT. We may include a factor of the number n of all accounts under consideration. When the number n is larger, the relative value of all accounts is lower as a whole. So, discount ratio D(t) must be introduced.

7. An official practice in the Security Camp 2016

The Security Camp is an event that is one of the workaround for security engineer education in Japan. It is organized by IPA. It is a camp for 5 days. Many people are invited who is expert for security. They have various classes. This event accepts applications from students in Japan and select participants about 50 peoples. Many of them are college students. High school students and junior high school students are sometimes selected. Ethical class is opened on the 1st day of the camp to prevent bad use of technique.

We performed trial contest before the Security Camp. It performed with cooperation of Irvine Inc. and student programming club SLP in Kagawa University (Nakaya 2017b). Its purpose is to find problems and to improve the system against competing. We got some feedback. Defenders need to read program code before the contest because of attackers' advantage. They also need to have inception before the contest. On the system side, organizer should prepare staging environment. Using sqlite3 is harder to maintenance without down time.

On the Security Camp, we improved these things. We gave the time for reading the program code and playing the game. It was 5 days before our class. However, they may be able to use the time for 1 day. Because they have to prepare for the camp, move and have other classes for 2 days. Therefore, we provided them before 5 days of our class. We also provided the staging environment for developing. Participants had some opportunity to talk with before our class. Therefore, we did not prepare extra inception time.

Our class has 4 hours. We performed 2 times of the CtFrog contest. First 30 minutes, we introduce the rule of the contest. Next 60 minutes, we performed the first contest. After 30 minutes rest time, we performed second contest for 90 minutes. Last 30 minutes, we discussed the result. We received questionnaire responses about their JavaScript skill level and which team (attacker or defender) they want to join. We organized 2 groups that has two teams, the attacker side and the defender side. Each team has 4-5 members and has at least one person who is good at JavaScript. We assigned almost of them to both attacker and defender on the 1st or 2nd contest. The team organization was changed at the 1st and 2nd contest.

8. The contest progress situation and the analysis of the result

At the 1st contest, attacker teams won on each group. Attacker teams got much point by level up cheat. Defender teams could not defeat them. At the 2nd contest, defender teams won on each group. Defender teams completed to fix the level up vulnerability at the initial time of the contest. Other vulnerabilities were also fixed. Attacker teams must do automation for the playing.

As the counter action for the level up cheating, some team removed the JavaScript code of level up function. However, the score server did not check the level up function. Therefore, the game server was judged as normal. As the result, they used the vulnerability of our score server. The score server also had a vulnerability that allows to ban the already banned account. Some team used it from shell command and got many points.

The attacker side executed JavaScript on the browser and performed various attacking. Some teams did automatically random moving and capture the frogs. It was easily noticed because blinking player character appeared on the game field randomly. As the counter action for this, the defenders set the some waiting code on every communication by using JavaScript function setTimeout. It limited every communication to have 1 second. This action was greatly effective to preventing attacker side playing and to getting defending point for normal operation. However, it had a problem to force players slower experience.

On the game client, some variables about player data or frog data were opened on the JavaScript global scope. Some attacker teams tried to use them for automation playing. It is required the coding skill. The success or failure of this attacking may be belonging to the skill. One of the team did completely automation that controls the player moving to the frog and capture and level up. However, the defender team inserted waiting time to all communication. Therefore, they could not get points in brief time.

On the 2nd contest, we made an extra group that organized by tutors. Their group tried to overwrite resource files on the game client. They made the frog image transparent. They also made the player character image to the frog image. Players could not find the frogs because of the transparent. Human thinks it is not normal, but the score server judged it as normal. It is a problem to judge by automatically checking.

Intermediate skilled students tend to enjoy the contest from their comment. However, high skilled students tend to be bored on the player side. Low skilled students are hard to do both attacking and defending. They initiatively observed the higher skilled students' performing and asked them the reason. The defender team could experience the impatience by the requirement to defense from the real time attacking. However, there are some comments that the score server automatically checking is optimistic and balance between attacking and defending is not good.

9. Conclusion

We proposed a CTF event "CtFrog" of attack and defense style. It treats a multiple online game "Capture the Frog". It is for training for web engineers and personal hackers. We developed a contest environment as a trial version. The contest organizer prepares an objective game website including several vulnerabilities as security holes. The contest is a battle between an attacker team and a defender team. Attackers are game playing users using some cheating actions. Defenders are website operators to fix bugs. The score of attackers is got by selling their accounts by character level in virtual RMT. The score of defenders is got by maintaining the server normally and banishing malicious accounts.

We carried out an official practice in Security Camp 2016. We gathered comments by the interview to participants. We summarized the server logs as participant actions. We considered the results for improvement. In the future work, we revise several functions and rules. We also plan to provide a virtual environment. We will carry out the system in some official events. By the performance, we must discuss educational effectiveness of our proposal in more detail.

Acknowledgements

The authors would like to thank participants and Mr. Okawa who assisted this practice.

References

1. USENIX, 3GSE '15., (2017),
   https://www.usenix.org/conference/3gse15/.

2. USENIX, ASE '16., (2017),
   https://www.usenix.org/conference/ase16/.

3. K. Boopathi, S. Sreejith and A. Bithin. Learning cyber security through gamification. Indian Journal of Science and Technology, 8(7), 642-649, (2015).

4. P. Chapman, J. Burket and D. Brumley, PicoCTF: A Game-Based Computer Security Competition for High School Students. In 3GSE, (2014).

5. Cisco, Cisco Cyber Range., (2017),
   http://www.cisco.com/c/dam/global/en_au/solutions/
   security/pdfs/cyber_range_aag_v2.pdf.

6. C. Cowan, S. Arnold, S. Beattie, C. Wright and J. Viega, Defcon capture the flag: Defending vulnerable code from intense attack. In DARPA Information Survivability Conference and Exposition, 2003. Proceedings (Vol. 1, pp. 120-129). IEEE, (2003).

7. CTFtime.org, CTFtime.org / All about CTF (Capture The Flag)., (2017),
   https://ctftime.org/.

8. C. Eagle and J. L. Clark, Capture-the-flag: Learning computer security under fire. NAVAL POSTGRADUATE SCHOOL MONTEREY CA, (2004).

9. Facebook, Facebook/fbctf., (2017),
   https://github.com/facebook/fbctf.

10. Hematite, CTF Kit., (2017), https://ctfkit.com/.

11. Ctf365.com, Houston, we have a problem!, (2017),
    https://ctf365.com/

12. M. Nakaya, T. Abe, M. Okawa and H. Tominaga, Problem Construction and Trial Practices using a Contest Management Server for a Hacking Competition CTF to Introduce Information Literacy and Security. The International Journal of E-Learning and Educational Technologies in the Digital Media, Vol.2, No.4, 181-188, (2017)

13. M. Nakaya, S. Akagi and H. Tominaga, A Practical Design of Group Competition as an Educational Event for Information Literacy and Security using a Hacking Contest CTF. Proceedings of WCTP, 116-123, (2015).

14. M. Nakaya, S. Akagi and H. Tominaga, Implementation and Trial Practices for Hacking Competition CTF as Introductory Educational Experience for Information Literacy and Security Learning. In The Fifth International Conference on Informatics and Applications (ICIA2016) (p. 57), (2016).

15. M. Nakaya, M. Okawa, M. Nakajima and H. Tominaga, A Support Environment and a Trial Practice of Hacking Contest. Proceedings of IEETeL, Vol.8, (2017).

16. PicoCTF, PicoCTF 2017., (2017), `https://picoctf.com/`.

17. A. S. Raj, B. Alangot, S. Prabhu and K. Achuthan, Scalable and Lightweight CTF Infrastructures Using Application Containers (Pre-recorded Presentation). In 2016 USENIX Workshop on Advances in Security Education (ASE 16). USENIX Association, (2016).

18. G. Vigna, K. Borgolte, J. Corbetta, A. Doupe, Y. Fratantonio, L. Invernizzi and Y. Shoshitaishvili, Ten Years of iCTF: The Good, The Bad, and The Ugly. In 3GSE, (2014).

19. K. Zhang, S. Dong, G. Zhu, D. Corporon, T. McMullan and S. Barrera, picoCTF 2013-Toaster Wars: When interactive storytelling game meets the largest computer security competition. In Games Innovation Conference (IGIC), 2013 IEEE International (pp. 293-299). IEEE, (2013).

Author Index

Printed in the United States
By Bookmasters